Approaches to Teaching DeLillo's *White Noise*

Edited by

Tim Engles

and

John N. Duvall

The Modern Language Association of America
New York 2006

85 Broad Street, New York, New York 10004
www.mla.org

To order MLA publications, visit mla.org/books. For wholesale and international orders, see mla.org/Bookstore-Orders.

The MLA office is located on the island known as Mannahatta (Manhattan) in Lenapehoking, the homeland of the Lenape people. The MLA pays respect to the original stewards of this land and to the diverse and vibrant Native communities that continue to thrive in New York City.

Cover art of the paperback and electronic editions: photoillustration by Javier Rodriguez

Approaches to Teaching World Literature 85
ISSN 1059-1133

POD 2022 (first printing)

Library of Congress Cataloging-in-Publication Data

Approaches to teaching DeLillo's White noise / edited by Tim Engles and John N. Duvall.
p. cm.—(Approaches to teaching world literature ; 85)
Includes bibliographical references (p.) and index.
ISBN-13: 978-0-87352-918-1 (alk. paper)
ISBN-10: 0-87352-918-9 (alk. paper)
ISBN-13: 978-0-87352-919-8 (pbk. : alk. paper)
ISBN-10: 0-87352-919-7 (pbk. : alk. paper)
1. DeLillo, Don. White noise. 2. DeLillo, Don—Study and teaching.
I. Engles, Tim. II. Duvall, John N. (John Noel), 1956– III. Series.
PS3554.E4425W4833 2006
813'.54—dc22 2005029240

CONTENTS

PREFACE TO THE SERIES

In *The Art of Teaching* Gilbert Highet wrote, "Bad teaching wastes a great deal of effort, and spoils many lives which might have been full of energy and happiness." All too many teachers have failed in their work, Highet argued, simply "because they have not thought about it." We hope that the Approaches to Teaching World Literature series, sponsored by the Modern Language Association's Publications Committee, will not only improve the craft—as well as the art—of teaching but also encourage serious and continuing discussion of the aims and methods of teaching literature.

The principal objective of the series is to collect within each volume different points of view on teaching a specific literary work, a literary tradition, or a writer widely taught at the undergraduate level. The preparation of each volume begins with a wide-ranging survey of instructors, thus enabling us to include in the volume the philosophies and approaches, thoughts and methods of scores of experienced teachers. The result is a sourcebook of material, information, and ideas on teaching the subject of the volume to undergraduates.

The series is intended to serve nonspecialists as well as specialists, inexperienced as well as experienced teachers, graduate students who wish to learn effective ways of teaching as well as senior professors who wish to compare their own approaches with the approaches of colleagues in other schools. Of course, no volume in the series can ever substitute for erudition, intelligence, creativity, and sensitivity in teaching. We hope merely that each book will point readers in useful directions; at most each will offer only a first step in the long journey to successful teaching.

Joseph Gibaldi
Series Editor

PREFACE TO THE VOLUME

Frank Lentricchia, one of Don DeLillo's earliest advocates, incisively labels the novelist's work an "anatomy" of contemporary American life (Introd. 1). Whatever his subject matter—from the subliminal power of the electronic media and advertising, through the pleasures and confusions of the blended nuclear family, to our national obsession with conspiracy and celebrity—DeLillo dives deeply, probing some of the innermost hideaways of the postmodern condition. For many American readers who lived through the 1980s, he plunged especially deep in *White Noise*, resurfacing with a steady grip on something recognizably pervasive, and yet also elusive, about American life. In particular, Jack Gladney's half-alert, half-lulled narrative depicted how it felt then to live amid, as the novel's resident semiotician and mystic Murray Jay Siskind puts it, "American magic and dread" (19).

Every generation has its own modes of dread, and as the wide-ranging essays gathered here demonstrate, teachers are using *White Noise* in a surprising array of contexts to elicit and examine contemporary apprehensions. In addition to fitting usefully into many different literature and composition courses, the novel can significantly contribute to a variety of American studies and cultural studies courses that make gender, race, the environment, or mediality rather than the literary the primary focus. Our forty-two survey respondents to an initial questionnaire about teaching *White Noise* listed the expected American literature and contemporary literature survey courses at all undergraduate and graduate levels, and the novel also showed up on syllabi for Introduction to Religious Studies, Postmodernism and Its Discontents, Machine Cultures, Literature and Medicine, The American Gothic, Multicultural Literatures, The History and Development of Communication Theory, Introduction to Ecocriticism, The Family in Fiction and Film, and Methods of Media Criticism.

Despite the novel's magic and utility in so many different settings, instructors repeatedly indicated that there is much about the novel that today's younger readers don't quite get. In our own classrooms, one persistent problem—though one hesitates to call it that—is the prophetic reach DeLillo often achieves with his anatomies. Many of the encroaching and disturbing American tendencies that he examines with satiric excess in *White Noise*, such as rampant consumerism, information overload, and obedience to the dictates of the mainstream media, have simply become the lived experience of most of our current undergraduates. As one such student said in class, "The way the media and its demands are seeping further and further into our lives might have seemed like something new and alarming in 1985, but it's part of my life. It basically *is* my life." Though such responses can be initially frustrating for instructors, they actually demonstrate one reason why *White Noise* is poised to become the avatar of postmodern American fiction. If today's undergraduate students experience its world as already known, having this world so graphically anatomized can help them achieve a more self-aware grasp on their daily lives. For those teaching the novel, of course, getting students to the point of self-reflection can be the biggest battle, and we're pleased that instructors in so many pedagogical contexts will find useful strategies here for meeting this challenge.

Given the complexity and thematic density of DeLillo's concerns in *White Noise*, it comes as no surprise that a different challenge instructors report is getting students beyond the novel's domesticated, ironic, and often humorous surfaces. "I want to help students see the humor," one respondent wrote, "but also see past the humor." Fostering student appreciation of the humor itself was also frequently listed as a difficulty; one respondent aptly described this problem as "getting the students oriented to contemporary satire in a culture that satirizes itself quite nicely, thank you." One solution to the humor problem comes about when instructors successfully contextualize the novel in contemporary and historical terms. The myriad supplementary materials and methods suggested throughout this volume for establishing such backgrounds generally echo those listed as most helpful by our survey respondents.

We have many people to thank for their help with this volume: the survey participants who offered such detailed responses to an MLA survey on teaching DeLillo's novels; our acquisitions editor, Sonia Kane, so quick and ready with advice and support; Hugh Ruppersburg, for extensive early support; Philip Nel, Mark Osteen, Joseph Conte, Arthur Saltzman, and other members of the Don DeLillo Society, for their steady interest, collegiality, and sustenance; Bill Prather, Patrick McCord, Sue Francis, and Allan Crandell, for challenging, illuminating conversations; and William J. ("Joe") Palmer, a former editor of *Modern Fiction Studies* who regularly teaches DeLillo's fiction, for a sympathetic ear when things went awry during the six years it took to bring this volume to fruition; and Curt Gardner, for his pioneering, ever-helpful Web site, *Don DeLillo's America*. We also appreciate our contributors' generous willingness to share their expertise and their patience throughout the many stages of this project. And most of all, we thank Don DeLillo for the meditation on American culture that is *White Noise*.

Part One

MATERIALS

Introduction

Since the early 1980s, scholars have been reading and teaching Don DeLillo's fiction, and its thematic depth has generated a great deal of critical interest. The centrality of *White Noise* in DeLillo's oeuvre is signaled by the publication of such volumes as Frank Lentricchia's collection of essays *New Essays on* White Noise (1991), Penguin's Viking Critical Library edition of *White Noise* (1998), and Harold Bloom's Modern Critical Interpretations volume *Don DeLillo's* White Noise (2003). In 1999, Penguin USA released a paperback version of the novel in its Great Books of the Twentieth Century series, one of three editions of the novel currently in print. Entering the words "Don DeLillo's *White Noise*" into an Internet search engine elicits hundreds of Web sites, including those for scores of college courses that include the novel. Our survey of Modern Language Association members who teach *White Noise* drew over forty responses, and many noted that the book has become a centerpiece in their teaching of postmodern American fiction.

The survey asked teachers to identify additional critical and contextual material that they find useful for their purposes, as well as material that they regularly assign to their students. Their answers provided much of the information offered here.

Readings for Students

Survey respondents have assigned or recommend to their students a broad range of reference and background materials covering topics represented in *White Noise*, such as consumer culture, mass media, postmodern and post-structuralist theory, family structures, and environmental and educational issues. As one might expect, teachers using the novel in undergraduate survey classes assign far less secondary material than do those using it in upper-level courses. Readings most commonly cited by instructors concerned with helping students perceive the novel's complex theoretical underpinnings include Jean Baudrillard's "The Precession of Simulacra" and *America* and Fredric Jameson's "Postmodernism; or, The Cultural Logic of Late Capitalism" (both essays are widely anthologized). Some instructors recommended reading all or portions of David Harvey's *The Condition of Postmodernity: An Enquiry into the Origins of Cultural Change*, Guy Debord's *The Society of the Spectacle*, Jean Lyotard's "Defining the Postmodern," and Walter Benjamin's "The Work of Art in the Age of Mechanical Reproduction." To clarify for students the forms of social change taken up in *White Noise*, some assign readings on contemporaneous social and cultural phenomenon. These include selections from Neil Postman's *Amusing Ourselves to Death: Public Discourse in the Age of Show Business*; Paul Slansky's *The Clothes Have No Emperor: A Chronicle of the American '80s*; and essays by Anne Norton ("The Signs of Shopping"), Phyllis Rose ("Shopping and Other Spiritual Adventures in America Today"), Scott Russell Sanders ("Speaking a Word for Nature"), Shawn Wilbur ("An Archaeology of Cyberspaces: Virtuality, Community, Identity"), and Mark Edmundson ("On the Uses of a Liberal Education: I. As Lite Entertainment for Bored College Students").

For situating the novel in general literary contexts, the most frequently recommended works were Linda Hutcheon's *Poetics of Postmodernism: History, Theory, Fiction*, Brian McHale's *Postmodernist Fiction*, and Cheryll Glotfelty and Harold Fromm's coedited volume *The Ecocriticism Reader: Landmarks in Literary Ecology*. For book-length critical work on *White Noise* and other works by DeLillo, instructors most frequently send students to Lentricchia's collections *New Essays on* White Noise and *Introducing Don DeLillo*; Tom LeClair's *In the Loop: Don DeLillo and the Systems Novel*; Douglas Keesey's introductory volume in the Twayne United States Authors series, *Don DeLillo*; and *Critical Essays on Don DeLillo*, edited by Hugh Ruppersburg and Tim Engles. The essays reprinted in Mark Osteen's Viking Critical Library edition of *White Noise* are also frequently assigned, along with its introduction and other helpful ancillary readings.

The Instructor's Library

Biographical Material

Because DeLillo is a living author and one who values his privacy, biographical resources are relatively scarce. Interested instructors can find information about him in the "Interviews, Profiles, and Essays" section that follows. A good starting point for information on the author's life is "Don DeLillo" (Civello). An especially helpful online source, Curt Gardner's *Don DeLillo's America*, contains one of the most imaginative biographical resources available. Posing a number of questions about DeLillo's life and background, Gardner then answers each by drawing on a number of published interviews with the author (this succinct summary of DeLillo on DeLillo may be accessed by clicking on "Bio"). The opening chapter of John Duvall's *Don DeLillo's* Underworld (8–20) provides an overview of DeLillo's life and uses published interviews with the author to survey the literary and intellectual influences on him. For a consideration of DeLillo's relation to his Italian American origins, see Fred L. Gardaphé's *Italian Signs, American Streets: The Evolution of Italian American Narratives* (172–92).

Interviews, Profiles, and Essays

Seventeen of DeLillo's interviews are collected in Thomas DePietro's *Conversations with Don DeLillo*. Of the forty-some published interviews with and profiles of DeLillo, the two containing his most extensive commentary on *White Noise* are "An Outsider in This Society" and Adam Begley's "Don DeLillo: The Art of Fiction CXXXV." Less central to *White Noise*, but significant nevertheless for their insights into the author and his craft, are Tom LeClair's interview with DeLillo and Vincent Passaro's profile "Dangerous Don DeLillo." See also *Don DeLillo's America*, clicking on "Interviews and Profiles"; it briefly summarizes and excerpts thirty-three interviews and profiles from 1978 to the present.

Instructors may also wish to use one or more of DeLillo's essays, which have appeared sporadically, in various publications. Three in particular offer much that illuminates the author's thinking about politics and art. The first, reprinted in Osteen's edition of the novel, is "Silhouette City: Hitler, Manson, and the Millennium" (1989). This essay is particularly pertinent because its subject matter, fascist impulses in contemporary American culture, dovetails with that of Jack Gladney's teaching subject, "the continuing mass appeal of fascist tyranny" (25). The other essay in which DeLillo writes about contemporary totalitarianism is "The Artist Naked in a Cage" (1997), which focuses on the imprisoned Chinese dissident writer Wei Jingsheng and speaks to DeLillo's sense of the role of the artist and the relation between politics and aesthetics. For those seeking a way to teach *White Noise* in a post–September 11, context, his "In the Ruins of the Future" (2001) is worth examining.

Bibliographic Sources

The fall 1999 issue of *MFS: Modern Fiction Studies*, devoted to DeLillo's fiction, contains Joseph S. Walker's complete bibliography of works by and about DeLillo up until that point. DeLillo's work continues to receive frequent attention in many scholarly journals devoted to American literature and culture. In addition to the standard *MLA Bibliography*, the most useful updates of DeLillo's writings and scholarly analysis of his work appear at two Web sites: *The Don DeLillo Society* (www.ksu.edu/english/nelp/delillo/), maintained by Philip Nel, and Gardner's *Don DeLillo's America*.

Critical Studies

Book-Length Studies

Many of the works instructors listed as readings for students were also recommended for those teaching the novel. In addition to LeClair's groundbreaking *In the Loop*, some full-length studies of DeLillo's work that include extensive, complex treatment of *White Noise* are Osteen's *American Magic and Dread: Don DeLillo's Dialogue with Culture*, David Cowart's *Don DeLillo: The Physics of Language*, François Happe's *Don DeLillo: La fiction contre les systèmes*, and Jesse Kavadlo's *Don DeLillo: Balance at the Edge of Belief*. In Arnold Weinstein's *Nobody's Home: Speech, Self, and Place in American Fiction from Hawthorne to DeLillo*, three chapters on DeLillo's work contain an extensive defense of *White Noise*'s depiction of family life. For overviews of critical responses to *White Noise*, see Osteen's introduction to the Viking Critical Library edition of the novel and the introduction to *Critical Essays on Don DeLillo* (Ruppersburg and Engles).

Journals and Collections

Four journals have devoted special issues to DeLillo's fiction. Lentricchia edited the first such issue for *South Atlantic Quarterly* in 1990. Reprinted as *Introducing Don DeLillo* a year later, this collection contains two influential pieces by Lentricchia (the volume's introduction ["American Writer"] and his essay on *Libra* ["*Libra*"]), as well as eight other analyses of DeLillo's work, an interview with the author, and a chapter from his novel *Ratner's Star*. The online journal *Postmodern Culture: An Electronic Journal of Interdisciplinary Criticism* followed with a "DeLillo Cluster" of four essays in 1994. In 1999, *MFS: Modern Fiction Studies* issued *Don DeLillo* (ed. Duvall), a special issue containing ten essays, an introduction by Duvall that assesses DeLillo's canonical stature, and Walker's bibliography mentioned above. In 2001, *Critique* devoted an issue to DeLillo's work with six essays (*Don DeLillo*).

Many survey respondents praised the accessibility and usefulness of Lentricchia's *Introducing Don DeLillo* and another collection edited by Lentricchia, *New Essays on* White Noise, for both students and instructors. His interpretations in these introductions are landmark studies, highlighting and clarifying for future scholarship several general concerns in DeLillo's work. *Critical Essays on Don DeLillo* (Ruppersburg and Engles) surveys the reception, by both reviewers and scholars, of each DeLillo novel through *Underworld*.

Electronic Resources and Other Teaching Aids

The most compendious and frequently updated online sources for information on DeLillo's work are the two sites mentioned above, *The Don DeLillo Society* and *Don DeLillo's America*. In the questionnaire responses, many instructors wrote of sending their students to these sites and of using them for their own purposes. As several others noted, Philipp Schweighauser's intricate online interface with his students regarding the novel could provide ideas for those wishing to integrate the Internet into their teaching (www.unibas.ch/anglist/delillo/index.html). One other online source noted by several respondents is a *New York Times* feature on DeLillo (www.nytimes.com/books/01/02/04/specials/delillo.html); this site contains links to reviews of each DeLillo novel, his article "The Power of History," and audio versions of his reading from his work and an interview with him by Terry Gross. Information about subscribing to an electronic discussion list devoted to DeLillo and his work can be found at *A DeLillo Mailing List*, run by Cal Godot (perival.com/delillo/delillo-l.html).

Many instructors listed narrative films that they teach in conjunction with the novel, including Sam Mendes's *American Beauty* (1999), for its treatment of middle-class white family life; Todd Haynes's *Safe* (1995), for its depiction of potentially toxic environments and postmodern paranoia; Stanley Kubrick's *Dr. Strangelove; or, How I Learned to Stop Worrying and Love the Bomb* (1964), Jayne Loader and Kevin Rafferty's *The Atomic Café* (1982), and Nicholas Meyer's *The Day After* (1983), for their concerns with nuclear weapons and overtones of Armageddon (one instructor uses an episode of *The Simpsons* that also treats this theme); and Ridley Scott's *Blade Runner* (1982) and David Fincher's *Fight Club* (1999), for their connections to the novel's concern with the Baudrillardian simulacrum, the postmodern problem of the real, and issues of masculinity and fascism.

One instructor suggested having a television tuned to an off-channel during class discussion to create a background filled with, of course, white noise.

Regarding Editions

Penguin publishes three paperback editions of *White Noise*, two of which are appropriate for classroom use. The original paperback, part of the Penguin Contemporary American Fiction (CAF) series, is fine for use in lower-division courses. For those teaching upper-division courses, the Viking Critical Library (VCL) edition, White Noise: *Text and Criticism* (ed. Osteen), is a good option to consider. Both the CAF and VCL editions reproduce the pagination of the first edition. The VCL costs slightly more, but it offers over two hundred pages of useful contextual and critical material, including excerpts from other DeLillo novels, DeLillo's essay "Silhouette City: Hitler, Manson, and the Millennium" (mentioned above in "Interviews, Profiles, and Essays"), contemporary reviews of *White Noise*, and seven essays on the novel published in the 1980s and 1990s. Teachers should avoid the Penguin Great Books of the Twentieth Century edition of *White Noise*, because it has different pagination. Page numbers cited for *White Noise* in the following essays refer to either the VCL or CAF edition.

Part Two

APPROACHES

Introduction

The essays that follow are arranged in five sections. The essays in the first, "Cultural and Theoretical Approaches," emphasize how the social text helps us read DeLillo's novel and how at the same time the novel provides a critical purchase for better understanding contemporary culture.

Randall Fuller discusses his use of *White Noise* at the beginning of an interdisciplinary honors course on American cultural studies to open a range of themes, including the myth of the West, American exceptionalism, middle-class hegemony, and the interrelation of advertising and consumption. Fuller finds that the eccentric professors of the Department of American Environments at the novel's College-on-the-Hill provide a richly ambiguous model for the very activity—the study of various manifestations of American culture—in which students are engaged. Thus DeLillo's portrayal of the scholarship in American Environments helps students discriminate between a critique and a celebration of American culture.

Margaret Scanlan addresses the uncanny in *White Noise* that grows out of references to the possibility of terrorist attacks. She raises questions about the limits of the novel's realism, particularly regarding the treatment of Jack's interest in Hitler studies, to help students understand the novel's America as a fictional construct. Her questions seek to direct discussion away from the matter of domesticity and toward a focus on allusions to the violent history and politics of the contemporary international scene. Scanlan suggests the classroom use of essays by Slavoj Žižek, Jean Baudrillard, and DeLillo himself that comment on September 11.

Paul Young puts DeLillo's decision not to represent the horrors of the Holocaust in his representation of Hitler studies in the broader context of two distinct traditions of texts that satirize the Nazi past. Looking first at Bertolt Brecht's play *The Resistible Rise of Arturo Ui* (1941) and Charlie Chaplin's film *The Great Dictator* (1940), Young reminds us of Theodor Adorno's critique of these satires—namely, that by trivializing the violence of the Nazi regime, they lose their intended political effect. Young places *White Noise* in a different tradition of using Hitler, one that includes Art Spiegelman's graphic novel *Maus* (1980–91) and Mel Brooks's film *The Producers* (1968). For Young this second tradition, while still implicated, provides a more adequate response to Adorno's call to express Nazi atrocity through a negative dialectic.

Louisa Mackenzie discusses the use of DeLillo's novel in an introductory course on ecocriticism. *White Noise* furthers her larger goal of encouraging students to think about nature as historically and culturally constructed while making clear that an ecocritical approach is not limited to nature writers such as Henry David Thoreau and William Wordsworth. She provides an overview of ecocriticism and also points instructors to specific essays, such as Lawrence Buell's "Toxic Discourse," for class discussion. An ecocritical context permits moments in *White Noise* to serve as a springboard for considering the role environmental racism plays in the larger construction of racial ideology.

Instructors interested in the issue of race that Mackenzie opens will find further material in Tim Engles's description of his use of the novel in courses devoted to multicultural literature. Working from a central tenet in the recent study of racial whiteness, that race matters for European Americans as much as it does for people of color, Engles explains that in a classroom composed largely of white students, a focus on the novel's portrait of middle-class white subjectivity can facilitate discussions of racial issues that students might otherwise avoid. Working with key quotations from theorists in critical whiteness studies, Engles and his students eventually credit the novel with an unusual attentiveness to some common features of late-twentieth-century European American subjectivity.

The second section, "Teaching *White Noise* in the Context of Electronic Media and Technology," gathers three essays that contextualize DeLillo's novel in the age of digital communication.

Timothy Melley details his use of short response papers, discussion questions, and electronic discussion list postings to examine with students DeLillo's critique of the ideology of scientific progress, an ideology that has profoundly (and often negatively) changed the relation of the individual to society and nature. Other elements of postmodernity featured in Melley's approach include the way *White Noise* points to people's larger inability to locate origin, nature, and the real itself when reality is thoroughly confused with its simulations; in such a mediated world, technology numbs the fear of death.

Kathleen LeBesco positions *White Noise* in a course on the history of communications theory. She uses DeLillo to illustrate how cultural criticism and theories about media go back to Plato's *Phaedrus* and Martin Luther's strategic use of early mass printings of the Bible. For LeBesco, *White Noise* challenges students to recognize what is toxic about contemporary media and consumer culture and to explore relations among electronic media saturation, consumer culture, and the functions of language. Her essay will be especially useful for teachers who seek to engage students' deeply rooted investments in television and other forms of the electronic media.

Turning from essays that focus on how *White Noise* thematizes media and technology to one that makes media and technology its very pedagogical basis, the section concludes with Philip Schweighauser's argument that, because the virtual world of the Internet is perhaps the ultimate site of simulacra so far, *White Noise* cries out for Web-integrated teaching. Schweighauser has created a useful Web site, *Thinking about DeLillo's* White Noise (www.unibas.ch/anglist/delillo/index.html), and his essay explains how students can use the Internet to elucidate such key elements of the novel as the media, simulation, commodification, and ecology. He encourages students to analyze the information and activities available at specific Web sites as a way of grappling with the novel's representations of postmodern media and culture.

The third section, "Surveying *White Noise*," discusses different ways that DeLillo's novel might be included in an American literature survey course.

Theron Britt argues for using *White Noise* as a capstone in a survey course on the American novel because it allows students to see both continuity with and difference from earlier American representations of the individual's struggle in society. Using such novelists as Mark Twain, Kate Chopin, Theodore Dreiser, Stephen Crane, and Ernest Hemingway, Britt traces changing conceptions of the self from the confident moral agency of realism, through the social determinations of naturalism, to modernism's alienated subject. The more fragmented subjectivity of DeLillo's Jack Gladney may be read as an instance of what postmodern theorists as various as Fredric Jameson and Gilles Deleuze have troped as cultural schizophrenia, in which the individual becomes merely a point through which media culture speaks. But while Britt sees the novel delineating the problems of a radically decentered identity, he also argues that DeLillo seeks a cure for this cultural malaise in the possibilities of belief, no matter how compromised a belief may be.

John Duvall examines the crucial role *White Noise* can play in defining, in a survey of American literature since the Civil War, the postmodern difference. Noting various definitions of philosophical, cultural, and aesthetic postmodernism, he argues that even when *White Noise* falls short of exemplifying postmodern aesthetics, it consistently works as a representation of First World postmodernity. Drawing particularly on the work of Fredric Jameson and Jean Baudrillard, Duvall shows how DeLillo depicts the hyperreality of cultural simulation and the impact such simulation and mediality have on personal identity.

Ted Billy places DeLillo's novel in a history of American subversive art, one critical of materialist impulses in the American dream. Starting with Ralph Waldo Emerson's and Henry David Thoreau's criticism of Benjamin Franklin's *Autobiography*, Billy ranges over texts such as Henry James's *The American*, Kate Chopin's *The Awakening*, Edith Wharton's *The House of Mirth*, and Theodore Dreiser's *The Financier* to create a thematic context for approaching DeLillo's novel. He also offers several practical suggestions to help students focus on the representation of consumption, leisure, and waste.

Together, the three essays in the third section provide a broader view of sites of classroom debate. Their complementary interests in postmodern identity lead both Britt and Duvall to examine Jack Gladney's encounter with Sister Marie near the end of *White Noise*. For Britt the meeting occasions the possibility of recovering belief; for Duvall it is another instance of DeLillo's presentation of postmodern simulation. Like Britt and Duvall, Billy sees *White Noise* as critical of contemporary culture, but he places that critique in the more conservative context of Christopher Lasch's communitarian perspective. Both Duvall and Billy point to F. Scott Fitzgerald's *The Great Gatsby* as a possible comparative touchstone but for quite different ends. For Billy the line from James Gatz to Jack Gladney is marked by continuity of materialist identity; for Duvall the pair marks a rupture, in which Gatz is an identity based on dissimulation and Gladney is an identity predicated on postmodern simulation.

Instructors interested in seeing how *White Noise* can be illuminated by a more in-depth approach to DeLillo should turn to this volume's fourth section, "Teaching *White Noise* in the Context of Other DeLillo Novels."

Michael Bérubé tells how he shows students connections between the significance of sports fandom depicted in DeLillo's *Underworld* and the repeated emphasis on plot and motive in *White Noise*. Finding that the detailed interest in baseball in *Underworld* eventually exposes as illusory both the straightforward certainty of sporting narratives ("The best players win") and the simplicity of the motives of those who act in them ("players play to win"), Bérubé uses selections of that novel to explicate the evasive complexity of the plots that move "deathward" in *White Noise*. He demonstrates how, by drawing on the interest of both male and female students in sporting events and their often controversial outcomes, instructors can help them understand the novel's obsessive concern with death and its potential meanings and the novel's sympathy for "how trying it is, outside of the worlds of sports, to live in a story without a plot, a narrative without a motive."

Mark A. Eaton relates how he uses *Mao II* in conjunction with *White Noise* to allow students to explore what he sees as DeLillo's debunking of the "secularization thesis," the widespread supposition that religious belief gradually declined in late-twentieth-century America. Eaton argues that in both novels DeLillo examines a contemporary tension between an actual increase in religious belief and the countervailing secularity of American culture. Eaton's goal is to help students reflect on their often ambiguous spirituality through novels that show how religion can be both a destructive force and a source of true hope.

Margaret Soltan uses other fiction by DeLillo to help students excavate some of the deeper philosophical issues lurking beneath the satiric surface of Jack Gladney's narrative. Warning that the more entertaining features of *White Noise* can distract from this effort, Soltan uses chapters from *Great Jones Street* and *The Names* to discover DeLillo's repeated call for a deeper attentiveness to experience and for a renunciation of the empty clamor of contemporary life. At the same time, like Eaton, Soltan sees an accompanying interest in more spiritual modes of existence. Her DeLillo is loyal to both reality and transcendence and constructs in each of these three novels a protagonist's movement toward a selfless, compassionate attentiveness to the suffering of others.

In this volume's final section, "Classroom Techniques and Strategies," instructors offer more-detailed accounts of their classroom praxis.

David Blakesley deploys a system derived from the work of the rhetorician Kenneth Burke for breaking down narrative elements. Blakesley suggests how key concepts from Burke's notion of dramatism can be used to help students tease out the novel's primary thematic concerns. He introduces and illustrates the use of Burke's system for narrative analysis to explicate scenes and to better describe the novel's illustrations of how the media mediate experience by encouraging us to interpret in certain ways what we perceive.

Philip Nel discusses DeLillo's careful attention to normalized social constructions of masculinity and femininity. Stressing the novel's depictions of gender roles as interpellated performance intricately shaped by culture, Nel offers several creative exercises for enabling students to question contemporary stereotypes of the sexes, including idealized female body types and the violence embedded in American masculine norms. Such exercises, he believes, help recontextualize the troubling implications of the novel's portrait of an "unrepentant sexist," Murray Jay Siskind.

Mark Osteen also investigates the novel's concern with societal influence on identity construction. Taking his cue from the commodity triads that punctuate the novel ("Visa, MasterCard, American Express"; "Krylon, Rust-Oleum, Red Devil"), Osteen explores with his largely upper-middle-class students connections between the novel's meditations on the blur and glut of American consumer culture and students' allegiances to various brand-names and products. In addition to presenting modes of textual analysis, he assigns ethnographic shopping trips to supermarkets and malls and arranges interviews with produce managers and corporate publicity operatives. The students channel this fieldwork into written biographies of the novel's commodity triads. In a useful appendix to his essay, Osteen addresses a lack in the scholarship on DeLillo's work by providing detailed analysis of these triads.

In the final essay of the volume, Valerie Wee and John Whalen-Bridge place DeLillo's novel in the context of their course on disaster narrative. Taking three different urges—to document, to satirize, and to inspire—that motivate producers of disaster narrative, Wee and Whalen-Bridge give a series of classroom exercises that allow students to better understand the relation between disaster and its aesthetic representation. Drawing on a range of filmic texts, from Steven Spielberg's *Schindler's List* and Claude Lanzmann's *Shoah* to two representations of nuclear apocalypse, *Fail-Safe* and *Dr. Strangelove*, Wee and Whalen-Bridge develop a classroom strategy that allows students to position *White Noise* amid the contradictory meanings that accrue in the cultural construction of the catastrophic.

As the essays collected here demonstrate, the stylistic and thematic complexities of *White Noise* make it amenable to many course contexts and pedagogical concerns. We hope the readers of this volume will see our groupings of the essays as provisional, and we invite instructors to seek alternative arrangements. For example, those who wish to teach conflict may want to contrast the different DeLillos represented in these essays: the postmodernist DeLillo of Britt, Duvall, and Melley; the secular humanist DeLillo of Billy; the spiritualist DeLillo of Eaton and Soltan. Instructors who are attracted to Young's use of Adorno and a range of films to teach *White Noise* will do well to look at Wee and Whalen-Bridge. Those who wish to draw on Mackenzie's ecocritical pedagogy will find useful Web resources in Schweighauser's contribution.

While it is impossible to exhaust all the approaches to *White Noise* in one volume, the essays collected here should increase awareness both of the cultural critique and of the manifold pleasures offered by DeLillo's incisive and affecting portrayal of late-twentieth-century America.

CULTURAL AND THEORETICAL APPROACHES

White Noise and American Cultural Studies

Randall Fuller

I teach *White Noise* in a series of honors courses that is devoted to American cultural studies and that employs an interdisciplinary approach to examine a wide range of American themes. In a given semester my students explore such topics as the myth of the West, American exceptionalism, manifest destiny, advertising and consumption, and middle-class hegemony—and they do so through a great variety of cultural artifacts, including film, graphic novels, advertising, architecture, and the Internet. My aim as a teacher is to provide students with approaches to American culture and to establish cooperative projects between academic areas so that ultimately they may more consciously examine American ideas and identities as well as their relations to power and authority. The course culminates for each student in an analysis of some artifact or aspect of American culture.

Taught in conjunction with the first chapter of Neil Campbell and Alasdair Kean's *American Culture Studies*, *White Noise* serves as an introduction to the course, and students invariably return to its potent narrative throughout the semester. The novel serves as a touchstone in part because it contains a rare fictional representation of people engaged in the same task that my students confront: the study of American popular culture. The "curious group" of professors at the College-on-the-Hill who labor "to decipher the natural language of the culture, to make a formal method of the shiny pleasures they'd known in their Europe-shadowed childhoods" (9), anticipates, albeit satirically, what we will attempt to do in class. While DeLillo expresses serious reservations about cultural studies in *White Noise*, his book is in many ways a compendium of cultural studies approaches, "a thesis," as Mark Osteen notes, "on the kinds and uses of intellectual, linguistic, commercial, personal, and televisual packaging" (167). If I eventually direct our discussion toward those aspects of cultural studies that DeLillo finds worthy of parody, I begin by arguing that the techniques and insights of cultural studies help DeLillo offer a nuanced analysis and interpretation of contemporary American culture. While I touch on the novel's narrative form, its postmodernism, its thematic concerns with fascism and family, and its overarching preoccupation with modern death, I focus most on how the close study of American culture's "incredible amounts of psychic data" (51) not only yields a better sense of cultural identity for the readers of *White Noise* but also awakens in us a better understanding of the ideological character of our national myths.

Ideology, myth, and hegemony are the three basic but key concepts outlined in Campbell and Kean's *American Culture Studies*, and I devote a class period to each as it is represented in the novel. In general I want my students to become familiar with the notion of myth as an attempt to confirm national attributes or qualities through stories; of ideology as those modes of perception and belief "that exist within and inform our everyday lives and connect us to power structures in the culture in ways that contribute to the sustaining of social power" (7); and of hegemony as the way in which a dominant class leads a society, often through moral, cultural, or intellectual leadership, so that a consensus is established in which all classes appear to support and subscribe to the ideologies and cultural meaning of the dominant class.

By using these terms and concepts to form an interpretation of DeLillo's novel, my students come to see that *White Noise* not only portrays a culture that has shaped their own beliefs and values but also reveals that culture to be, in James Clifford's words, "an assemblage of texts, loosely and sometimes contradictorily united" (41). If our task as American cultural studies scholars is to analyze and interpret these texts, we must also recognize our "own imbrication in white noise" (Osteen 190). Indeed, by the end of our discussion of DeLillo's novel, I hope my students have begun to see that cultural studies necessarily involves the kind of "complicitous critique" described by Linda Hutcheon in *A Politics of Postmodernism* (2) and enacted throughout DeLillo's ambivalent portrait of contemporary culture.

Myth

I usually begin any discussion of *White Noise* by locating its place in contemporary American literary history. This locating is important, because many students experience déjà vu when first encountering the book's subject matter: the heavily mediated experience of late-twentieth-century consumer culture. DeLillo's novel, published shortly after they were born, seems to the millennial generation a rehash of themes already dramatized in recent movies (*American Beauty*, *The Ice Storm*, *Fight Club*, and *Welcome to the Dollhouse* are the films that most often come up in our preliminary discussion). But it is against an American literary tradition that belatedly came to grips with the impact of mass consumer culture that *White Noise* takes on its meaning. After briefly describing the style of 1980s working-class fiction and domestic realism by authors such as Raymond Carver, Anne Tyler, and Richard Ford, I call attention to the names of towns scattered throughout DeLillo's novel, suggesting that Blacksmith, Iron Town, Glassboro, and Farmington represent an American literary landscape recently unmoored from earlier modes of production. More important, the self-conscious use of these names hints at a landscape recognized as such by its author, one understood in the text as created by large and historically grounded forces, especially those related to late capitalism. Concerned with modern life in America's postmodern consumer culture, *White Noise* characterizes that culture less by authentic production than by an endless flow of signifiers, a culture where signs often seem more real than reality.

During our first meeting, my class usually spends some time discussing DeLillo's tone and his anthropological list making; we especially consider the day of the station wagons that opens the novel. I ask my students why DeLillo chose to begin his work in this manner and have them reflect on what the list of belongings and food items in the first chapter suggests about the values and beliefs of Jack Gladney's students. What is it about these items that enables the parents to see themselves as "a collection of the like-minded and the spiritually akin, a people, a nation" (4)? How similar is the list in the novel to the ones my students could compose in describing their own recent return to campus? Finally, what do their own lists suggest about the beliefs and assumptions they may or may not be aware they possess? After discussing the opening scene at the College-on-the-Hill, we explore other instances of DeLillo's anthropological description—the scenes of "sheer plenitude" (20) of the supermarket, the mall, and the Gladney household, where the television is portrayed as an omnipresent guest or even a part of the family.

From this cursory examination of *White Noise*'s principal settings, or "power haunts" (6), I ask my students to extrapolate any myths that seem to arise. Usually they are quick to point out the "fullness of being" and the sense of "security and contentment" (20) Jack experiences whenever he shops. For a generation of students raised on television and yet deeply skeptical of the media's truth-value, the search for "peace of mind in a profit-oriented context" (87) articulates all too clearly a late-capitalist ethos equating identity and well-being with consumer goods. This impression is bolstered by DeLillo's depiction of the "New York émigrés," the College-on-the-Hill's cultural critics, whose strikingly uncritical fascination with the ephemeral artifacts of American consumerism is made most clear by Murray Siskind's remark, "I understand the music, I understand the movies, I even see how comic books can tell us things. But there are full professors in this place who read nothing but cereal boxes" (10). DeLillo's parodic description of the American Environments

Department allows students to begin discussing two important issues in the context of the novel as well as of the classroom itself: first, the commodification of higher education; second, the issue of complicity, which we return to in greater detail during our last class discussion.

Having identified the myth of self-realization through consumer culture, my students are reminded of Campbell and Kean's assertion that national myths are valuable primarily for their ability to "explain complexities and to banish contradictions, thus making the world seem simpler and more comfortable for us to inhabit" (7). Jack—and, by proxy, DeLillo—resists myths that too obviously minimize ambiguity and streamline complexity for the sake of well-being. Listening to the doomsday prophecy of the born-again Christian in the disaster shelter, for instance, Jack wonders skeptically, "Is this the point of Armageddon? No ambiguity, no more doubt" (137). Moreover, his recognition that "all plots lead to death" can be taken in part as a refusal to subsume the contradictory nature of American life into simple narratives. But if Jack resists the teleology of tabloid narratives and religious doctrine, he is more susceptible, as are the rest of DeLillo's characters, to the deeply embedded narratives of television, to its identity- and consciousness-shaping social myths. As Murray points out, television is "like a myth being born right there in our living room" (51). Its power is illustrated best in the scene when Steffie talks in her sleep, articulating a commodity-driven dreamworld by mumbling "*Toyota Celica.*" What I point to in this passage isn't so much the interpenetration of the natural language of the culture with Steffie's subconscious—that comes later—but Jack's response to the troubling phenomenon. Realizing that his daughter's dreams are the stuff of advertising slogans and product placement, Jack does not simply fail to lament his daughter's utterance; he in fact experiences it as though it were "a moment of splendid transcendence" (155). Myths aspire to such transcendence—from time, from history, from politics, from society. If time permits, I ask students to isolate more passages where such seemingly transcendent myths are born in DeLillo's fictional world.

Ideology

The next class is devoted to recognizing the ideological character of the cultural myths articulated in *White Noise*. For this discussion it is helpful to return briefly to recent American literary history, especially to the mainstream writers of the past twenty years, noting, as Frank Lentricchia has, that DeLillo's writing stands in "harsh judgment against American fiction" through its assertion that broad political and economic forces are responsible for American culture ("American Writer" 6). I also rely again on Campbell and Kean for a definition of ideology as "those modes of feeling, valuing, perceiving and believing that exist within and inform our everyday lives and connect us to wider structures of power in society in ways that contribute to the maintenance and reproduction of social power" (7). I tell my students that most of us, whether we're aware of it or not, live by a variety of ideologies, the most prominent one perhaps being liberal humanism. Through interrogating ideological myths, I explain, we can begin to discern the complex ways in which privileged groups structure, often quite unconsciously, preferred meanings to experience. *White Noise* reveals how any compelling social ideology, as Terry Eagleton points out, must engage with "deep-seated a-rational fears and needs" (20). To help make this point, I have students spend most of this class attending to "The Airborne Toxic Event."

In this section of the novel, events intrude on the members of the Gladney family in a dramatic way: they are forced to evacuate their home for nearly two weeks or risk exposure to a menacing toxic cloud. Even before they depart, however, their ideas about disastrous events have been structured by the myth-making apparatus of television. DeLillo is especially good at showing our reliance on conventionalized narratives that at first seem empty of ideological content. He portrays the victims of a potential plane crash lingering in the airport terminal to reenact their horrifying experience through a communal narrative. He describes the uneasiness felt by the family when they see Babette on television—for according to the norms of television, the familiar and the uneventful are not fodder for the medium. Yet reality and narrative rub up against each other during the airborne toxic event. Jack's insistence that disasters aren't for college professors but rather "for people who live in mobile homes out in the scrubby parts of the county, where the fish hatcheries are" (117) suggests his reliance on conventionalized narratives, as does his earlier discussion with the New York émigrés about the appeal of natural disaster footage ("We want them, we need them, we depend on them," the chair of the cultural studies department explains. "As long as they happen somewhere else" [66]). But these narratives also reveal—if not to the characters then at least to the novel's readers—the ideological alignment between the Gladney family and the medium that has structured its understanding of reality.

By turning human disasters into glitzy packages of ephemeral consumption, television obscures the actual lines of power behind such occurrences. If the airborne toxic event takes on the characteristics of a romantic revolution, releasing "a spirit of imagination in people" (153) and later producing "postmodern sunset[s], rich in romantic imagery" (227), it does so at the expense of provoking community outrage or even inquiry into the source of the problem. Heinrich's conspiracy theories may seem comic in their extremity ("If they released the true findings [of the toxic event], there'd be billions of dollars in law suits. Not to mention demonstrations, panic, violence and social disorder" [173–74]), but they do have the virtue at least of throwing into relief a narrative largely ignored by the media and those who consume it: the story of how "a whole bunch of things thrown together that are byproducts of the manufacture of insecticide" came into use in the first place (131). That such by-products usually affect "poor people who live in exposed areas" (114) is lost in the white noise of the consumer culture's dominant narrative about itself.

When this point has been made in class, I ask my students to think about other actualities mystified by the conventionalized narratives of purchase and consumption. I refer back to the names of the towns in *White Noise*, suggesting that my students try to identify where the products purchased by the Gladney family are actually manufactured. I ask what it might mean that one of Jack's former wives, a Waspish woman married to an intelligence operative, has almost the same name as a prestigious mutual-fund company (Tweedy, Browne). Is DeLillo suggesting a basic connection between government and business too often obscured in the public discourse of advertising? Our discussion of ideology usually ends with a close analysis of the final scene of "The Airborne Toxic Event." Here we see concern for social issues replaced by another, seemingly trivial preoccupation. As a final assignment for the day, I ask my students to analyze the ideological content of the nameless man's outraged speech about the scant airplay afforded the harrowing event: "There's nothing [about the event] on network. . . . Even if there hasn't been a great loss of life, don't we deserve some attention for our suffering, our human worry, our terror? Isn't fear news?" (161–62).

Hegemony

White Noise portrays a nation that embraces consensus at the expense of opposing or contestatory points of view. Tim Engles has shown how at times the novel itself seems to portray a dominant consensual narrative in which "the brief presences of racialized others can be difficult to detect" (171). But the concept of hegemony, which I initially describe to students as a master narrative told by a dominant group to justify its actions, can be brought into sharp relief through a cursory examination of the frequent allusions in *White Noise* to Hitler and Nazism. Less interested in Hitler's coercive international policy, DeLillo focuses instead on his domestic agenda, seeing in its trappings "a geometric longing, the formal notation of some powerful mass desire" (26) that has its analogs in contemporary American culture. (In his essay "Silhouette City," he describes Nazi lore as a "rich source of material to be consulted in the service of fantasy and self-fulfillment" [29].) Fascist tyranny was the most obvious result of Germany's consensual longing, and DeLillo hints throughout his novel at the United States' imperialist aspirations (e.g., most of Jack's former wives are involved in covert operations). But his primary concern is America's dreamlike rush toward consensus (the repeated references to uniforms, whether the black robes of the professoriat, the Mylex suits of the toxic waste workers, or the complex camouflage outfit that Heinrich wears, are telling here).

I ground our final discussion of *White Noise* in Campbell and Kean's definition of hegemony as the way in which a dominant class leads a society so that a consensus is established in which all classes appear to support and subscribe to its ideologies and cultural meaning (13). I begin by asking my students to identify several dominant classes or interest groups in *White Noise*. After some discussion, we usually come up with three interrelated sectors of society that could be said to be dominant: business, media, and the government. Most noticeable about the responses of DeLillo's principal characters to these three sectors is their almost total absence of skepticism. Few in the Gladney household question the presence of SIMUVAC workers or the omnipresence of television advertising. Discussing the disaster workers in Mylex suits, Babette dismisses their implicit threat—if these men need protective suits to patrol the town, everyone else probably does—by saying, "This is what they wear on duty. . . . It doesn't mean we're in danger" (173). Even more telling is Murray's response to the cultural matrix: inevitably one of celebration, of childlike wonderment. Purchasing generic products, he feels he's "not only saving money but contributing to some kind of spiritual consensus" (18). This consensus, reinforced by "marketing surveys aimed at determining current levels of consumer desire" (48), is experienced by Jack most obviously when he checks the balance of his bank account at an ATM and taps into a grid of communal belief and validation:

> The figure on the screen roughly corresponded to my independent estimate. . . . Waves of relief and gratitude flowed over me. The system had blessed my life. I felt its support and approval. . . . I sensed that something of deep personal value, but not money, not that at all, had been authenticated and confirmed. . . . The system was invisible, which made it all the more impressive, all the more disquieting to deal with. But we were in accord, at least for now. The networks, the circuits, the streams, the harmonies. (46)

If we have time, I like to discuss how DeLillo's characters experience an endless but rapid cycle of dread and relief encouraged in one form or another by consumer capitalism. "Terrifying data is now an industry in itself," Jack proclaims (175), and my students are good at noting how that dread is shown to be assuaged by shopping binges, bids for celebrity, and pornography, all of which in turn produce experiences of depletion and longing. But the crucial point of our final discussion of *White Noise* is the willing submission of DeLillo's characters to a system they dimly understand. If the characters in the novel submit to and are even grateful for this system, it is DeLillo's goal to make his readers more aware of their own willing participation in it. That is, *White Noise* not only reveals the workings of hegemony but ultimately problematizes hegemonic analysis by critics who live and work in the culture they are critiquing.

It is helpful to return to Jack Gladney's professional career for this point.

Jack's understanding of Nazi culture—summed up in a "course of study designed to cultivate historical perspective, theoretical rigor and mature insight into the continuing mass appeal of fascist tyranny" (25)—is accomplished without mastery of the language of his field of study. In some ways, his comic inability to learn German is what allows him to keep his subject of study forever exotic, at arm's length. But as American cultural studies students, we haven't this distancing effect. I hope to impress on students early in the semester how the world we see is in part a function of the language we speak. If it is possible, as Giles Gunn has asserted, for us to think and imagine against the grain of our dominant culture (1), if not entirely resisting then at least subtly altering the terms and values provided by that culture, it is nevertheless impossible to do so beyond the options provided by language itself.

This conundrum is best exemplified by Murray Siskind and the other New York émigrés, who respond "as children" (50) to American culture because they cannot extricate themselves from its natural language. While my students at times find Murray to be the novel's center of gravity, his theoretical—but ultimately uncritical—musings exempt him from this role (Murray's adjuration that "TV is a problem only if you've forgotten how to look and listen" [50] prefigures the theoretical sophistry that will eventually have him propose that Jack murder someone). DeLillo's strongest condemnation of an unreflective approach to one's culture occurs when he writes of Alfonse Stompanato, the chair of the American Environments Department, that "When he talked about popular culture, he exercised the closed logic *of a religious zealot*, one who kills for his beliefs" (65; my emphasis).

This line has interesting ramifications for our understanding of *White Noise*'s plot, of course. But as it relates to my students' beginning forays into American cultural studies, it suggests a pitfall to be avoided even as we come to realize our limitations as critics immersed in and shaped by the cultural language we wish to study. I agree with Osteen that "the most bracing feature of DeLillo's work is that he satirizes postmodern cultural forms not from some privileged position outside the culture, but from within those very forms" (3). If this strategy has led to radically differing critical interpretations of the novel, it also makes DeLillo's cultural critique more trenchant, I would argue, by suggesting ways in which aspects of American culture may be appropriated in order to critique its less desirable aspects. Ultimately, by placing in the fore the complicitous nature of life in "the networks, the circuits," *White Noise* allows for self-reflexive analysis. Calling on its readers to discriminate between a critique and a celebration of American culture, DeLillo's novel enables my students to become readers and interpreters as opposed to unreflective producers and consumers of white noise.

"Hijacked Jet Crashes into White House": Teaching *White Noise* after September 11

Margaret Scanlan

For several years, beginning in the early 1990s, I taught a course in terrorism and fiction, Dostoevsky to DeLillo, gathering material that eventually made its way into a book. Inevitably, the DeLillo novel in that course was *Mao II*, the author's most extended meditation on the kind of terrorism that leaped into the American consciousness on September 11, 2001—foreign terrorism, the invasion of New York City by aliens who master our technology in order to destroy us in the name of an apparently incomprehensible ideology. *Mao II* is about an American writer obliterated by the Islamic fundamentalists with whom he had hoped to negotiate, about his fear, and DeLillo's, that televised news of terrorist incidents is replacing the novel: "Beckett was the last writer to influence the way we think and feel. After him, all the major work is done with midair explosions" (*Mao II* 157).[1] In *Mao II*, the dominant images of fundamentalism are a hysterical mob at Khomeini's televised funeral, snatching his body away from the pallbearers, and an evangelist strongly resembling the Reverend Sun Myung Moon presiding over the mass marriages of young American women to Korean men in shiny blue suits. Terrorists and fundamentalists of the homegrown variety, Timothy McVeigh or David Koresh, the "men in small rooms" who drive DeLillo's *Libra* (181), receive the briefest of glances.

In the wake of September 11, we Americans were continuously bombarded by media narratives of Islamic fundamentalism and terrorism. To be more precise, we were told by a series of conservative authority figures, from George Will to President Bush, that September 11 was a wake-up call summoning the nation to face terrorism's reality. The reality to which we were summoned, however, proved indistinguishable from the narrative of Islamic terrorism that had been a Hollywood staple since Palestinians bombed the Super Bowl in the film *Black Sunday* (1976). In life as at the movies, innocent civilians died en masse because they were in a place that symbolized the American way of life. For Will, September 11 was "the Great Refutation" of "the notion that everything can be understood as the emanation of this or that culture, no one of which is superior to any other" ("Great Refutation"). In the bleak aftermath of the attacks, claimed Will, Americans learned that understanding does not entail forgiveness; rather, "to understand our enemies is to know they must be smashed." Freed of academic tentativeness, "the postmodern plague of quotation marks," the newly resolute American public came to understand that unflinching realism requires a huge defense budget, stricter immigration controls, and a more powerful surveillance system. Realism demands the Patriot Act, a Terrorism Information and Prevention System (TIPS), and the detention of suspected terrorists at Guantánamo Bay without the protection of either the Geneva Conventions or the United States Constitution.

In this atmosphere, and in all that will follow it, how can we still teach *White Noise*? Isn't it the archetypal postmodern novel, an exemplary text for tenured radicals who ironize everything and treat the whole world as a giant simulacrum? And isn't its underlying message that the real threat to America is our own technology, mass disaster with a corporate sponsor, a manufacturer of pesticides? If we must teach that "bad citizen" DeLillo, wouldn't it be better to assign *Mao II* or one of his several other novels that directly engage terrorism (Will, "Shallow Look")?[2] Well, perhaps. But if we do teach *White Noise*, out of something more than habit, I think we will find that the novel offers us ways of talking about anxieties that have haunted America since the attacks of September 2001. *White Noise* speaks to the terrible contradictions in a consumer culture prone to deny its connections to history, to politics, to the global community, yet driven by the fear that some external force is secretly bent on its destruction. The novel can do so, however, only if we recover its political and historical content, if we trace the links among Jack Gladney's peculiar obsession with Hitler, his preoccupation with death, and the repression of politics and history generally that the novel attributes to Americans. But first we must rethink the rather insular way this novel tends to be read, and doing so can help to highlight the affinities between *White Noise* and *Mao II*, DeLillo's most extended meditation on international terrorism.[3]

A brief lecture could characterize the role of terrorism in these novels, particularly the theme of the terrorist as the novelist's rival in *Mao II*. It would be helpful also to assign DeLillo's essay on September 11, "In the Ruins of the Future," where he reiterates his claim that "the world narrative belongs to terrorists" and goes on to explain that "parts of our world have crumbled into theirs, which means we are living in a place of danger and rage" (33). As many other observers did, he commented on the irony of the al-Qaeda members' extended stay in Florida and their participation in suburban routines. He imagines a terrorist pushing his shopping cart, glancing up at "a woman pushing a stroller." Does the terrorist see her? That he does not, writes DeLillo, is his "edge": "there is no defenseless human at the end of his gaze" (34).

This terrorist in the supermarket is no stranger to DeLillo's fictional world, where menace often lurks beneath familiar surfaces. Even in *White Noise*, where the reader never encounters a terrorist, the supermarket's bright colors and overflowing produce bins mask anxieties their customers hope to allay: "Everything was fine . . . as long as the supermarket did not slip" (170). Shoppers buy Glass Plus and generic peanut butter at the same checkout counter that stocks Babette's favorite tabloids, on whose pages Elvis lives even as Armageddon looms, and where one day she learns about trials for Dylar, the drug that prevents its users from fearing death.[4] Thus what is most superficial in their lives, the celebrity trivia and the take-out fried chicken, is a defense against something deeper, a lost sense of agency, perhaps: Jack's simple trip to the ATM is disturbed by a glimpse of "a deranged person . . . escorted from the bank by two armed guards" (46). He maxes out his credit card, intoxicated by the sense that he is discovering and expanding himself, locating "a person I'd forgotten existed" (84). By the end of the novel, we can gauge the anxiety that the supermarket is expected to assuage in the "panic . . . the aimless and haunted mood" that a rearrangement of its shelves induces (325–26). This repressed fear as an American emotion is not, of course, the same thing as experiencing political terrorism or living under the constant threat of bombs or a sniper's bullets. But it does invite us to see continuity between *White Noise* and DeLillo's more overtly political novels; furthermore, it invites us to see the repression of the political, or the historical, as a key to the novel's power. The question is not, "Why is the American consumer so dumb?," but, "What are these people afraid of seeing?"

A good entry point into discussion of the link between domestic surfaces and politics is to ask just how realistic *White Noise* is. Most students already know something about literary realism as a set of conventions, and most can tell, or work toward, the difference between documentary or statistical accuracy and the encouragement a fictional text gives us to see its characters as representative human beings in recognizable settings doing things that under the circumstances are fully believable. But the degree of realism in *White Noise* has never been easy for my students, even with this minimal sophistication, to assess. Everyone can point to objects, conversations, and situations in the novel that are familiar: Babette's gray sweatsuit, Jack's insecurity around men who know about "gaskets and washers, grouting, caulking, spackling" (245); the family meal in the kitchen, children and parents foraging the cupboards and refrigerator companionably, each finding something different in the collection of boxes, bags, and Saran-wrapped plastic. Yet, with a little prodding, the class can also identify touches of the bizarre and the improbable, the satirist's exaggerations: Steffie wondering how she will recognize her mother, Jack's department chair urging him to gain weight to ensure tenure, Murray's deadpan attribution of a shoulder separation to "an old sexual injury" (293). More perplexingly, one of the book's most realistic motifs, television as background to daily life, also invites us to confuse the Gladneys with a sitcom family. That they seem as much a unit as the Cleavers, even though Jack is not two-year-old Wilder's biological father and no two children in the family have the same set of parents, may stem from the frequency with which we see them in settings equipped with the products most widely advertised on television. Or perhaps it's the television convention of the happily blended family, like the Partridges and Bradys? The first time I taught the novel, a student argued that the scene in chapter 14 where the children assemble on Jack and Babette's bed is especially lifelike and then caught herself citing an episode of the *Cosby Show* as evidence. Toward the end of the book, when Jack starts giving away his possessions, we were all torn between the view that he is acting suicidal and the view that he is acting out the signs of suicide as described by every school counselor ever interviewed on television.

Once students realize how vexed the question of realism is in *White Noise*, they are prepared to look at the novel's America as a deliberately fictional construction. It is helpful at this point to talk a bit about the decidedly different settings of *Mao II* and *White Noise* so that everyone understands that DeLillo does not take Blacksmith for America, although many of the characters in *White Noise* do. We constantly hear Jack and Murray go on as if the supermarket, television, and the tabloids constitute the American consciousness, with Nyodene derivative the unintended by-product of our ingenious efforts to replace nature with technology. The novel constructs a compelling version of America, but how does this fictional world compare with ours? Is the America where wives teach classes in sitting and walking, or where children spend school holidays flying back and forth between parents in Indonesia and London, in some sense the ultimate America, the one toward which even the bagger at the supermarket is moving? My South Bend students, for whom Iron City is more familiar than Blacksmith, can be counted on to object whenever a writer seems to take an upper-middle-class ambience as the American norm. But if they accept Iron City and Babette's handyman father as evidence that *White Noise* acknowledges the existence of working-class America, then they are ready to ask why DeLillo chooses to focus on the upper middle class. Is upper-middle-class ambience as close as real life comes to the idealized consumer world of situation comedy and the television commercial? Surely an America with Dristan and Glass Plus but no president, weather forecasters but no one watching for an economic collapse that might cost millions of jobs, is not the world we all live in. But an America where politics is about image, where a presidential spokesperson compares his boss selling a war with a car salesman introducing a new model line, is all too familiar.[5] After the corporate scandals of 2002 and 2003—World Com, ImClone, Martha Stewart under indictment—and to students who have seen Alex Gibney's *Enron: The Smartest Guys in the Room* (2005), the vision of the large American corporation as a flimflam scheme, of computers generating electronic deposits of money for which there is no corresponding product but only speculation and hype, is almost too obvious.

The whiteness of *White Noise* is equally problematic. Where in contemporary America can one find a college with no African American students, no Asian American faculty members? Is the typical Euro-American college professor as clueless about the origins of his non-Anglo-Saxon neighbors as Jack is? For Jack, his son's best friend, Orest, "might have been Hispanic, Middle Eastern, Central Asian, a dark-skinned European, a light-skinned black. . . . Was he a Samoan, a native North American, a Sephardic Jew?" (208). Chun Doc, the "Asian baby" whose adoptive mother the Gladneys meet at the supermarket, is equally mysterious: "Everyone referred to the baby by name, almost in a tone of proud proprietorship, but no one knew who Chun belonged to or where he or she had come from" (39). Is America's biggest racial problem that white college professors worry that it's "hard to know what you [can't] say to people" (208)? This line of questioning may prompt some students to argue that colleges remain in thrall to the Anglo-Saxon heritage. Even if students do not, the instructor can refer back to the previous discussion of DeLillo's America and ask why in this novel DeLillo chose to depict an America without the vital ethnic communities where many of them grew up. Because they are disappearing? Because television advertising doesn't target Guatemalan or Hmong communities? Because the author is interested in the disappearance of history and the repression of difference it requires?

For students who crave simple realism, the discovery that the novel's America is more unlike their own than they first thought can become an excuse to dismiss the novel. For this reason, the point needs to be made, though obvious to others, that *White Noise*'s America is a meaningful, critical construction. Since the author wishes us to see the denial of history, the transformation of what actually happens into an attractive myth, as a key feature of American life, we need to pay close attention to the one public historical figure the novel considers: Adolf Hitler or, rather, the construction Murray calls "Gladney's Hitler" (11). Even students whose knowledge of the Third Reich is derived from popular entertainment can quickly see how ahistorical this Hitler is. He's powerful and demonic but never explicitly connected with World War II or the Holocaust. Gladney's Hitler is all Nuremberg and no Stalingrad, "with special emphasis on parades, rallies, and uniforms" (25). What is his appeal to Jack? Why does Jack carry his dog-eared copy of *Mein Kampf* around like a security blanket? What evidence is there for Murray's argument late in the novel that Jack used Hitler to protect himself from knowledge of his own death but failed because he also wanted to use him to "grow in significance and strength" (287)? Do some Americans share Jack's view of Hitler? And what should we make of chapter 15, one of the book's major tours de force, in which Murray and Jack lecture contrapuntally on Elvis and Hitler? What possible set of values leads one to see the King and the Führer as comparable?

To begin with the obvious, the perspective from which Hitler and Elvis resemble each other is indelibly American; one can hardly imagine a Czech or a Pole entertaining it. One might add, as examples of that perspective, the distinctively American versions of Bible stories or American quasi-historical myths that have European roots. In an American literature course one might already have talked about R. W. B. Lewis's American Adam or about the adaptation of the Exodus story to the African American experience. In a genre course, one might point to the myth of the Kennedy White House as Camelot. Since Americans fought in World War II, it is hardly surprising that we have developed our own distinctive accounts of Hitler, the Nazi Party, and the fall of Berlin. But the Holocaust has a special place, since it destroyed or dispersed most of the European Jewish population against which it was directed and since the United States, along with Israel, became the survivors' new home.

Although we often claim to be shocked by our students' ignorance of history, most know more about the final solution than about any other event of World War II. In Indiana high schools at least, Anne Frank's diary is the most widely taught text of the era. Films from *Schindler's List* (1993) to *Life Is Beautiful* (1998) to *The Pianist* (2002) similarly perpetuate a popular consciousness of the Holocaust. To add a more critical edge, one can refer to the general arguments made in Hilene Flanzbaum's *The Americanization of the Holocaust* and Tim Cole's *Selling the Holocaust: From Auschwitz to Schindler, How History Is Bought, Packaged, and Sold* (see also Novick; Finkelstein). These scholars point to tensions between the Holocaust as an event in European history and the Holocaust as it has been reconstructed in popular American books, films, museums, and memorials. Flanzbaum and Cole both identify distortions that result not only from factual errors but also from the imposition of American conventions, such as emphasizing the survival of a small group of valued characters to produce a happy ending. Bruno Bettelheim's widely anthologized "The Ignored Lesson of Anne Frank" is also a good resource. His criticisms of the popular dramatic version of the diary, and more generally of the American public's enthusiasm for the Franks as representative Holocaust victims, underscore how emphasizing one authentic text at the expense of others produces distortion. We can certainly find more positive reasons than Bettelheim does for the popularity of Anne's diary, but his point seems incontrovertible that its domesticity and inevitable restriction to her innocent, pre-Auschwitz perspective make it congenial to American values. A discussion could follow of how one might define a distinctively American view of the Holocaust and of how films like *Schindler's List* and *Life Is Beautiful* both amplify what one learns from Anne Frank and ratify her innocent perspective. What do American universities, which have institutionalized Holocaust studies, do to challenge such popular histories?[6]

Hitler studies in *White Noise* is an anti–Holocaust studies, a memorialization of the killers and their survival in our popular culture and political imagination. "We couldn't have television without [Hitler]," as Jack tells Denise (63). Hitler studies can be mastered by an American professor who neither reads nor speaks German, because some part of Hitler has become American. The cult of the celebrity dead; the sense that life is defined by images and style, by aesthetic rather than political or moral choices; the appreciation of disaster and violence as satisfying spectacles—these have all become as American as, well, cinematic car crashes. Hitler studies as Jack teaches it doesn't lead to quarrels over evidence or passionate debates about the connection between daily life and historic massacres; it leads to the crowd, to nostalgia for a power so absolute that it shields us from death. DeLillo's question in a 1989 essay, "Is there something missing from your life which the imagination of the Nazis can helpfully provide?" is, of course, rhetorical ("Silhouette City" 345).

Once we've established the centrality of Hitler studies and the notion of a

Nazi imagination to *White Noise*, we are prepared to consider how the novel alludes to other political and historical issues, even as television, the mall, and the supermarket offer powerful distractions from them. Again, the way to unearth such references, which few students will identify in a first reading, is to connect them to that sense of nameless lurking disaster that characterizes the novel long before the toxic cloud is airborne. One technique I've found helpful is asking students to get in small groups, each assigned some section of the text, and flip through it backward, looking for allusions to the international scene, to history or politics or violent death. Then we make a random list, which might include:

> Heinrich's mother lives in an ashram now. She has taken the name Mother Devi. . . . The usual rumors abound of sexual freedom, sexual slavery . . . mind control . . . monkey-worship, torture, prolonged and hideous death. (25)
>
> airline bag with a handgun and two kilos of uncut heroin (60)
>
> closed logic of a religious zealot . . . who kills for his beliefs (65)
>
> Malcolm and I once took tea with Colonel Qaddafi. A charming and ruthless man, one of the few terrorists we've met who lives up to his public billing. (88)
>
> they didn't prepare us for this at the death simulator in Denver (90)
>
> Barring mechanical failures, turbulent weather and terrorist acts . . . an aircraft traveling at the speed of sound may be the last refuge of gracious living and civilized manners known to man. (93)
>
> Is this the point of Armageddon? No ambiguity, no more doubt. (137)
>
> Members of an air-crash cult will hijack a jumbo jet and crash it into the White House in an act of blind devotion to their mysterious and reclusive leader. . . . (146)
>
> no more bodies had been found (222)
>
> Officer Walker, a Vietnam vet, said the bizarre scene reminded him of helicopter crews throwing Vietcong suspects out the door. (234)
>
> Most people don't burn to death. . . . They die of smoke inhalation. (239)

Once we've discussed the connections of these passages to politicized terror, we need to ask how DeLillo manages to smuggle so many references to terrorism into a novel that takes place mostly at home, the supermarket, and the mall. One answer is that such remarks float through the air, random utterances from a television set that seems always to be on, even when it isn't being watched. Another is that some are lines from the tabloids that Babette reads to the blind. Another is that several are associated with Jack's ex-wives, all of whom had "ties to the intelligence community" (6), a bizarre and improbable fact that seems linked to his need for Babette's homelier comforts. Another is that such images frequently pop up in the novel's metaphors, where the most mundane tasks merit desperate analogies, where Steffie, lining wicker baskets with small plastic bags, assumes "the quiet and conscientious air of someone who does not want credit for saving lives" (101). And some of them come out of the characters' fears—for example, Babette's fear that Heinrich "will end up in a barricaded room, spraying hundreds of rounds of automatic fire across an empty mall before the SWAT teams come for him with their heavy-barreled weapons, their bullhorns and body armor" (22). By now, we may not even need to point out how those fears have been given shape by mass journalism.

This exercise reminds students how much of a novel's meaning eludes a simple summary of its plot and setting. It provides a window into the issues that Jack and Babette are suppressing every time they go shopping, confirming that they really are as frightened of death and disaster as they tell each other they are. And because all these allusions point to something familiar, the tabloid headline or the *Dateline* special report, they lead us to reflect on how our daily lives are marked if not shaped by the background of doom and disaster that the news provides. Given how the September 11 attacks shocked all of us and apparently caught the CIA, FBI, and United States military unprepared, what should we make of DeLillo's parody of a tabloid prediction of suicidal pilots crashing a jet into the White House? I would ask students if they can think of other references from literature or popular culture that seem to predict September 11. Some will know the album cover that the hip-hop group Coup selected months before September 11, an image of the World Trade Center exploding that is uncannily similar to photographs of the subsequent attack (Glasner). A discussion is sure to produce other examples, including a whole list of disaster movies of the last fifteen years in which Los Angeles, New York, and Washington, DC, have repeatedly been firebombed, flooded, and destroyed by aliens and runaway asteroids. What, one might ask, can we make of this eerie similarity between imagined scenes and the historical events of September 11?[7]

Popular culture often poses such questions, leaving them half answered but suggesting that God or an occult force provides messages for us to read, not only in the stars and Nostradamus but also in rock lyrics and coincidences. An instructor could develop some alternative analyses by summarizing responses to September 11 by two European theorists, Jean Baudrillard and Slavoj Žižek, who both stressed the parallels between the terrorist acts and the apocalyptic vein in American culture that DeLillo examines in *White Noise*. For Žižek, the nearly universal response that the broadcast images of planes crashing into the World Trade Center looked like a scene from a movie proved the extent to which our reality has become "virtualized." We long for a "return to the Real," but "The Real which returns has the status of a(nother)semblance: *precisely because it is real, that is, on account of its traumatic/excessive character, we are unable to integrate it into (what we experience as) our reality, and are therefore compelled to experience it as a nightmarish apparition*" (*Welcome* 19). Students who have heard Jack complaining to Murray that "there's something artificial about my death" will recognize the move (283).

Baudrillard, on the other hand, managed to enrage many readers with his comment that the attacks represented the fulfillment of a collective wish: "they [the terrorists] *did it*, but we wished for it" (*Spirit* 5). Would it be reasonable to assume that Coup wanted the World Trade Center to go up in flames? That the moviegoers who flocked to *Deep Impact* and *Armageddon* wanted to see an asteroid crash into the Eiffel Tower? Can we believe that the Gladneys, gathered around the TV watching "whole villages crackle and ignite in a mass of advancing lava," want a volcano to erupt in Montserrat (64)? I try to elicit a range of opinions rather than a simple no. Some students will think that hip-hop promotes the destruction of mainstream American culture. But recognition should follow of the difference between wanting these disasters in the abstract and welcoming them in reality and of the complex interchange between our fears and our desires. If someone argues that the movies are just entertainment or, as Peter Murphy puts it in a response to Žižek, that "everybody over six knows the difference between movies and real life," Žižek's rejoinder is helpful: "the most elementary paradox of the psychoanalytic notion of fantasy [is that] the greatest shock is when that which we were fantasizing about effectively takes place" ("Slavoj Žižek").

This line of reasoning should allow everyone to make the transition from analyzing references to popular culture in *White Noise* to analyzing the novel's own apocalyptic set piece, the airborne toxic event. I talk about how DeLillo himself makes the transition from the familiar materials of domestic fiction to this unexpected disaster. After showing how the work we've done on the novel's allusions to violence, terror, and death reveals this unforeseen contingency as a visible embodiment of the culture's ill-suppressed fears, I shift discussion to what happens after the event. What's important about the failure of the national media to carry the story? Why does Jack simultaneously seek out monthly checkups and lie to the doctor about his exposure to Nyodene D? In what ways do coping mechanisms, such as going to the supermarket, break down? And what connection do we find between the disaster and Jack's one act of violence, the shooting of Willie Mink?

When the class has thought about how DeLillo links the novel's domestic and academic scenes to the toxic cloud and to Jack's confrontation with Willie, they might discuss the ways they and the culture around them have responded to, absorbed, or evaded the September 11 attacks, the anthrax deaths, and the prospect of similar terrorist acts in the United States. Again, the point is to encourage them to read *White Noise* as, at least in part, a work of cultural criticism, which they can compare with their own experiences. There are obvious differences: the saturation television coverage of September 11; the danger coming not from foreign terrorists but from a toxic by-product of American manufacture. But similar themes emerge: the strong suspicion that the weaponized anthrax was made at Iowa State, the Bush administration's advice to the American people to go shopping as a way of combating terrorism, the urge to kill as a reflex of self-defense that we find in some of the more violent vows of revenge. The novel certainly does not tell us what to do about al-Qaeda, but does it tell us anything valuable about how we coped with color-coded terrorism alerts or the movement of United States troops to Afghanistan and Iraq? There is no single answer to such questions, but at this point students should be able to talk about how we integrate a violent political reality with daily life in a domestic or academic setting.

I would give Murray the last word. This character has always frustrated and puzzled me, since I can see defending him as the novel's *raisonneur* while also conceding that there's much to be said for John Duvall's argument that Murray is its "true villain," who "encourages and fosters the worst in Jack" ("[Super] Marketplace" 443). In this blandly Anglo-Saxon world, he is the one character seen at any length who is definitely marked by ethnicity, as if to play in the novel the same role he plays in his rooming house where, as puts it, "I'm the Jew" (10).[8] How does someone who labels himself as the Jew fit into the novel that gives us Hitler studies, and what could it possibly mean for him to be its villain? I cringe from asking this sort of question in the classroom, wanting neither to face a repetition of the occasional anti-Semitic response I've got to similar questions in the past nor to put the few Jewish students in my class on the spot. These are deep waters, but we cannot do the novel justice without wading into them. Is Murray the outsider? the perennial critic? someone so assimilated that he really does think of Hitler and Elvis as comparable figures? On the other hand, if in some sense he is Jack's enemy, may he not have reason to be? At any rate, this uncomfortable character makes a comment linking war to nostalgia that, in the light of the celebrations of old-fashioned patriotism that followed September 11, is one of the novel's most unsettling observations. Murray and Jack are discussing nostalgia, as they often do, but for once specifically in the context of Hitler studies. Having described Albert Speer's plans to build structures that "would decay gloriously, like Roman ruins," Jack notes a "certain nostalgia behind the power principle, or a tendency to organize the longings of future generations" (258). Class discussion will have touched on nostalgia already, but if the point has not been made, we should distinguish it from history, much as we have distinguished Hitler studies from Holocaust studies. In daily speech, nostalgia is usually a harmless sentiment, and we can provide some examples of that evocation in the text; the New York émigré's obsession with childhood, Jack's pleasure in old black-

and-white family photos, the "beamish old folks in hand-knit sweaters" chatting with their daughters-in-law in some undefined space between Blacksmith and a telephone company commercial (272). But what might make nostalgia more problematic? What must we suppress about the past in order to enjoy nostalgia? When Murray says, "The more powerful the nostalgia, the closer you come to violence. . . . War is the form nostalgia takes when men are hard-pressed to say something good about their country" (258), is he on to something?

Some students may sense a connection between late-twentieth-century celebrations of the moral clarity of the "last just war" and the flag-waving that followed September 11. They may find a nostalgia for 1941 in the analogy made between Pearl Harbor and the September attacks or in the expansion of the war on terror to Iraq. But other students have every right to argue that the parallel between Pearl Harbor and September 11 is compelling and that Murray is too willing to distance himself from Jack's exposure to Nyodene D, that Murray is the academic who sits on the sidelines talking about ideas when the world needs action.

If the discussion is sufficiently intense, it will demonstrate that the apparently free-floating anxieties of *White Noise* have roots not only in such timeless constructs as the human condition but also in the history and politics of late-twentieth-century America. Students will understand that the juxtaposition of the supermarket and the fear of death, or of family rituals and a television set constantly issuing reminders of disaster and violence, is as significant in their world as it is in DeLillo's fictional America. Commentators on both the left and right have marked September 11 as the date when Americans realized that their economic dominance and cultural visibility meant they were "directly involved" in global antagonisms from which they had felt "exempt" (Žižek, *Welcome* 49). For Baudrillard, September 11 tells us:

> [T]errorism . . . is everywhere. . . . It is at the very heart of this culture which combats it, and the visible fracture (and the hatred) that pits the exploited and the underdeveloped globally against the Western world secretly connects with the fracture internal to the dominant system.
> (*Spirit* 10)

White Noise does not anticipate September 11, but "the unreliable menace" it locates at the domestic heart of America (184) suggests that the terrorist attacks were the realization of a nightmare that had lurked in it for decades.

NOTES

[1]In a 1993 interview with Maria Nadotti, DeLillo mused, "The news is fiction, the news is the new narrative–particularly the dark news. . . . I think that from this kind

of news people find a kind of narrative with a tragic stamp which in another time they found in fiction" (92).

[2]Will famously accused DeLillo of "bad citizenship."

[3]We should also teach these sensitive issues with a good deal of mindfulness to the political and emotional differences among our students. If we want students to pay closer attention to texts and events, we must persuade them that we too listen, are shaken by major catastrophes, and can criticize our own premises as well as other people's. We need to be up-front about our questions and hesitations and willing to keep the classroom open to views we dislike. There are no perfect formulas for this complex negotiation. I suggest trying to build a mutually sympathetic and respectful relationship with students before challenging their politics. Small-group work gets the teacher out of the spotlight and helps students work out conflicts and defuse the sense that the instructor is overly invested in one response. I try to keep in mind that, to paraphrase E. M. Forster, a good book interrogates us as much as we interrogate it (see *Passage* 245). While we all retain the right to judge whether *White Noise* gets America wrong, we will learn more if we first let the novel ask us what our own blind spots are.

[4]Or as Babette puts it later, "It is all a corporate tie-in. . . . The sunscreen, the marketing, the fear, the disease. You can't have one without the other" (264).

[5]"From a marketing point of view, you don't introduce new products in August" was in White House Chief of Staff Andrew Card's statement on the timing of George Bush's campaign for United States military intervention in Iraq, quoted by Democratic Leader Tom Daschle in a speech on the Senate floor ("Text").

[6]Students unfamiliar with Holocaust studies may need to be told about such things as the Yale oral history project or the intense debate over Daniel Goldhagen's *Hitler's Willing Executioners*. That is, they need to understand the scrupulous care required to create an archive of what memories and information survived the Nazis. They need to see how difficult it is to interpret the motives of historical figures; to see the questions of evidence that come up when one tries to make an argument for or against the view that ordinary Germans collaborated in the Holocaust; to see at least part of what is at stake in Goldhagen's argument that millions of Germans actively participated, without apparent qualms, in the persecution of Jews, which took place not only in concentration camps and Polish ghettos but also on German streets and in German schools and was integral to everyday activities such as buying groceries or riding trams. For more information about the Fortunoff Video Archive for Holocaust Testimonies, see www.library.yale.edu/testimonies/about/index.htm. Started in 1979 by a grassroots organization to preserve the testimony of eyewitnesses to the Holocaust, the collection now holds over 10,000 hours of videotaped testimony by more than 4,100 survivors.

[7]Harry Youtt points to a number of such apparent premonitions in popular culture. In one particularly striking example, he notes that *Microsoft Flight Simulator* opens with dialogue in which a flight instructor jokes about how "it would be cool" to fly a plane into the Empire State Building. After September 11, the company removed the phrase from future editions, along with images of the Twin Towers. Owners of previous editions could download a free patch at the company's Web site that would allow them to delete the World Trade Center from their games.

[8]The point is made again when Vernon, Babette's working-class father, arrives for a visit. Jack explains that one of his friends believes that people go on vacation "to escape the death that exists in routine things." "What is he, a Jew?" Vernon asks (248).

No One Sees the Camps: Hitler and Humor in *White Noise*

Paul Young

White Noise still makes me laugh—out loud—even though I've read it at least seven times in twice as many years. It's unlikely that many people who think highly enough of DeLillo's novel to teach it would challenge my amusement, but my freshmen and sophomores, bless them, sometimes have a hard time finding anything funny about the book. Some don't recognize that DeLillo is engaging in satire—a mode of humor they tend to find wanting unless it elbows them rather harshly. Granted, his prose doesn't cut this group much slack. His alternately flowing and telegraphic style, which exudes such profundity in a work like *Libra*, makes it almost impossible for him *not* to tell a joke with a straight face. In addition, students are reading a satire aimed not so much at them as at the very academics who teach it. We are the Jacks and Babettes to their eye-rolling Gladney brood; they are the postmodern kids who, like Steffie and her half siblings and stepsiblings, have grown up navigating an ionosphere of televisual and digital signifiers that is as real to them as any reality they could name.

Though they don't initially recognize their own precociousness and media savvy in these aging children, students warm quickly to the satire of suburban home life when asked to compare their childhood experience of TV watching and pretending not to hear smoke alarms with how the Gladney family alternately distrusts and clings to the technologies that engulf them. After I hit (accidentally) on the idea of inviting such comparisons, I began to teach the hyperbolic humor of *White Noise* directly, as DeLillo's way of drawing readers' attention to their own quotidian acts of absurdity. This approach gives students license to enjoy the book instead of complaining about how unlikely the characters' behavior seems.

But before we get very far with the satire question, DeLillo challenges our desire to laugh by introducing, in the role of Jack's unattainable idol, the unfunniest showman of the twentieth century: Adolf Hitler. Students can be excused for finding little to laugh at—let alone sympathize with—about a protagonist who uses Hitler to make his academic reputation. Paul Cantor's essay "Adolf, We Hardly Knew You" goes a long way toward redeeming DeLillo's Hitlerian imagination for an ethical critique of postmodernity, but students still have more than reasonable questions about the appropriateness of the subject matter. I believe that focusing on DeLillo's humor means confronting those questions directly, and this focusing can be done only if we invite students to stare Hitler in the face with a directness that Jack can never muster. In Jack's struggle to repress any but the barest acknowledgment of Hitler's crimes, the same crimes that give the twenty-first century no option but to remember Hitler, lies what I'll call, for want of a better name, Hitler humor, an evolving tradition of undercutting the Führer and his followers. This humor must be contextualized if the full impact of Hitler's legacy on *White Noise*'s uniquely postmodernist satire is to be understood.

The logic of Jack's exploitation of Hitler, and of his lack of concern with the Holocaust, plays off Hitler humor in a particularly self-conscious way. The tradition of this humor goes back at least to Bertolt Brecht's 1941 play *The Resistible Rise of Arturo Ui*, in which Brecht recasts Hitler as a petty gangster who establishes a "cauliflower trust" over Chicago's greengrocers, and Charlie Chaplin's film *The Great Dictator* (1940), a fantasy about a Jewish barber who bears an uncanny resemblance to Adenoid Hynkel, the fascist leader of Tomania, and infiltrates Hynkel's regime in order to warn the world. As Theodor Adorno argued to devastating effect in his 1962 essay "Commitment," this brand of humor denies the most visceral signified of the signifier "Hitler" and the closest thing there is to a referent for this despicable sign: Hitler's murderous cruelty and violence.

Adorno chastised both Brecht and Chaplin for portraying Hitler as a mere gangster or bumpkin and for suggesting that these representations constituted an adequate critique of absolute fascism.

> Against every dialectic, the ridicule to which Ui is consigned renders innocuous the fascism that was accurately predicted by Jack London decades before. . . . *The Great Dictator* loses all satirical force and becomes obscene when a Jewish girl can hit a line of storm-troopers on the head with a pan without being torn to pieces. For the sake of political commitment, political reality is trivialized; which then reduces the political effect. (184–85)

(One wonders how Adorno would have reacted to the very idea of the film *Life Is Beautiful* [1997], in which the director and star Roberto Benigni uses comic pranks to reasssemble his son's perception of life in a concentration camp into an elaborate game of make-believe.) Adorno argued that human atrocity on the Hitlerian scale can be expressed adequately in art only by the negation of that atrocity. Hitler and his thousands of accomplices left wounds in the sensibilities of the postwar world, wounds so gaping that a return to beauty or a literal representation of suffering could never suture them shut. Instead, a work of art must remove any trace of what caused these wounds while continually recognizing and examining them with such formalist means as those employed by Franz Kafka before the war or Samuel Beckett afterward. Only by conspicuously absenting both the atrocities of the war and the humanist faith in the essential goodness of humankind represented by beauty in art can the wounds themselves be confronted, fully and honestly, as the monumental loss they forever represent.

I ask students to consider whether Adorno's criticism of Chaplin and Brecht applies to *White Noise*. One possible answer is that DeLillo indeed obeys Adorno's warning against representing the Holocaust. That Jack ignores the Holocaust altogether in his lessons and conversations about Hitler invites the reader to wonder at its absence. I try not to begin on this point, however, because negative dialectics make better conclusions than tools for investigation, at least where undergraduates are concerned. A good way to move the discussion in that direction is to draw attention to the parallels the novel draws between the simulacral logic of Jack's existence and the "society of the spectacle" (to borrow Guy Debord's term) that Hitler made of Germany. By enlisting Hitler as the patron devil of *White Noise*, DeLillo makes it possible for us to consider that postmodernism's victory over the sign has much in common with Hitler's triumph over empirical reason, in that both Hitler and postmodernist consumer culture unhook signifiers from their historical contexts and discard that core of material history like so many fruit pits. Hitler managed to prettify mass murder by pitching it as a necessity for the collective good—of gentile Germans. To paraphrase Murray Jay Suskind's advice to Jack on becoming a killer instead of a dier, the Germans fell into line behind a singularly objectifying and mythifying policy: Better them than us.

A relatively painless next step to take toward uncovering *White Noise*'s place in this discourse is to delve into the connection between semiotic violence and the novel's obsession with death. The novel's particular brand of gallows humor—best exemplified by the "Better you than me" theme, in which people regard the deaths of others as a spectator sport that allows them to savor their own survival—comes to light when Jack's family gets engrossed one Friday evening in watching televised disasters. To Jack's remark that people like his family can't get enough video footage of anonymous victims running from earthquakes and mud slides, Alfonse Stompanato, chair of College-on-the-Hill's American Environments Department, responds, "We need an occasional catastrophe to break up the bombardment of information" (65). Rather than take the typical Pavlovian swipe at media violence and its numbing effects, Alfonse offers us the much more insidious idea that people's fascination with the misfortune of others is less prurient than it is simply self-interested: the significance of the violence they view begins and ends with its value to them as a remedy for information overload.

With Alfonse's remark, DeLillo begins to develop the idea that the characters suffer more profoundly from violence done to the relation between sign and referent, in Ferdinand de Saussure's sense, than from watching violence in itself. The nameless, foreign subjects who withstand TV disasters are to Jack just victims who live elsewhere than Blacksmith—a subspecies of empty signifieds to whom avalanches and mud slides happen—whereas he feels that because he's the "head of a[n academic] department," he can't possibly have to evacuate his home when the novel's central, man-made disaster strikes. Evacuation is "for people who live in mobile homes out in the scrubby parts of the country, where the fish hatcheries are" (115).

It makes perfect sense to say about this hilarious moment of denial that Jack has begun to view even his physical surroundings as if they were part of a television show, a National Geographic special that he ought to be allowed simply to observe from the safety of his recliner. But here I would stress that, in keeping with the spirit of Alfonse's assessment, Jack's incredulity at this most inappropriate disaster indicates how completely Jack has come to see actual events less as moments of material history than as signs that exist for him and him alone, to interpret as he sees fit. TV and radio's transformation of real tragedies into docudramas has made him indifferent to even the most urgent, most immediate physical referents, including the descending chemical mist that may soon cloud his eyes, invade his lungs, attack his pores. His tendency to cast others as characters who perform for his detached eye may boomerang on him and damage his own body—a possibility that becomes a probability when he exits his station wagon to pump gas, thereby exposing himself to the Nyodene D cloud and catalyzing the events of part 3 of the novel.

To explain why fleshly human beings take up so little space in Jack's empathetic imagination (if he still has an imagination that supports empathy), it helps to focus more generally on the disappearance of referents from *White Noise*'s semiotic universe. An effective way to do this is to use Jack and Murray's visit to the Most Photographed Barn in America as the anchor for the discussion. While they watch tourists snap photos of the barn, Murray, ever the Baudrillardian semiotician, tells Jack, "No one sees the barn. . . . They are taking pictures of taking pictures" (12). To paraphrase Roland Barthes's "The Photographic Message," a photograph, when understood as a sign among other signs rather than the purely indexical sign it pretends to be, refers to a highly structured signified—an idea or attitude about the referent being photographed—that denotes this referent only in the most equivocal and connotative way. The barn's use value as a tourist attraction helps demonstrate the slippage between index and referent here. Since the tourists do nothing with or to the barn except take pictures of it, it no longer functions the way barns have traditionally functioned (to store straw, to pen horses, etc.). Instead, it has accrued a new signified that takes precedence over its past functions: if every photo of the barn is, as far as its consumers are concerned, nothing more nor less than a photo of the Most Photographed Barn in America, then for all intents and purposes there is no longer a barn where the barn sits but only the Most Photographed Barn in America—an object the collective perception (and thus, epistemologically speaking, the existence) of which depends solely on the snapshots and postcards that circulate its image.

It's difficult not to imagine DeLillo sneaking peeks at Jean Baudrillard's theories of the simulacrum while writing this scene. In fact, where I used to introduce *White Noise* with a few pages from one of Baudrillard's best-known essays, now I let the barn do all the talking. Two pages on the barn and the plethora of further examples throughout *White Noise* suffice to impress on undergraduates the transformation of the simulacrum into the only world in which Westerners fully live. To sum up (and it's important to review the point, since not every undergraduate has seen *The Matrix* recently): What it means to say that no one sees the barn is that, to the perception of its visitors, there's no longer a historical, material barn there at all. The precession of simulacra has outstripped it.

The flexible relation between the subjects who snap photos of the barn and a barn as material object presents a lens through which to view other narcissistic interpretations of material events in the book. That lens helps students grasp the implications of perceiving TV disaster victims as Disaster Victims, signifiers of Disaster rather than suffering human beings, and letting that mode of perception bleed into one's perception of others in the physical world. The novel's most chilling joke on the simulacrum comes when the town's insane asylum—so called because the citizens of Blacksmith agree that it looks like an insane asylum rather than a mental hospital—catches fire. Jack and Heinrich experience the fire not as a tragic event that gives them an opportunity to perform some civic duty but as a male bonding ritual. Watching the firefighters and victims dash about before the blaze awakens feelings of "appreciation" in them, particularly when a burning woman in a white gown literally explodes in flames: "How powerful and real," Jack intones (239). Father and son may as well be performance art spectators, grateful patrons who glean from this feat of human immolation only what the show means to them: what Barthes might call its *fireness*, something you can "look and look" at, Heinrich says, "just like a fire in a fireplace." But when an "acrid" smell hits the nostrils of the appreciative crowd, they "feel betrayed." Clearly it is the material reality of the fire that betrays them here, but DeLillo leaves it intriguingly uncertain what, exactly, the "burning material" they smell might be. Jack guesses that some kind of insulation has caught fire and speculates that the spectators feel betrayed because they've "been forced to recognize the existence of a second kind of death. One was real, the other synthetic" (240). Considering how unreal reality has become for these people, however, I can't help but wonder whether Jack calls this smell "synthetic" only because he cannot (or cannot allow himself to) recognize the horrifying stench of the real, and by "the real" I mean burning flesh. The crowd came not to watch a fire with material effects, functions, and consequences, or to help the injured, or to protest the poor safety record of the hospital, but to watch it the way they watch TV. The smell sends the crowd home, disappointed that their enjoyment of someone else's mortality has not, in the end, allowed them to deny their own.

To make matters worse for our opinion of Jack, he does exactly the same thing with his personal icon. He exploits Hitler as his personal blank signifier, which he fills up with what Hitler means to him. In this, Jack relates to his mass-murdering meal ticket both as empty signifier and as role model, his mentor in doing violence to the signifier. Hitler manipulated signifiers to eliminate the human referent from the discourse of genocide. He made himself a media star with the help of Joseph Goebbels and of course Leni Riefenstahl's staged documentary *Triumph of the Will* (1934), in which Hitler appeared as the beloved subject of Germany's collective, hungry gaze on the rest of the world, a living signifier for the reunification of Germany and for an exclusively Aryan future. He also sponsored the architectural designs of Albert Speer, some of which were intended (had they seen fruition) to crumble and become signifiers not of a real Nazi regime but of Germany as a reincarnation of ancient Rome, complete with majestic and mythical ruins—as Jack himself notes (246).

Murray's statement to Jack during their final encounter, as they discuss Jack's (apparently) impending death from exposure to Nyodene D, solidifies the connection between, on the one hand, Jack's desire to ignore the traditional signifieds and referents of everything from household smoke alarms to fire victims and, on the other, the disappearing bodies that populate his televisual and live-and-in-person disaster shows: "Better you than me" (293). This remark drives home the idea that, for Jack, Murray, probably Babette, and likely the entire America of *White Noise*, the death of another human being functions as a guarantee that you are not the one dying. No death but your own, in the novel's only slightly twisted universe, has any irreducible meaning; others' deaths are meant to be exploited for your emotional, psychological, or authoritarian benefit, to aid in, and signify, your survival.

By having Jack and Murray superimpose Hitler onto Elvis during their joint lecture, as if Hitler were merely a star like Elvis, or Elvis a world-historical figure like Hitler (70–74), DeLillo makes clear the absurd results of emptying the dead of their histories and filling them with whatever self-serving fodder one chooses. One gets the impression that the barest mention of the Holocaust at a moment like this would kill Jack's hero-worshipping buzz; indeed, by allowing his characters to nod significantly over the coincidences that link the Führer to the King during this dialogue, DeLillo makes it impossible for us not to notice the absence of the Holocaust from this discussion. By getting inside Hitler's head, exploring the dictator's exploitation of himself as a signifier for whatever signified he chose, Jack can dismiss the finite existence of Jack Gladney: he can identify with, even use (as Murray notes with some admiration [274]), the twentieth century's most reviled killer to bolster himself. He can thus avoid becoming what Murray calls a "dier"—someone who, by falling victim to a killer, loses all meaning and instead merely confirms the vitality of the person doing the killing. Following this cracked logic, what better way to avoid dying than to identify with the man responsible for some eight million deaths in concentration camps, not counting the casualties of World War II?

What brought these pathetic, relatively smart people to such a crux? To claim that Jack merely suffers from some vaguely motivated midlife crisis—an answer students reach for pretty quickly—is to ignore the more intricate formal connections that DeLillo constructs between the characters' greatest fear, their fear of death, and their greatest pleasure: shopping for the commodities that radio and TV ads continually tempt them to buy, between images of volcano eruptions and audio-evangelical reports on the impending End of Days. Jack escapes one confrontation with his mortality—a chance encounter with a colleague who describes him as "a big, harmless, aging, indistinct sort of guy"—by shopping voraciously at the mall, "seeing himself unexpectedly in . . . reflecting surface[s]" everywhere he goes (83); and he begins to throw things away in a similar frenzy once he's certain that his Nyodene exposure will kill him. Having failed to procure the drug for treating fear of death from his beloved Babette, who slept with the shadowy Mr. Gray for the right to try it, he scapegoats the discarded objects in his attic for chaining him to mortality: "I bore a personal grudge against these things. Somehow they'd put me in this fix. They'd dragged me down, made escape impossible" (280).

If Hitler is the novel's most visible example of Jack's semiotic hubris, these scenes of Jack tossing his material history into the garbage give us fleeting but crucial glimpses of the logic that sponsors his transformation of everything, from bodies to history, into objects, victims of his reifying gaze. When Jack indicts what he discards—coasters, paintbrushes, old candles, even his academic credentials—for pulling him into an unnameable quagmire, he unconsciously indicts himself for the pleasures he takes in his objects and, by analogy, for his reification of bodies both living and dead. While Jack gets closer, over the course of these scenes, to discovering the "fix" he's in, DeLillo the moralist implies that Jack would be better off to stop pinning the rap on his commodity fetishes and instead to inspect more carefully the way he treats the connotations of objects as if they were objective and manifest truths. He might then see how this relation leaches into his perceptions of everything and everyone, even his family, whose lives he threatens by refusing to acknowledge that chemical disasters affect departmental chairs too.

But Jack lives in denial of his universal fetishism, for to accept it as a failing would be tantamount to accepting the damning implications of his success as an academic—not just any academic but the chair of a department of Hitler studies, a field he founded himself and without which he would be nothing more than the sagging, indistinct old man that his colleague hails in the hardware store. Jack's exploitation of the world's most photographed Austrian to generate his own cult of personality marks the novel's most disturbing example of a sign severed from its referent. By disconnecting Hitler from the utterly objectifying Holocaust, Jack exposes himself as a permanently lost consumer who can never admit his lack of empathy without also admitting that his career depends on, if not Holocaust denial, then on focusing exclusively on Hitler's career as a master semiotician.

DeLillo's concern with the Hitler industry—wryly expressed in Jack's assertion to Denise that Hitler is "always on [TV]. We couldn't have television without him" (63)—puts him in the company of yet another incarnation of Hitler humor, in which exploiters of Hitler's legacy take as much heat as the man himself. In Mel Brooks's film *The Producers* (1968), Zero Mostel fronts a musical called *Springtime for Hitler*, with help from Gene Wilder's naive accountant. *Springtime*'s transformation of the Führer into a stoned flower child, played by a hippie nicknamed LSD, pokes fun less at Hitler than at those who would profit from him, not to mention at the musical's spectators, who prove they would do anything for a little decadent entertainment by laughing the musical into a hit. *The Producers* presents the titular Svengalis' exploitation of anti-Nazi sentiment as the ultimate example of winning as losing: because the producers have oversold stock in the production and banked on its failure in hopes of retaining the investors' contributions, the success of *Springtime for Hitler* spells their ruin. As in *White Noise*—where Jack pays for his semiotic carelessness and ethical failings by getting shot by Willie Mink, his wife's sexual partner and drug supplier—Mostel and Wilder get their just deserts for having used Hitler for personal gain: a prison term that contains (but scarcely quells) their desire to produce terrible musicals.

When Mink pulls the trigger of Jack's Zumwalt pistol in the novel's climactic scene, the impact of the bullet jerks Jack into the reality of bodies through the pain of his own. It's as if the scent of death that drifts under the surface of his semiotic and iconic Hitler can no longer be contained once he feels pain and recognizes it in another. Jack suddenly sees Mink not as a gray, indistinct, televisual blur but as a creature with the definite identity of a suffering body that deserves his compassion.

If we're watching carefully, however, we can see that DeLillo has been prodding death back toward the novel's surface all along. It speaks itself, if not overtly, then in coincidences that pop through the chaos of randomized signifiers from time to time, such as the fact that Jack has to travel to Iron City's Germantown district in order to kill Mink with a German gun. That the name of Nyodene D, the insecticide by-product that makes up the novel's toxic cloud, resembles the name of one of the insecticides used to gas the victims of Hitler's camps—Zyklon B—implies that history clings to even the most random collisions of signifiers in the present. Perhaps the airborne toxic event is a form of poetic justice dealt by a postmodern deity, a means to punish Jack's reifying imagination that gives him at least an inkling of the terror and uncertainty that the Nazis inspired in those interred at the concentration camps.

Does DeLillo succeed in chastising Jack without indicting himself as an exploiter of Hitler in the process? Though Bruce Bawer argues that no "moral distinctions enter into [DeLillo's] appraisal of any human act" (41) and uses the Hitler of *White Noise* as proof, Cantor's essay makes clear how DeLillo holds the postmodern fragmentation and commodification of history responsible for "moral indifference to Nazism" (40, 41). Yet even Cantor does not recognize the degree to which it is the postmodern transformation of perception—how we frame history and tell it to ourselves in the present—that empties Jack's historical imagination. He seems to miss the point when he argues that DeLillo has inappropriately projected postmodernism onto the history of Catholicism when the German nuns confess that they only pretend to believe in God. In fact DeLillo demonstrates here the depth of his sensitivity to the philosophical parameters of his era. By teasing Jack for expecting them to believe in a God they cannot see, the nuns show how postmodernism's incredulity toward metanarratives can and must undermine any aspiration to pure faith.

Despite any such defense of DeLillo's choices, a lesson plan that stresses his use of humor still must scrutinize other potential effects of his narratorial cynicism, so that students can decide if *White Noise* falls prey to the twin risks of Hitler humor, that of cheapening Hitler's crimes on the one hand and of exploiting them on the other. While pursuing a debate on this topic, one might offer students a few pages of Art Spiegelman's graphic novel *Maus* (1980–91) and ask how the obvious representational choices that Spiegelman makes compare with DeLillo's decision never to mention the Holocaust. *Maus*, a decidedly unfunny but extremely affecting comic book about the experiences of Spiegelman's father in Eastern Europe and Auschwitz during World War II, treats the exploitation of mass suffering in a similarly ambivalent way. Artie, Spiegelman's semifictionalized version of himself, interviews his father in order to draw an account of his experiences in comic-book form. Like Jack and Brooks's producers, Artie profits in a backhanded way from Hitler's existence, but he also punishes himself for this profiting and frets over his decision to use broad signifiers—cats and mice straight out of *Tom and Jerry*—to signify complex identities wrought less out of race than out of webs of racist and fascist perception that made the Jews into mice for the Germans' predatory cats.

While such a debate can be fruitful, it can also degenerate into a one-sided and simplistic defense of Holocaust victims and survivors against any representation of them, and especially one undertaken for profit. This is the point in the discussion where negative dialectics come in handy. As I have discussed, Spiegelman and DeLillo (and even Brooks) adhere in their own ways to Adorno's interdiction on representing the Holocaust. At the same time, they implicate us as potential collaborators in their exploitation of Hitler, precisely because in reading either of these works, we do what DeLillo's characters can never stop doing: we consume world-historical suffering as a narrative for our contemplation and distraction. Spiegelman forces us to think about the stakes of Holocaust signification by refusing to envision its human sufferers as human. He concentrates instead on what they signified in the semiotic economy of Hitler's Europe, and thus he drags the reader into the Nazis' ideology, its way of seeing Jews as vermin—as if human social relations were a kind of revisionist cartoon to be resolved at last in favor of the predator rather than the weak but wily prey. DeLillo, of course, implicates us more pointedly than Spiegelman as the Gladneys' fellow consumers of tragedy. But each in its way, *The Producers*, *Maus*, and *White Noise* all point to consumer culture as the most dangerous terrain on which to approach Hitler's legacy. The minute Hitler goes up for sale on the open market, whether as the star of a breezy musical comedy, as the shadow cast over a funny animal comic about mass extermination, or as a solipsistic academic's goose(stepper) who laid the golden egg, he becomes a magnet for unpredictable connotations that will inevitably cast the signifier "Hitler" adrift in a sea of signs whose current carries it ever farther from its historical referent. Commodities and consumption are funny that way.

Not to say that *White Noise* ought to be understood as simply DeLillo's condemnation of a tribe of horrible people or a comedy that punishes us for laughing. Jack may be delusional, but at least he attempts to determine what's missing from his life, and to a certain degree he succeeds. I teach Jack as an every-American whose representative nature DeLillo gets across in everything from his domestic-sitcom surname, Gladney, to the fact that his town of Blacksmith exists only in a region of the United States (apparently the Northeast), not in a specified state. Like most Americans of the 1980s and today, Jack negotiates his identity with the only means the omniscient economy offers him: by engaging with the same consumerist, technologized, sign-saturated environment through which he experiences his life.

We would be remiss, I assure my students, were we not to read Jack's desires as compromises that American consumers must strike with the simulacrum sooner or later rather than as capitulations to it. Indeed, the humor of the novel is merely snide and contemptuous if we believe that DeLillo simply derides Jack, as if DeLillo owned an unpoisoned, objective position with respect to the cloud of floating signifiers that no American can ever avoid breathing in. But just as Jack never knows whether or not the Nyodene will kill him, neither does *White Noise* tell us whether the fog of signs must be avoided or breathed all the more deeply if we are to reach the others that the fog obscures behind endless reflections of our desires.

Hope does come to DeLillo's world, in the form of Wilder, Babette's young son by a different marriage and the only character braver than Murray about confronting the Medusa of unhinged signifiers. Unlike Murray, who cuts his path through cultural static by taking notes on everything he hears and sees, Wilder has a bona fide strategy: by refusing to increase his vocabulary past a few words, he avoids signification itself with the determination of one who fears being tainted by it. Instead of adding more words to the graveyard of meaning, he stares into things. He looks into the car radio, a pot of boiling water, and other technologies and household objects as if to see past their connotations and even what they look like, feel like, and do. Their surfaces, it seems, would distract him from discerning their true nature. But what matters most about his studied gaze is that it refuses to be distracted by signs at all, whether they signify fashion or use value. It seems far from accidental, once we note the conspicuous absence of the Holocaust in this book, that on the day the child begins to cry uncontrollably, Jack catches him staring into the window of the Gladneys' oven (75). Wilder's deep and penetrating gaze, accompanied by a wail of grief that he seems to not so much produce as channel, is as close as anyone in the novel gets to the ovens that Jack can never bring himself to mention, let alone peer into with such intense desire to know and understand what no surface can reveal.

An Ecocritical Approach to Teaching *White Noise*

Louisa Mackenzie

In a strange moment in *White Noise*, Jack Gladney experiences a sensory epiphany: during a trip to the supermarket, his awareness and appreciation of his surroundings are suddenly and almost psychedelically heightened:

> I was suddenly aware of the dense environmental texture. The automatic doors opened and closed, breathing abruptly. Colors and odors seemed sharper. The sound of gliding feet emerged from a dozen other noises, from the sublittoral drone of maintenance systems, from the rustle of newsprint as shoppers scanned their horoscopes. . . . (168)

Such moments of intense sensory connection with place have a long tradition in Western literature. But the space of sensory heightening, in this tradition, is almost always what we would call nature. Consider for example Henry Thoreau's famous evening walk in the woods at Walden:

> This is a delicious evening, when the whole body is one sense, and imbibes delight through every pore. I go and come with a strange liberty in Nature, a part of herself. . . . [A]ll the elements are unusually congenial to me. The bullfrogs trump to usher in the night, and the note of the whippoorwill is borne on the rippling wind from over the water. (*Walden* 129)

Both Thoreau and Gladney experience a heightened receptivity to their environment. In fact, DeLillo seems to displace onto consumer society some elements of the canonical trope of a Thoreauvian restorative relation with nature—with important differences, of course. What is missing from the supermarket moment is the association, common in nature writing, between sensory heightening and spiritual awakening. Nevertheless, the supermarket is the place in which the Gladney family finds emotional sustenance, where all becomes right again in the world. One critic has even posited a resemblance between the supermarket and paradise, albeit a postmodern paradise of "prepackaged commodities . . . suppression of origin and labour" (Kerridge 183). Grocery shopping, mutatis mutandis, is arguably the closest experience to a religious ritual to be found in the novel, and the supermarket becomes a postmodern Walden Woods.

I propose here that DeLillo's almost parodic displacements of known literary topoi from the canon of nature writing make *White Noise* a particularly provocative addition to a class on nature writing and ecocriticism, challenging some of ecocriticism's less examined assumptions; I also propose that the other texts one might read in such a class allow a unique set of questions to be raised about DeLillo's novel. In other words, an ecocritical reading of *White Noise* is interesting not only in terms of what the novel does or does not say about nature but also for the articulations between the novel and texts that are more likely to be standards in a class on ecocriticism, such as *Walden*, and that find themselves postmodernized by the proximity to *White Noise*. Richard Kerridge argues that "DeLillo uses the environmental crisis to interrogate postmodernism, but does not offer the reader any route out of postmodernist self-consciousness and irony" (182). One might push further Kerridge's analysis and make the interrogation two-way: postmodernism is used to interrogate the environmental crisis just as much as vice versa, and still with no way out, leaving a "condition of passive waiting" (194).

Ecocritical pedagogy, since it encourages interrogation of the relations between text, writing subject, and represented space, is particularly illuminating in *White Noise*. Nature in DeLillo's novel is largely absent, so a standard ecocritical response is that DeLillo must be condemning the alienation of modern consumer society from the natural world. But *White Noise* resists such a reading in interesting ways, one of which is the above-mentioned displacement into urban and commercial space (such as the supermarket) of the standard nature-writing themes of connection and contentment. Another challenge posed by *White Noise* to normative ecocritical readings lies in the novel's treatment of themes of risk and toxicity: many ecocritical responses to representations of exposure to toxicity read these representations as protests against the environmental degradation caused by consumer society, but the text gives no such condemnation.

The novel can thus be offered as a challenge to ecocriticism to expand the kinds of spaces (and textual mediations on them) with which it is concerned, ecocritics having for the most part focused on figurations of the natural world. A notable exception is Lawrence Buell, whose *Writing for an Endangered World* posits an "environmental unconscious" that orders man-made and natural landscapes alike, encouraging modern culture to go "beyond the conflation of 'environment' with 'nature' " (22). *White Noise* encourages us to consider how the human subject negotiates a distinctly postnatural environment, thus pushing the boundaries of first-wave ecocriticism in directions suggested by Buell.

When putting together a syllabus entitled Introduction to Ecocriticism for a writing and composition class in a comparative literature department, I thus had high hopes for the role that *White Noise* would play. Classes with an ecocritical approach are almost always given in English departments in the United States, and syllabi usually feature at least two of the greats of American nature writing, in whose number are Thoreau, Ralph Waldo Emerson, Edward Abbey, Aldo Leopold, John Muir, Wendell Berry, and Walt Whitman. Indeed,

American environmental and nature writing is a huge field in its own right, but by no means is it coterminous with ecocriticism, which my class purported to introduce. As Patrick Murphy has noted:

> Ecocriticism can be employed in studying any literary work insofar as that work reveals or reflects something about nature and humanity's place in, with, or against it. But that does not automatically make any work that can fruitfully be interpreted by means of ecocriticism a type of nature-oriented literature. (1)

White Noise can usefully be analyzed under both Murphy's optics: as ecocriticism and as "nature-oriented literature." The second classification may be harder to maintain, but Murphy's taxonomy of the genre of environmental literature contains at least three descriptives that can be applied—at least as hypotheses—to *White Noise*: observation of crisis, environmental crisis and resolution, and dystopia (11).

In order to explore the outer reaches of ecocriticism and also because, like most comparative literature departments, this one had breadth requirements, I ended up with a syllabus that was generically as well as nationally diverse. Besides *White Noise*, we read some classic American nature-oriented literature: Rachel Carson, Thoreau, and Emerson. We also read an ancient Greek epic (the *Odyssey*), a French Romantic novel in translation (Bernadin de Saint-Pierre's *Paul et Virginie*), and a selection of tales and poetry in translation from various cultures (Elder and Wong; Farrell). *Paul et Virginie*, an idyll that has lovers living on a tropical island in communion with their natural surroundings and that presents a Rousseauesque philosophy of nature as educator, illustrated ways in which many modern views of nature, including American transcendentalism, have been molded by European Romanticism. Carson's *Silent Spring*, with its haunting first chapter describing a transition from pastoral utopia to environmental dystopia, provided a particularly interesting articulation with *White Noise*. The fall into a post-Edenic world of contamination is a powerful and familiar narrative in our culture (I brought in Ovid's description of the golden age to show how far back the theme of a lost ideal relation with nature goes), and this narrative is a tempting one to impose on *White Noise*. The novel, of course, reveals itself to be more slippery than at first appears: one could argue that it is not about ecocatastrophe at all, that it is not simply a fictional realization of Carson's environmental holocaust but uses such catastrophic discourse in ambiguous ways. How does *White Noise* expose or challenge what ecocriticism tries to do with texts?

To answer this question in detail, it is necessary to take a short detour to define some parameters of ecocriticism as practiced both in the classroom and on the page. For some, the teaching of ecocriticism is motivated by the notion that literary studies must assume responsibility, in the face of escalating ecological threats, for bringing students' attention back to the workings, the needs, and the beauty of the real world. Ecocritical practice in the literature classroom is in this case conflated with the teaching of a type of nature writing that presents edifying models of human experience in nature or cautionary tales about the dangers of indifference to the health of the biosphere. In a high-profile article in the *New York Times Magazine* in 1995, Jay Parini suggests that the entire academy is "greening," witnessing not only a growth in environmental studies as a science but also a concomitant turn in the humanities toward aesthetically pleasing descriptions of nature, "the actual universe of rocks, trees and rivers that lies behind the wilderness of signs." "Green" teachers of literature, he and his interviewees claim, are dismissing "theory's more solipsistic tendencies" in order to "return to activism and social responsibility" (52).

Other ecocritics—by now the majority—are less euphoric about ecocriticism's potential to actualize social change, although for the most part they share the conviction that there is a material world beyond social fabrication. A happy, or not so happy, medium is being sought between theory and the material world (Campbell); we are realizing the basic truth that to represent nature at all is to produce cultural discourse, of which theory is a subset. Cheryll Glotfelty, in her useful introduction to *The Ecocriticism Reader*, writes:

> Ecocriticism takes as its subject the interconnections between nature and culture, specifically the cultural artifacts of language and literature. As a critical stance, it has one foot in literature and the other on land; as a theoretical discourse, it negotiates between the human and the nonhuman. (xix)

Ecocriticism, like any other academic school, is becoming increasingly rigorous in the examination of its own tenets. Arguably there is still a tendency to accept a post-Romantic notion of the definition of nature and in particular a human being's place in and relation to this nature (selections from Elder and Wong go some way toward presenting alternative cultural conceptions of nature).

Still others suggest going beyond the study of texts to a sweeping revision of how we teach, elaborating pedagogical theories of ecology in the classroom—that is, models of collaboration, connection, and responsible knowledge. David Orr envisions a generation of "ecologically literate" students who are taught that "they are a part of or apart from the natural world." The university would be structured not along disciplinary lines but rather as "transdisciplinary laboratories" (90). With respect to the teaching of the humanities, he proposes an alternative reading list to Allan Bloom's great books (109–14). Orr's list is composed of books on ecology, thermodynamics, and environmental ethics. Although there is much to recommend Orr's model and others like it (Bowers 164–69), they risk being just as prescriptive as the models they propose to replace: even if *White Noise* figured in such a curriculum, it would arguably be there only as a cautionary tale of toxicity as the by-product of consumer culture. The application of ecocriticism's tenets to the classroom would hinder the teaching of *White Noise* or reduce the novel to one prescriptive kind of reading.

Because my class was intended for first-year students, our engagement with ecocriticism's constantly shifting frontiers and self-stylings was limited. Use of ecocritical perspective was concerned more with representation and roles of nature in texts in which the notion of nature and the natural varied greatly. The greater goal of the class was to encourage students to question nature's status as an absolute by asking why nature is figured in certain ways at particular times by particular cultures. Ecocriticism understood as a set of concerns about cultural manufacturing of notions of the natural does allow for directed engagement with particular moments in *White Noise*, such as the toxic event, as I illustrate below.

Given this directive to study constructions of nature, *White Noise*, a landmark of postmodern consciousness, may seem an odd addition to the syllabus. Indeed, asking students what they thought the novel was doing on the syllabus proved to be a productive first question, since it articulated the confusion many of them felt on encountering a text that excluded most of what we understand as the natural world. Where is nature? How can one talk about its construction in a text from which it is conspicuously absent? The most obvious answer, of course, is that one talks about nature in terms of its absence or commodification, as "submerged into the depths of silence and instrumentality" (Manes 17): in *White Noise*, nature does not speak; it is abundantly spoken for. The natural world is commodified ("CABLE HEALTH, CABLE WEATHER, CABLE NEWS, CABLE NATURE" [231]) or understood as a kind of public utility, part of the network of power and water that supplies urban communities:

> "Mountains are always upstate," Denise told her. "This way the snow melts as planned in the spring and flows downhill to the reservoirs near the cities, which are kept in the lower end of the state for exactly this reason."
>
> I thought, momentarily, she might be right. It made a curious kind of sense. (235)

Nature is "enframed" and transformed into "standing reserve" in the Heideggerian sense (Moses 65), mutated by technology into a consumer item. Gone is any Thoreauvian delight in a natural world understood to be pristine. The closest the Gladney family come to a contemplation of their nonhuman environment is watching the sunset from a freeway overpass, a sunset that is a comically gross distortion of itself, since the sunsets become "unbearably beautiful" after the toxic event (170). This scene stands out as the only moment of contemplation of nature's beauties, and it presents a familiar Romantic literary tradition as already poisoned. The possibility of a relation between a human observer and a pristine environment is negated by the toxic by-products of modern society.

Or is it? An ecocritical reading would say yes, yet DeLillo is silent on the question of the cause of the toxic event. Nyodene derivative, unlike DDT, whose effects are denounced by Carson in *Silent Spring*, is a nonexistent toxic agent. DeLillo's narrator points out that there was no "measurable connection" (170) between the toxic event and the changed sunsets. At this key moment, *White Noise* refuses to impute causality. It invites us to read the toxic event and the sunsets ecocritically but will not back up such a reading, challenging many of ecocriticism's processes. Even if, as Ursula Heise has argued, the whole novel maps out a modern "riskscape" (751), can one pass from this observation to the imposition of any environmental value judgment?

That *White Noise* resists being read as a warning about ecocatastrophe makes it a rich addition to an ecocriticism class, which is often concerned with locating messages about the contamination of nature. A dialectic can be established between the rhetoric of ecocriticism and the resistance of DeLillo's text to any prescriptive reading. Teaching *White Noise* in a class on ecocriticism, where students may read authors such as Emerson and Wordsworth, reveals DeLillo's engagement with, and transformation of, literary clichés about nature and our place in it. After reading such scenes as the sensory epiphany in the supermarket, students might go back to a text like *Walden* more critically, questioning the naturalization of a certain type of relation with nature. In other words, *White Noise* acts as a foil in an ecocriticism class, preventing the imposition of an environmental approach to texts to the exclusion of other approaches.

From the students' first contact with *White Noise*, there was no consensus about the correctness of an ecocritical reading of the novel. It was hard for students to find an explicit condemnation in DeLillo's presentation of the Gladneys' alienation from nature. Some observed that the Gladney family seem to enjoy being together. Others argued that DeLillo could not be presenting a gloomy environmental dystopia, since the family appear close and find humor in most situations. Human relationships are somehow recuperated. The Gladneys are perhaps not presented, as some ecocritics would have it, as enablers of a wasteful and destructive consumer culture; their relation to this culture is more ironic and self-aware, and more comfortable, than is allowed by a reading that pushes environmental themes to the forefront and ignores other narrative clues. Students detected what Naomi Klein, in her brilliant study of forms of resistance to corporate branding of physical and mental space, has called "semiotic shadowboxing" (296): an attempt, successful or not, to preserve identity and human bonds despite the constant and bewildering presence of consumer culture, both its white noise and its sometimes toxic by-products. For Klein, an important facet of recent Western consumer culture is "ironic consumption" (77). Savvy, disabused consumers maintain a distanced, ironic attitude to advertising, capable to a certain extent of deconstructing commercial messages or at least of producing for themselves a "cozy, protected, self-referential niche" (79) from which to negotiate the barrage of marketing images. This notion proved to be of great help in the class: students saw their own negotiation of commercialism mirrored in the Gladneys', and instinctively brought to the text the same level of critical awareness that they are used to bringing to corporate messages. DeLillo's representation of family relations, and of the individual's relation with the commercial world, is not necessarily catastrophic, even if forever on the brink. This balance enabled some students to respond critically and thoughtfully to ecocritical articles and to find the ideological motivations and blind spots in them.

Our use of three short articles as guides for discussion about the centrality (or not) of toxicity illustrates how *White Noise* and ecocriticism can be put into dialogue and productive disagreement. These essays deal precisely with the novel's relation to ecocriticism. Scott Russell Sanders argues that by almost completely excluding the natural world from the mental and physical landscapes of his novel, DeLillo presents a harsh commentary on the degree of modern alienation from nature and its processes (193). For Cynthia Deitering, themes such as commodification and the abundance of waste are harnessed by a discourse according to which *White Noise* reveals the psychosocial roots of modern environmental deterioration and encourages us to raise our environmental consciousness (202). Her essay refers to the scene where Jack goes through his family's compacted garbage and proposes that modern identities are figured by our relation not just to the products of consumer culture but to the waste of those products: "we have begun to comprehend our seminal role as producers of waste" (198).

Both these pieces have in common an assumption dear to many ecocritics: any representation of human life as alienated from nonhuman nature is necessarily a condemnation of this life and a call to a renewal of a "deep awareness of nature" in cultural discourse (Sanders 192). After students read these two short essays, they were asked what the narrative function of the toxic event was. Armed with Sanders and Deitering, many saw the toxic event as an inevitable result of the type of society portrayed, a metaphor for the general decay of human-natural relations.

But Lawrence Buell's article, a somewhat longer and more theoretically sophisticated piece, asks whether ecodiscourse carries any weight at all in *White Noise*. Buell concludes that the "recontainment of the toxic event" is not an "awakening"; rather, the threat of toxicity is invoked only to be eclipsed, a narrative red herring ("Toxic Discourse" 663). The possibility of inferring a moral lesson from the ecocatastrophe is thus denied, and toxic discourse is exposed precisely as discourse—that is, the opposite of action. Buell's article gave many students insight into Heinrich's copious production of speech right after the event, in which the boy shares vast amounts of scientific knowledge but fails to offer any solution or suggest action, fails even to attribute blame (130). Discourse becomes its own sanctuary, a reason for not doing anything beyond critical appraisal of the problem (Buell, "Toxic Discourse" 662).

Although the language of Buell's article was challenging for many students, the article allowed us better to critique some of ecocriticism's teleology. Ecocriticism is concerned with the increasing gap between human beings and their natural environment: it poses this gap as a problem. *White Noise*, while it illustrates the rupture, does not necessarily problematize it. Because the Gladney family refuses to engage the consequences of the toxic event and DeLillo's narrator also refuses, the reader is left wondering what material effects the spill did have. It is not even clear that DeLillo offers a judgment about this refusal, and here lies the core of *White Noise*'s challenge to ecocriticism in general.

Environmental approaches to this text acted as a springboard to many other levels and types of discussion instead of closing off the text to anything but ecocritical concerns. Most first-year students are at least minimally aware of the existence of environmental movements and the arguments made for and against them, whether or not they have thought through their own positions on the issues. They have an ideological framework to the text that at least seems familiar, an approach that facilitates the eventual introduction of terms such as *postmodern* or *alienation*. Since our relation to and conception of nature are products of our culture, discussion about the former almost always leads to conclusions about the latter.

One might, for example, construct a discussion around the media presentation of risk in public discourse. The same class given today would have to include recent work by Heise that elegantly and gently engages Buell, placing toxicity closer to the center of the novel's concerns. Using risk analysis as a tool for reading toxicity in *White Noise*, Heise points out that the toxic event is not a singularity but part of a "riskscape" that includes domestic products, radiation, drugs, hair loss, and an evacuated school. She argues that the novel presents different forms of subjectivity in risk assessment, exploring the boundary between "realism and hyperbole" (756) instead of either acting as a simple documentary of modern risk types or mocking perceptions of risk as hyperbolic. Risk assessment can be related to environmental concerns as well as to students' experience processing media representations of risk. One might ask students how they process media messages about risks to human health and safety. Do they seek second opinions? To which kind of authority or rhetoric are they more likely to lend credence? How does their response differ if they perceive the risk as being directly to their person or country rather than to others and abroad? Do they perceive risk as a class issue, or do the major risks of today transcend class? How (if at all) do they protect themselves against risk? These last two questions would be best addressed with reference to Gladney's confidence that belonging to the middle class insures him against disaster, like the well-heeled parents who exude a vague air of "massive insurance coverage" (3).

Our class talked less specifically about risk, but we did engage the question of personal responsibility for ecological disaster. After reading the second section, "The Airborne Toxic Event," and before turning to the critical material discussed above, students were asked if they could recall any significant toxic disasters. Some mentioned *Exxon Valdez*; a few had heard of Three Mile Island. At the time, in January 1999, there had just been a large oil spill in the English Channel that was attracting a lot of press. Students generally felt that these were regrettable incidents but perpetuated by others; they did not see any causal connection between their own behavior and large environmental catastrophes. This response illustrates a point made by many academics who encourage students to connect their reified personal experience to a broader political and theoretical engagement. The discourse of the self, of private experience, has become so commonplace in our culture that it is replacing relational (and thus political) thought. Here, ecocriticism can challenge the individuated notion of the personal by encouraging students and readers to consider as a kind of ecosystem the entire network of human and nonhuman events taking place on the planet.

Some students admitted that environmental catastrophes may have affected their lives, but they resisted thinking in the other direction—that is, from themselves to such catastrophe. They began to think about the consequences of individual behavior only when asked whether the Gladney family was in any way responsible for the toxic event in the novel. Many said yes. Although they did not immediately understand their impulse, the difference between their appraisal of causality in a text and in their own lives was obvious to most. At this point, the notion of narrative function was introduced: the idea that details in a text exist for a reason, that the author has put them there to establish a connection, and that part of what we do as readers is to enter almost unconsciously into a contract by which we must interpret narrative events as related. DeLillo, by placing description of human interactions in the same textual space as the toxic spill, implies a connection between them. Through a series of such connections, some students concluded that the Gladneys are presented as a cautionary example of the kind of indifferently consumerist mentality that tacitly enables the economic powers that produce toxic spills. The scene in which Gladney goes through the family garbage can be revisited from this angle. He expresses surprise at the realization of his and his family's role in the production of this "dark underside" of modern life: "Was this ours? Did it belong to us? Had we created it?" (259, 258).

From such questions about the answerability of our personal, everyday choices emerged a more general discussion on the relation between DeLillo's characters and their world, at which point notions such as fragmentation and alienation took on meaning for the students. But *White Noise* still did not seem a cautionary narrative about the dangers of overconsumption. It was soon concluded that DeLillo implies a link between the Gladneys' consumerism and the toxic event the better to frustrate it. Here again, *White Noise* resists attempts to be read ecocritically, and it is in the interrogation of that resistance that meaning is found.

The Most Photographed Barn in America episode further illustrates the rich dialogue that can be established between the novel and ecocriticism. A landmark is singled out from the environment for particular attention, then represented in simulacra. The episode is doubly significant, first, for the arbitrary nature of the object chosen to be photographed; second, for the displacement of that object by its representation in visual media—the barn is important not in itself but in the number of times it has been photographed (Lentricchia, "Tales" 88–91). The construction of experience through distancing and the mediation of media, particularly images, is of concern to ecocritics and postmodernists alike. In addition, the nature-culture division that still underlies much ecocritical work is revisited, since the attraction could as easily be a waterfall or granite cliff. The slippage between the actions of visitors and the object of their admiration illustrates the arbitrary nature of any place's becoming a tourist attraction, whether a barn, the Taj Mahal, or Niagara Falls. When asked why Yosemite, for example, could not be substituted for the barn in this episode, students explained that natural beauty is something one instinctively wants to capture, but the barn has no such intrinsic beauty and the iteration of the experience is thus worthless. But, I asked, is it not possible that DeLillo's characters have an experience similar to that of the reverential visitor in Yosemite? After all, photographing the barn is described by one character as a "spiritual surrender . . . a religious experience in a way" (12). The visitors have a sense of connection to a greater community of photographers, whose presence past and present confers an authority on the place, just as nature writers describe an experience of connectedness with the environment and the flow of time when viewing a scene of natural beauty.

On what exactly is our modern appreciation of nature based? Are we conditioned to have certain reactions in front of certain types of landscape (Byerly 53), in much the same way that different ages have varying standards of beauty in human-produced culture? In writing from the European Middle Ages, mountains were usually considered not beautiful but frightening; and Rubens's ideal woman was far from the feminine ideal today.

Most students were reluctant to let go of an ideology so deeply ingrained that it passed for an absolute: the beauty of wild places. But when we had worked through the question some more, with help from Alison Byerly's essay and extracts from Max Oelschlaeger's *The Idea of Wilderness*, they started to accept the possibility that the intrinsic or absolute beauty associated with the natural world by many environmentalists and nature writers may be culturally dependent—in other words, that nature is culture or at least always already constructed by it. The barn thus brings into question cultural aesthetics in general. If no beauty is intrinsic, what determines the success of a work of art—including a novel such as *White Noise*? The critical notion of social construction was also brought in at this point, better illustrated by a discrete episode than by a purely theoretical introduction.

The barn episode can be usefully read under the optic of ecocriticism, but it also questions an idea close to the hearts of some ecocritics and deep ecologists in particular such as Arne Naess, George Sessions, and Bill Devall. The idea is that we must return to an essential connection with nature, from which contemporary technology and culture have alienated us, in order to find our lost spirituality. DeLillo denies, in this and other episodes, that spiritual epiphanies can happen only on contact with unmediated nature. In fact, the one time the word *wilderness* is used in *White Noise* is as a metaphor for fear, when the narrator describes panic as "the god of woods and wilderness" (224). Primal nature as a catalyst for discovery of a precivilized, elemental self is not contained by the world of *White Noise*; the possibility of such discovery is mentioned only once, by Winnie in her example of the grizzly bear, the sight of which "gives you a renewed sense of yourself. . . . The beast on hind legs has enabled you to see who you are as if for the first time" (229). But the process she describes is still that of fear, as the bear on the alert is a distinctly threatening view of untamed nature. The characters of *White Noise* get their nature through cable television: "by way of technology reducing nature to a postmodern *simulacrum* (a copy with no original), 'CABLE NATURE,' . . . man assumes sovereignty over a reality that was once understood to transcend man himself" (Moses 65).

The issue of economic and class distinction was easily approached from an environmentalist point of view: Jack Gladney expounds at some length on how toxic spills are not supposed to affect nice middle-class families such as his (114, 117). A well-behaved toxic spill should stay within the boundaries inhabited by the urban poor. Only a few miles north of Berkeley, California, where I was teaching, were the oil refineries of Richmond, situated in a primarily African American neighborhood prey to frequent noxious leaks. "Environmental racism" is the term used by Richmond activists to describe the willful ignorance of the primarily white middle class toward the plight of those inhabitants. That middle class ironically included many environmental activists. Ecocritical pedagogy is not the only way in which environmental classism may be raised, of course. Gladney's "These things happen to poor people" cries out for commentary in any classroom. But read in conjunction with Buell's article, Gladney's remarkably stark avowal of "eco-inequality" (644) raises questions about the relation among different types of environmental awareness and in particular about the role of academic environmentalisms, including ecocriticism. (Gladney, a college professor, maps out the conceptual distance between academia and ecocatastrophe: "I'm the head of a department. I don't see myself fleeing an airborne toxic event" [117].) Buell pits a privileged, academic, often solipsistic environmentalism, pastorally yearning for safe suburban spaces and preserved areas of natural beauty, against "green activism among the nonprivileged" (642). Environmental classism and racism thus problematize the more elitist tendencies in academic environmentalism, challenging it to embrace more than the safe spaces epitomized by Gladney's academia and his comfortable middle-class neighborhood.

After spending two weeks with *White Noise*, I showed a film that complemented it well, Todd Haynes's *Safe*. Our consideration of this film continued and deepened the discussion of environmental classism. *Safe* is ostensibly about environmental illness: chronic allergies spontaneously developed by some people to almost any artificial product. But Haynes leaves unresolved the question of whether the illness is psychosomatic or not. The main character is a wealthy white woman whose main occupation is the decoration of her enormous home. Her neighborhood is presumably safe not only from crime but also from the kinds of pollution inflicted on poor neighborhoods. Yet she develops a set of symptoms that she decides indicates environmental illness. Many students saw the film as a tale of the ennui of wealth, opining that the woman was inventing her illness because she had nothing else to do or wanted to make her empty life interesting. Others saw it as a story of just retribution: a member of the social elite whose money creates environmental devastation becomes allergic to the toxic world she has participated in creating. The film is a good example of what Deitering, with reference to *White Noise*, has called a "toxic consciousness" in cultural discourse since the mid-1980s (196). As in DeLillo, there is no real recourse to nature: the strange archetypal retreat into nature at the end of the film is deeply disturbing rather than comforting, thwarting the viewer's attempts to place the whole in a comforting narrative of error and redemption, where one misuses then turns back to nature for forgiveness and an authentic, unpoisoned life. Both novel and film present a truly postmodern relation to nature that questions even the category of nature itself and refuses to admit any absolutes. This pairing of novel and film needed no explanation to students.

Activities and presentations based on our reading of *White Noise* were inspired mainly by the omnipresent themes of commodification and control. Students looked, for example, at the packaging of certain commercial products, particularly at advertising, to identify ways in which notions of the natural were being manipulated and commodified in order to persuade us to buy. The theme of desire for control over and absolute understanding of natural forces inspired one student to play a videocassette recording of a weather forecast and compare it with the obsessive discussion of weather in DeLillo's text.

For the class of first-year students, immediate reading and discussion of *White Noise* proved preferable to beginning with a theoretical preface. Some sophisticated questions arose as we examined the novel, but they came much more easily from text-based discussion than from an exterior theoretical framework. Ecocriticism, although it began by rejecting a summarily understood theory, has of course itself produced a veritable industry of theorizing. Much of that theory is useful for my preparation and ongoing understanding but not particularly useful in a lower-division course syllabus. I do not often refer students to Web sites, but those interested in ecocriticism per se were referred to the Web site of the Association for the Study of Literature and Environment (ASLE), which I wholeheartedly recommend also for interested educators (Philippon). The searchable bibliographies, discussion list archives, resource lists, and syllabi provide a wealth of information for research and teaching alike. The site is designed with pedagogy in mind and is helpful whether one is familiar with or entirely new to the field. It is slanted toward literature from the Anglo-American tradition, but this shortcoming is of the field rather than of the Web site, although significant progress is being made to embrace a more multicultural agenda.

"[A]ll ecological criticism shares the fundamental premise that human culture is connected to the physical world, affecting it and affected by it" (Glotfelty ix). Students too participate in this physical world; whether it is conceived of as the natural world or the world of supermarkets and credit cards matters less than the concept of interaction and interrelation. One does not teach ecocriticism to convert students to environmentalism or persuade them that everything is ultimately about nature. The many ways in which *White Noise* resists econormative readings enable a healthy distance from, and critical appraisal of, ecocriticism itself. Teaching a text from an ecocritical point of view invites students to use their intuited relation with the physical world to come to see how a text, too, can be a product of and in dialogue with an experiential reality. What is more, a text such as *White Noise* offers so many recognizable elements from the students' experiential world that they find themselves making the connections and "doing literary criticism" with relative ease.

Connecting *White Noise* to Critical Whiteness Studies

Tim Engles

Although I have taught DeLillo's *White Noise* in American literature survey courses, I find, surprisingly enough, that it serves a crucial function in a course on multicultural literature. I teach the course Multicultural American Literature to an almost exclusively white student population at Eastern Illinois University. Including a novel by a white writer is part of my broader attempt to enhance this course with the insights of critical whiteness studies, a recent offshoot of academic inquiry into race. A guiding presumption amid this recent flurry of study is that racial whiteness has come to function in the United States not as a particular, specified racial status but rather as an invisible, unspoken norm. As George Lipsitz writes in an oft-quoted formulation of this phenomenon, "As the unmarked category against which difference is constructed, whiteness never has to speak its name, never has to acknowledge its role as an organizing principle in social and cultural relations" (1). I include *White Noise* in a course designed to highlight racial minority literature precisely because race seems, especially to white readers, to matter so little in the lives of the novel's white, middle-class characters. Jack Gladney would seem to be, as one such character puts it, just a "big, harmless, aging, indistinct sort of guy" (83), but DeLillo subtly marks and scrutinizes Jack's social position in terms of race, class, and gender. The novel thus anticipates recent scholarly and pedagogical efforts to highlight overlooked features of majority membership. Teachers can heighten and enrich student understanding of matters of race by addressing with *White Noise*, and with other texts, some of the insights that critical whiteness studies has brought to the study of race.[1] Doing so can also alleviate some of the difficulties that inevitably arise during serious classroom discussion of contemporary racial realities.

I have found that getting students to the point where they can appreciate DeLillo's analysis of racial whiteness calls for placing the work late in the semester and for prefacing it with periodic extraliterary readings and discussion on the history and ramifications of American racial formation. I open multicultural literature courses by asking why such relatively new classes exist and what students think of having a white person like me teaching them. These questions provoke discussion that is useful on its own terms, but my effort is to steer them toward consideration of the overwhelming, ongoing whiteness of the received literary canon. On the first day, I also ask students to jot down names that pop into their heads when I say the phrase "great author"; I then ask them to call out the names of such authors, which I write on the board. Shakespeare usually appears first, followed by, almost always, another eight or ten white, male British and American authors (Toni Morrision and Virgina Woolf sometimes come up; DeLillo has not yet). When I ask what these authors all have in common, someone soon points out that they are all white and male. I then ask students to write for five minutes about why, despite the end of slavery, despite universal suffrage, the civil rights movement, the advent of politically correct language, the recent retiring of many racially offensive sports team mascots, and even the awarding of the 1992 Nobel Prize for Literature to an African American woman—why is it that, despite all this apparent progress toward recognition and celebration of America's diversity, almost no great authors come to mind who are not white and male?[2]

When I ask some of the students to summarize what they have just written, some occasionally venture intelligent guesses about the race and gender of those critics and teachers who initially established the canon. A discussion about canon formation may ensue, but my aim at this point is to crystallize their recognition of how a presumption of white superiority continues to influence our collective consciousness, including our normalized conceptions of the canon. To further illustrate hidden, related presumptions of white centrality, I give them another thought experiment. I ask them to close their eyes and let an image of someone come to mind when I say a certain phrase. I then say, "All-American girl," and when they open their eyes, I ask them to call out adjectives describing the girl who came to mind. *Young*, *beautiful*, *cheerleader*, and *blonde* usually come up, but almost never the adjective *white*. Students usually acknowledge, though, whether they are white, black, or otherwise racially positioned, that the girl who came to mind for them did happen to be white. One student argued that some women of color, such as Jennifer Lopez and Halle Berry, receive widespread acclaim for their beauty. Others soon countered that while these women who are not white are indeed considered beautiful, their racial backgrounds clearly separate them from the wholesome, all-American looks of such white icons as Jessica Simpson, Hillary Duff, and Jennifer Aniston.

I then write on the board Toni Morrison's assertion from her pioneering study *Playing in the Dark: Whiteness and the American Literary Imagination*, "American means white . . ." (47).[3] When we discuss what Morrison could have meant by such a claim and why she would make it, students of course recognize that America contains many citizens who are not white. It is a short step then to add that America also contains many nonwhite girls who are thoroughly American as well as many nonwhite authors who are certainly great. Yet, as the students have just demonstrated, broader collective conceptions of all-Americanness and of literary greatness continue to register, at least initially, as white. While conceptions, preconceptions, and stereotypes of others are not problems that white writers typically examine in their works, they are precisely what so many minority writers consciously attempt to counter in the works by them that we will read in this course.

On the first day, including some direct discussion of the paradoxically hidden centrality of whiteness helps explain the existence of separate multicultural courses, by highlighting both the dominance of white writers in the received canon and the default status of whiteness that lies behind that continuing dominance. Such discussion also establishes useful concepts for students' later reading of a white writer who does address matters of race in the lives of seemingly ordinary (white) people, Don DeLillo. From the first day of this course, white students are more engaged than they were in multicultural courses where I did not discuss whiteness, and their own racial status, whether taken for granted or not,[4] has been marked as something that will be under consideration in this course. The few students of color in my classes have also expressed appreciation for periodic discussion of whiteness throughout the semester, primarily because it leads white students to some forms of awareness that students of color tend to have already.

We spend about the first third of the semester on readings that begin in precolonial times and progress quickly to the start of the twentieth century. An understanding of the ongoing effects of white-supremacist ideology, effects that are reflected in both minority texts and white-authored texts, is deepened, I believe, by literary and extraliterary readings that provide historical and sociological insight into American racial formations. Literary readings include occasional pairing of works that enables comparative consideration of privilege and disadvantage on either side of the color line; extraliterary readings include chapters culled from the efforts of various recent historians (e.g., Howard Zinn's *A People's History of the United States*, Ronald Takaki's *A Different Mirror*, and Reginald Horsman's *Race and Manifest Destiny*). Though I do not by any means match every minority text with an ostensibly white one, productive pairings have been transliterated Native American songs and chants with excerpts from Cabeza de Vaca's sixteenth-century account of Spanish and aboriginal contact, excerpts from Frederick Douglass's slave narrative with Mary Rowlandson's captivity narrative, and short stories by Chinese American Sui Sin Far with excerpts from Italian American Constantine Panunzio's memoirs. As we occasionally read works by white authors, we search for ways that being categorized as white matters in the lives of the characters and of the authors, how it automatically increases their options and decreases their problems, and how little they often seem to appreciate the benefits of white racial membership (despite their heightened awareness at the time of this membership).

The next two-thirds of the course is taken up with twentieth-century literature and further outside readings.[5] Studying Morrison's *The Bluest Eye* at some point shortly before *White Noise* has proved especially valuable for anticipating much of what I emphasize in DeLillo's novel. With her poignant, painful depictions of the internalized racism borne by black girls, Morrison helps students conceptualize America's normalization of white standards and the consequent erasure of white specificity. As Rafael Pérez-Torres writes in his discussion of teaching *The Bluest Eye*, "The novel . . . scrutinizes how white most often is considered not a category in the text (or in our society) but, rather, a nonrace, a norm, a universal standard" (24).[6] Morrison's novel illustrates how deeply rooted and devastating the effects of racialization can be on the formation of individual minority identities, and an attentive reading of the part played in this process by unspoken white beauty standards provides solid groundwork for the interest in majority identity displayed in *White Noise*.

To increase our focus on the significance that race can have in shaping identity formation to both people of color and whites, I hand out near the end of our reading of *The Bluest Eye* the following quotation by the whiteness studies theorist Ross Chambers:

> In contrast to minorities, whose identity is defined by their classificatory status as members of a given group, whites are perceived as individual historical agents whose unclassifiable difference from one another is their most prominent trait. Whiteness itself is thus atomized into invisibility through the individualization of white subjects. Whereas nonwhites are perceived first and foremost as a function of their group belongingness, that is, as black or Latino or Asian (and then as individuals), whites are perceived first as individual people (and only secondarily, if at all, as whites). Their essential identity is thus their individual identity, to which whiteness as such is a secondary, and so a negligible factor.
> (192)

This quotation takes a bit of unpacking, but by this point in the semester, the "invisibility" of whiteness having been one of our recurring course themes, most students quickly see Chambers's point and register agreement with it. Chambers also provides here a way into discussion of how power is afforded those whose group membership seems to go unnoticed. As Timothy Barnett puts it, "Whiteness maintains its power by presenting itself as unraced individuality, as opposed to racialized subjectivity that is communally and politically interested" (10). Some students have astutely noted, though, that Chambers's statement begs the question about who is doing the perceiving and where. An African American student pointed out that while whites may see themselves as individuals, many blacks, herself included, often see whites as white. She added that white people sometimes speak and act in ways that nonwhites see as "typical white behavior." Many of the white students grew visibly uncomfortable, and some eventually explained why (these are polite midwesterners—open, heated debate, especially about race, rarely occurs in our classrooms): they felt that any such generalized assessments of white behavior were unfair and untrue. As a result, though, the sudden awareness that many had just experienced of how it feels to be categorized and then judged accordingly gave them some sense of the discomfort, frustration, and outrage expressed in the readings by many minority authors and characters.

More significant, these white students have gained the further understanding that their being white does often place them in a group in the eyes of others, which counters the illusory sense of individuality that was heightened in those whites who were raised, like most of my students, in largely white settings. Some white students did remark, in discussing Chambers's quotation, that when they attended high schools with a high percentage of minority students, they often felt themselves perceived as whites rather than as individuals. This point adds to the realization that the perception of group membership depends on who the perceiver is. Our discussion of Chambers's claims concludes with a limiting of them to environments largely populated by whites, much like the environment depicted in DeLillo's novel. Again, though, the larger gain here is getting white students to see that race matters not only for people of color but also for themselves and thus that the color-blind, liberal individualism subscribed to so dearly by most of them impedes perception of the group-bound realities of both oppression and privilege.

As we proceed with our reading of *White Noise*, I give students a one-page, overnight writing assignment: "Connect Ross Chambers's quotation in any way you can to any of the novel's characters." Their written responses, which I ask some to summarize in our next session, have been widely varied and often insightful. Many focus on the protagonist, of course, noting that so far in our reading Jack Gladney has never thought of himself as white and that race seems to matter little, if at all, to him. (Some point out the irony of his inattention, given the centrality of racialized thinking to Hitler and the Nazis, Jack's supposed area of academic expertise.) By now, students have read Peggy McIntosh's foundational essay "White Privilege and Male Privilege: A Personal Account of Coming to See Correspondences through Work in Women's Studies." In perhaps the most widely cited (and lauded) work in recent critical whiteness studies, McIntosh examines with penetrating clarity the ramifications of whiteness in her own life, giving forty-six concrete, quotidian examples of privilege that would not have been afforded her had she not been white. Thanks in part to this reading, in part to our periodic recognition in most texts of specific instances of white advantage as the underacknowledged counterpart to racial oppression, students often list additional advantages enjoyed by Jack that would be unavailable in his social setting to a person of color.

Especially productive discussions arise when we consider the racial status of Jack's colleague, Murray Jay Siskind. Students often recall that Murray identifies himself as Jewish, something he seems to joke about when describing in caricatured detail the denizens of his apartment building (when Jack asks, "And which one are you?," Murray answers, "I'm the Jew. What else would I be?" [10]). Being Jewish is of course not a racial status, at least not in contemporary America. I ask if Murray's religious identity nevertheless separates him from whiteness somehow. If whiteness is a norm or normal and Christianity is as well, can a Jewish person be a normal white person? Reference to Karen Brodkin's sociohistorical analysis *How Jews Became White Folks and What That Says about Race in America* has been especially helpful in these discussions. Part of Brodkin's argument is that while overt discrimination clearly kept Jewish Americans outside the privileged realms of whiteness before the Second World War, Hitler's racialization and abuse of the Jews, along with high-profile immigrant Jewish success, opened the doors of the white club to them when the war ended. As a perquisite of club membership, Jewish American families were in part enabled by what Brodkin aptly calls "the biggest and best affirmative action program in the history of our nation," the Servicemen's Readjustment Act (or as it was popularly known, the GI Bill) (27). She explains that discriminatory allocation practices limited most of the act's benefits to European American men, making it a de facto affirmative action program for whites, one that returning Jewish American veterans were by and large welcomed to take part in. Most Jewish Americans have now been absorbed by what Brodkin labels "an expand[ing] notion of whiteness" (Sephardic Jews are an occasional exception), to the point where a person like Murray has become unremarkably "white" in this novel's setting (36). Few characters seem to notice his religious difference, least of all the one person who should be most aware of its historical significance in terms of racial discrimination, his friend and confidant, Professor Jack Gladney.

When such discussions are interwoven with efforts to discover the novel's many other thematic concerns, it becomes evident that despite the tendency induced by unremarked whiteness to think of oneself in more individualized terms, membership in the white race does matter in the characters' lives. The next question I raise is whether DeLillo has any overt authorial interest in the racial status of his characters. After all, in nearly every work students have now read by authors of color, race and its ramifications have been of central concern to the characters, clearly because these matters are of central concern to the authors. I introduce students to another of Morrison's insights, a concept that I encapsulate for them with my own label, "relational identity formation." Throughout *Playing in the Dark*, Morrison analyzes the ironic dependence of individualized, unremarked white identity on figurations of black otherness. For instance, in a discussion of early American literature and its intellectual context, she writes:

> Eventually individualism fuses with the prototype of Americans as solitary, alienated, malcontent. What, one wants to ask, are Americans alienated from? What are Americans always so insistently innocent of? Different from? As for absolute power, over whom is this power held, from whom withheld, to whom distributed? Answers to these questions lie in the potent and ego-reinforcing presence of an Africanist population. This population is convenient in every way, not least of which is self-definition. This new white male can now persuade himself that savagery is "out there." (45)

I sometimes assign Morrison's book in these courses, and in those where I do not, I hand out this quotation during our reading of *White Noise*. As we consider it together, I ask students if they can think of instances when someone they know evaluated or described the features or qualities of another person. As they try to remember such instances, I also ask if the describer was implicitly identifying himself or herself as different from the person being described, particularly in an opposite way. When students volunteer examples, we use Morrison's quotation to articulate this process of implicit self-assertion as relational identity formation, a term that I write on the board. I then divide students into pairs and ask them to spend ten minutes searching together for moments when characters in *White Noise* size up other people while simultaneously bolstering a comparative conception of themselves.

Some students struggle with this task, but others realize that DeLillo has embedded many such incidents in the novel, beginning with the opening scene of the day of the station wagons, where the parents of college students look around and see in other parents "images of themselves in every direction" (3). Such moments occur elsewhere in terms of race and other categories. Students have twice pointed to Jack's refusal to leave his house as the cloud of toxic chemicals looms. Explaining to his family, Jack says, "I'm not just a college professor. I'm the head of a department. I don't see myself fleeing an airborne toxic event. That's for people who live in mobile homes out in the scrubby parts of the county, where the fish hatcheries are" (117). This scene illustrates his tendency to see his surroundings through the lens of a media-induced construction of social relations. It also illustrates his use of specific categories of people to assert something about himself. As he ponders fleeing the toxic cloud, Jack fearfully and absurdly hopes that because he has seen lower-class people fleeing from disastrous events on television, a professional, middle-class person such as himself will be spared similar trauma.

In other scenes, Jack's detailed recognition of an other and his implicit, simultaneous registering of himself as the opposite of that other occur specifically in terms of race. There is an encounter with "a black family of Jehovah's Witnesses" (132); another with the "middle-aged Iranian" who delivers his newspaper (184); another in a jungle-like hardware store, replete with people speaking in "Hindi, Vietnamese, [and] related tongues" (82); and, most spectacularly, another with Willie Mink, a man whom Jack labels a racial "composite" and who is the only character in the book to identify Jack as racially white (307, 308).[7] If instructor and students have been mindful of the novel's racial undercurrents, the scene with Mink functions climactically in terms of both race and story line. Earlier in the hardware store setting, Jack's conceptions of the racialized others hovering at the margins of his perception take on a sinister cast when students realize that Jack conceives of these others as part of an ersatz, sharply racialized, colonial backdrop, against which he asserts himself (albeit ridiculously, by shopping) as a masterful and ineluctably white male. His regular use of racial otherness to bolster a flagging sense of himself finally culminates in his shooting of his sexual rival, a man with an "odd, concave," nonwhite face (305). Our earlier considerations of whiteness as the default all-American category usually resurface with Mink's confession that when Babette visited him incognito, she kept a ski mask on "so as not to kiss my face, which she said was un-American" (310). DeLillo pulls together in this scene nearly all the novel's thematic threads. The dependency of white racial identity, in this instance on a watching, perceiving, and conveniently racialized other, is crucial, helping to bring off the novel's satiric take on embittered, besieged American white masculinity.

As these and other scenes demonstrate, Jack tends to assert himself as an individual by claiming or perceiving his difference from another type of person. Yet as he does so, he implicitly and ironically places himself in an opposite category. The irony is that he fails to perceive his own categorical membership. In racial terms, *White Noise* contains repeated instances of what Valerie Babb calls "the recurring pattern of using nonwhiteness to give whiteness form" (66). Babb, Morrison, and others have problematized Euro-American authors' usage of objectified racial otherness in order to flesh out and individualize white central characters. DeLillo's figurations of otherness, however, seem quite different from those in Willa Cather's *Sapphira and the Slave Girl* or Ernest Hemingway's *To Have and Have Not*, texts used by Morrison to illustrate her thesis in *Playing in the Dark*. Such repeated, acutely detailed scenes in *White Noise* demonstrate DeLillo's unusual awareness (unusual for a white writer) of the use whites often make of racial otherness to define themselves relationally. His novel repeatedly satirizes this process of majority identity formation.

It is important to acknowledge that everyone tends to think of others in terms of categories, as this or that type of person (be it stranger or acquaintance, friend or enemy, man or woman, American or foreigner, and so on). What we object to, of course, is when people assume that the occupants of a category all think or behave in a particular way. When discussed in a comparative context, with reference to issues and concepts raised in minority literature and some helpful outside readings, *White Noise* can shed light on the ubiquitous tendency to categorize people. It shows that to avoid categorizing oneself in the process is a habit especially instilled by racial whiteness, when, in a social environment such as the one in this novel, its members constitute the demographic majority. Majority membership can also occur in terms of class, gender, sexuality, religion, and so on. The larger the majority, the less aware its members tend to be of their membership.

Such a discussion can reach a level of abstraction beyond the grasp of some students; pausing to search with the class for more examples with categories other than race can help. For instance, my university has a large special education program. Some students with this major have pointed out how membership in the abled majority can make it difficult to keep in mind that the abled enjoy membership in a group, complete with perquisites unavailable to the disabled; they lack self-awareness *as* abled people. McIntosh's essay also offers a brief list of heterosexual privileges worth calling to mind as a way of talking about similar consequences for identity formation of the presumptive normality of heterosexuality. In both cases, it has been helpful to discuss instances in students' lives or in the mainstream media when abled or heterosexual characters encounter people who are their categorical opposites. In such encounters, the minority figure is often referred to or conceived of in ways that reveal something of the opposite in the majority figure. (For example, a student remembers a cruel classmate in elementary school who laughed at a disabled child to bolster his own "low self-esteem"; a young man on campus is overheard complaining about "fags" as a way of asserting his own, tougher masculinity.)

Multicultural literature courses serve the worthy goal of highlighting and recognizing the merits of minority literatures, but the many insights such courses offer students into the complex, ever-shifting significance of race can be enhanced considerably with an analysis of whiteness. There is of course the danger of overemphasizing whiteness and thereby recentering it. Periodically addressing the issue from various angles more fully engages white students in discussions of race, prodding them into an awareness that most students of color already have—that race signifies in every American life.

Working with insights from critical whiteness studies has proved to me that in a multicultural literature course, addressing the significance of minority group membership for minority authors and characters without addressing whiteness tends to leave intact an erroneous pair of assumptions: that when we talk about race, we should automatically talk about the issues that people of color have and that, as a corollary, race doesn't much matter in the lives of most whites. Including works by Euro-American authors can help counter such notions, if an instructor is alert to the significance that majority racial status has in the settings of particular works and to the standard ways that white authors address (or do not address) matters of race. Several teachers have noted that it is tricky to address whiteness in relation to racial oppression without demoralizing and effectively paralyzing white students with feelings of guilt or resentment.[8] Conceiving of some common white tendencies as analogous to common majority tendencies can reduce such counterproductive emotions. In *White Noise*, instructors and students can appreciate a white author who clearly seeks understanding of the myriad ways that race works.

NOTES

[1]Especially useful introductory sources on critical whiteness studies are Delgado and Stefancic; Fine, Weis, Powell, and Wong; Frankenberg, *White Women* and *Displacing*; Hill; Lopez; Lipsitz; and McIntosh. Note that the McIntosh article listed in this volume's works-cited list is the longer (and more useful) of two commonly reprinted versions (the other is usually entitled "White Privilege: Unpacking the Invisible Knapsack").

[2]When I eventually ask for the names of famous "minority" authors and add them to the list, several arise, including Hurston, Wright, Ellison, Walker, Angelou, and others, invariably African American. Of course, if my classes had more students of color, such names might arise more frequently.

[3]Morrison's full sentence reads, "American means white, and Africanist people struggle to make the term applicable to themselves with ethnicity and hyphen after hyphen after hyphen" (47). I take it as a good sign that many students find Morrison's claim troublesome and even objectionable—such responses indicate that they are already engaged with the complexities of some fundamental multicultural issues. To shift the discussion toward Morrison's crucial focus on standard conceptions of ordinary Americanness, I usually insert quotation marks around two words in her claim when I write it on the board, so that it reads, "American" means "white."

[4]For further discussion of varying degrees of white student self-awareness qua white, see Gallagher; Perry.

[5]Apart from further outside readings that illuminate the sociohistorical contexts for twentieth-century minority works, McIntosh's foundational article on white privilege is especially useful for direct discussion of white subjectivity and for the ramifications her insights have for white authorship and characterization. I have also had students conduct comparative analysis of two Web sites, that of the Center for the Study of White American Culture (www.euroamerican.org/) and that of *Race Traitor: Journal of the New Abolitionism* (www.postfun.com/racetraitor/). The second can be read as inflammatory, and student responses to it should be dealt with extensively and carefully. I have also found viewings of period maps useful for discussing the concept of Eurocentrism and its impact on canonicity and historiography. If instructors have computers available in the classroom, entering the words "world map" into *Google*'s Images section will produce dozens of maps, nearly all of them literally Eurocentric. For maps that illustrate alternative views of the world, see *The Upsidedown Map Page* (www.flourish.org/upsidedownmap/) and Roediger's essay "Plotting against Eurocentrism: The 1929 Surrealist Map of the World" in *Colored White* 169–76.

[6]The essay by Pérez-Torres offers solid, pragmatic advice for promoting comprehension of *The Bluest Eye*'s depictions of the power that unspoken whiteness can have. He also writes, "For a class of predominantly white students, the novel can help highlight the deracialized status of Caucasians. The book focuses on the 'ugliness' of Pecola Breedlove, an ugliness fostered by a society that values blond hair and blue eyes as standards of beauty. *The Bluest Eye* can be unsettling because it traces the racial identity American society has erased for so many of our students" (22). This type of "unsettling," I argue, is something that *White Noise* can further provoke, in productive ways.

[7]I examine several such scenes in further detail in another article ("Who Are You"). For further consideration of racial whiteness as depicted in *White Noise* and of the unexamined racialized perspective of many of DeLillo's scholarly critics, see Cunningham's chapter "His Complexion" in *Race-ing*. Wesley examines DeLillo's depictions of racial whiteness elsewhere.

[8]Of course, much of what I recommend would play out differently in settings less homogeneously white and with teachers who are not themselves white or male. A good deal of helpful writing has appeared on the difficulty of addressing racial whiteness pedagogically, much of it from subject positions other than white or male and some of it about classrooms where white students are not in the majority. Particularly useful are Beech; Daly; Keating; McIntyre; Giroux; Barnett; Bernstein; Fox; A. Harvey; Kincheloe; McKinney; and several of the essays in Kincheloe, Steinberg, Rodriguez, and Chennault; Rodriguez and Villaverde; and TuSmith and Reddy.

TEACHING *WHITE NOISE* IN THE CONTEXT OF ELECTRONIC MEDIA AND TECHNOLOGY

Technology, Rationality, Modernity: An Approach to *White Noise*

Timothy Melley

White Noise is one of the outstanding novels of the postwar period and among the most enjoyable texts I teach each year. Even though it mocks some of my own investments (cultural studies, for instance), I find its satire of contemporary American life genuinely funny and its diagnosis of modern technology brilliant. My students regularly report that the novel deeply affects their view of the world.

The central insight of DeLillo's novel is that, through an ever-expanding commitment to modern rationality, contemporary Western societies have generated increasingly paradoxical relations to the natural world. *White Noise* makes these relations visible in a stunningly comprehensive way by linking the proliferation of technology to the broader assumptions of modern scientific consciousness. By understanding technologies as constructs that mediate between human beings and the natural world, DeLillo brilliantly articulates the links among mass media, machine technology, and modern technological rationality. This approach correctly depicts machine technology as merely one element of a sweeping technical ideology—an unspoken celebration of rational progress that has thoroughly transformed our social and environmental relations.

My central goal in teaching *White Noise* is to help students see how DeLillo connects media, technology, and modernity so that they can respond to his vision of contemporary American society. My aim is not to provide them with a particular interpretation of the novel but to move them toward a position from which they can launch a more sophisticated interrogation of their own. I want them to struggle with questions I myself find difficult. Does DeLillo's novel offer a solution to the unchecked advance of a technological worldview? What does the novel imply by portraying angst—the dread fear of mortality—as an inescapable and healthy part of "the human condition"? In its anxious vision of technological progress, does the novel ultimately celebrate a regressive form of humanism? What is its ultimate position on postmodern ideas and developments?

For students to address such questions, they must first understand how DeLillo connects the themes of runaway technology, mass-mediated social controls, modern angst, and postmodern groundlessness. What links these apparently disparate issues is the self-aggrandizing ideology of technological progress. Jürgen Habermas has called this ideology and its effects "the project of modernity"—the ongoing Enlightenment attempt to enrich and prolong human existence through objective science, rational social organizations, and the technological domination of nature (3). Students must also understand the novel's satire of certain postwar intellectual postures: the growing influence of cultural studies in university humanities and the even more pervasive skepticism about philosophical grounds, metanarratives, origins, and reality.

To ensure that students can interrogate DeLillo's depiction of these developments, I provide them with a number of important intellectual contexts. In post-1945 American literature and culture courses, where I most often teach *White Noise*, I offer introductory lectures on modernity and postmodernity early in the term. These talks distinguish the sweeping intellectual and economic features of modernity from the formal aspects of modernist and postmodernist art. They sketch the underlying values of modernity: its commitment to individualism, universalism, technical progress, and scientific rationality. To illustrate the logic of rationality and its progressive disenchantment of the world, I summarize Max Weber's account of bureaucracy and charisma. So that students can engage with various theories of postmodern culture, I introduce them to the approaches of David Harvey, Fredric Jameson, Jean-François Lyotard, Linda Hutcheon, and Brian McHale. Jean Baudrillard's "Precession of Simulacra" is particularly important in helping students understand DeLillo's sense of an evanescent real—visible in everything from "virgin acrylic" (49) and "IRREGULAR PEANUTS" (18) to the practice of simulated evacuation (SIMUVAC) drills. While presenting postmodernity and postmodernism as concepts still under construction, I suggest that much of the ongoing critical debate over modernist and postmodernist representation concerns the degree to which these artistic movements reject—or embrace—the values of modern rationality. This framework is valuable for reading *White Noise*, because the novel repeatedly dramatizes debates about whether rationality produces mainly positive or negative effects.

But note that I present such material as context for an entire course, not simply for *White Noise*. Furthermore, the way I introduce students to this context depends on the course I am teaching. In an introductory survey of twentieth-century literature, I summarize most or all of this material. In an upper-division course, where my syllabus often focuses on postmodernism or some more specific cultural phenomenon, I summarize some material but also have students read and discuss certain key texts before they work on DeLillo's novel. In American Literature since 1945, for instance, in addition to signal essays on postmodernism I sometimes assign sections from other obvious sources for the novel, such as Richard Slotkin's *Regeneration through Violence* and Max Horkheimer and Theodor Adorno's *Dialectic of Enlightenment*. Advanced students appreciate Michael Valdez Moses's superb essay "Lust Removed from Nature," which is also a useful resource for anyone attempting the approach outlined here. But none of these supplementary readings is essential for my approach to *White Noise*; my choices depend as much on the rest of my syllabus as they do on my use of DeLillo.

Before describing my class discussion plan, I want to counter an impression the above description of background material has undoubtedly created: I neither lecture much nor am interested in passing along a pet reading to appreciative, passive students. I believe in making students responsible for their own learning and expect student questions to influence my classroom activities. I invest considerable time teaching students how to ask good questions, how to turn their initial observations and confusion into coherent lines of inquiry, how to pursue and complicate those lines of inquiry, how to locate and analyze evidence relevant to their questions, and how to reflect this intellectual process in their writing. My students prepare daily discussion questions, exchange comments on an electronic discussion list, and write a number of short response papers that are due *before* we address a text in class. I allow all these responses to shape my classroom agenda, and I often photocopy selected responses for general discussion.

What follows, then, is meant to be not a rigid plan of instruction but a flexible framework for harnessing and connecting typical student responses to DeLillo's novel. The framework contains four topics: the ideology of technological rationality; DeLillo's depiction of that ideology's paradoxical effects; its relation to postmodernism; and, finally, DeLillo's humanist critique of modern technological values. Because student observations obviously do not often emerge in this order, my classes rarely work through the novel as efficiently as my summary suggests. Nor is there anything magical about the passages cited below; while they arise frequently, others work equally well. Yet technological rationality has such broad explanatory power for this novel that the framework to follow easily accounts for the elements of the novel most important to students: consumerism, late capitalism, simulation, omnipresent television and mass media, fear of death, technological failures, cultural relativism, the contemporary academy, violence, fascism, and superstition.

Technological Rationality

I begin classroom discussion of DeLillo's novel by focusing on student questions about technology. Students frequently understand this term as a mere synonym for *machines*, especially complex machines like computers, airplanes, and power plants. I press them for a more capacious definition. What, I ask, are the features of a technology? I supplement their high-tech examples with more primitive ones: eyeglasses, pencils, clothing, the chalkboard. When they define technology as a tool, I inquire about more complex tools. What about communicative or representational tools, such as writing systems? What about systems of organization, such as bureaucracies? What do these things have in common with refrigerators, televisions, drugs? Through what binary oppositions do we typically conceive of technology? What is its relation to the natural, the real, the supernatural, the human?

After some discussion along these lines, we are able to sketch some conventional conceptions of the technological. From one point of view, technologies are artifacts that prosthetically extend the capacities of the natural human body. Television allows our eyes and ears to register distant events; writing and recording technologies supplement our memories; drugs enhance our immune response, and so on. From another perspective, technologies are instruments that permit us to convert natural objects into products for our use. Dams and freezers, for instance, extend our capacity to consume natural resources. Common to both these ideas is that technologies mediate between us and the natural world. As they do so, they tend to change our view of nature. As Heidegger observed in his influential essay, technology "enframes" the natural world, turning it into a "standing-reserve . . . at our command" (16).

It is crucial for students of *White Noise* to see that, because technology mediates our experience of the natural world, technologies are media and media are technologies. DeLillo's novel insists on this relation. It also insists that technology be understood as an array of ideas and attitudes as well as a set of material devices. In other words, it suggests that the concept of technology is inseparable from the ideology of technological rationality—the pervasive, unspoken celebration of standardization, objectivist science, and rational technique.

Students can begin to see this connection by considering the category of technique—a technical approach that may require no material apparatus for its effect. DeLillo relentlessly catalogs technical colonization of basic natural acts: standing, speaking, eating, and sexual intercourse. Jack's wife, Babette, teaches an adult education course on posture and is preparing another called "Eating and Drinking: Basic Parameters." "People," she explains, "need to be reassured by someone in a position of authority that a certain way to do something is the right way or the wrong way, at least for the time being" (171–72). Later she reveals the rationalist assumptions underlying her courses:

> I think everything is correctible. Given the right attitude and the proper effort, a person can change a harmful condition by reducing it to its simplest parts. You can make lists, invent categories, devise charts and graphs. This is how I am able to teach my students how to stand, sit and walk, even though I know you think these subjects are too obvious and nebulous and generalized to be reduced to component parts. I'm not a very ingenious person but I know how to break things down, how to separate and classify. We can analyze posture, we can analyze eating, drinking and even breathing. (191–92)

This statement articulates the fundamental assumptions of the modern project: first, that all aspects of human experience can be improved by rationalization (better living through technology); and second, that reductionist analysis is a sound basis for such rationalization.

Once aware of these assumptions, students can locate them in DeLillo's novel. The German lessons Jack takes with Howard Dunlop, for instance, are absurdly technical in nature, focusing not on a holistic experience of the language but on "tongue positions" during "the pronunciation of consonants, diphthongs, long and short vowels" (54). Dunlop places his face inches from Jack's mouth to monitor his oral technique and even, in one "strange and terrible moment," "reache[s] in with his right hand to adjust [Jack's] tongue" (173). Jack is subject to equally reductionist analysis by his son, Heinrich, who tries to improve his cooking with a time-motion study:

> Did you see what you just did? You took the coffee can with you to the counter. . . . You could have left it by the stove where you were standing and then gone to the counter to get the spoon. . . . You carried it in your right hand all the way to the counter, put it down to open the drawer, which you didn't want to do with your left hand, then got the spoon with your right hand, switched it to your left hand, picked up the coffee can with your right hand and went back to the stove, where you put it down again. (102)

When Jack protests that "a little waste doesn't hurt," Heinrich argues that over a lifetime Jack could "save tremendous amounts of time and energy" and thus "live longer" (102). This final argument—that rational technique has the primary benefit of extending human life—is the ultimate promise of modernity and the central subject of DeLillo's novel. Once students have identified this technological benefit in such passages, they are ready to consider DeLillo's critique of it.

The Technological Paradox

In *White Noise*, the grand promise of technology is forever undercut by technology's mediating function. As technology enhances human capacities, it simultaneously erodes other capacities and experiences: it intervenes between our senses and the world, mystifies formerly mundane tasks, and creates new forms of human dependence and ignorance. I introduce this issue by asking students to consider Jack and Heinrich's argument about whether it is raining.

> "It's going to rain tonight," [said Heinrich].
> "It's raining now," I said.
> "The radio said tonight." . . .
> "Look at the windshield," I said. "Is that rain or isn't it?"
> "I'm only telling you what they said."
> "Just because it's on the radio doesn't mean we have to suspend belief in the evidence of our senses."
> "Our senses? Our senses are wrong a lot more often than they're right. This has been proved in the laboratory." (22–23)

The debate swiftly develops into a tour de force parody of familiar philosophical positions, Heinrich taking up so-called postmodern relativism and social constructionism against Jack's commonsense analytic empiricism. As I allow students to identify these positions, I make sure they grasp Heinrich's assumption that mass-mediated messages are more authoritative than personal sensory experiences. I then ask where this assumption resurfaces in the novel. Because DeLillo obsessively depicts the abdication of decision making to technical systems, students readily locate other examples. After the toxic spill, for instance, Denise and Steffie develop each potential symptom immediately after it is reported on the radio. In a number of other scenes, characters decide that their traumatic experiences are insignificant, because those experiences are not documented by the mass media (92, 162). It is difficult but important for students to identify the logic of such scenes: in each, individual human judgment is subordinated to judgments or ideas circulated by mass media.

Once students appreciate the relentlessness with which DeLillo documents the transfer of authority, decision making, and human agency to technical systems, they can explore the factors that cause such transfer. DeLillo traces the problem to an increasing dependence on technology, which has not only eroded our capacity to know the world directly but also mystified technology itself. A useful passage to explore in class is Heinrich's despairing rant about human ignorance during the airborne toxic event. "[A]fter centuries of progress," he asks:

> Name one thing you could make. Could you make a simple wooden match that you could strike on a rock to make a flame? We think we're

> so great and modern. Moon landings, artificial hearts. . . . What good is knowledge if it just floats in the air? It goes from computer to computer. It changes and grows every second of every day. But nobody actually knows anything. (147–49)

Students identify with Heinrich's thinking. They quickly (and sheepishly) acknowledge that they can't "make a refrigerator" (147) or explain the machines they use daily. But they must also see how this ignorance mystifies technology, giving it a sense of agency traditionally accorded only to humans or deities. When Jack successfully obtains money from an automatic teller, for instance, he is overcome by "[w]aves of relief and gratitude": "The system had blessed my life. I felt its support and approval. . . . The system was invisible, which made it all the more impressive, all the more disquieting to deal with" (46). After exploring such examples, I point out that Jack's view reverses Weber's account of modernization, in which charismatic authority becomes routinized, rationalized, and bureaucratized; here, by contrast, the mechanisms of rationalization have become mystified, accorded the magical or charismatic properties once located in God and God's ordained. I call this sort of reification postmodern transference—the imaginary reassignment of human agency to social systems and technologies—and in most classes I am able to show that it is a significant feature of postwar American writing.

Identifying this form of reification is the first step in illustrating DeLillo's critique of technology. The second is to focus students on DeLillo's sense of technological paradox. Students will understand this paradox when asked to consider the school evacuation early in the novel. Investigators cannot determine what sickened students and teachers, although they suspect microcomputers, the ventilation system, insulation, wiring, adhesives, and synthetic finishes. To narrow the list, experts wearing Mylex suits and respirators conduct a series of tests. Yet, Jack notes, "[b]ecause Mylex is itself a suspect material, the results tended to be ambiguous and a second round of more rigorous detection had to be scheduled" (35). The simultaneously protective and threatening nature of Mylex epitomizes DeLillo's vision of advanced technology.

Nearly every major character in the text makes a similar point. "Every advance is worse than the one before," says Babette, "because it makes me more scared." "The greater the scientific advance," Jack adds, "the more primitive the fear" (161). Willie Mink tells Jack that although there may eventually be an effective medication for fear, it will be "[f]ollowed by a greater death. More effective, productwise" (308). Murray Siskind understands the paradox by reifying death, treating it as a powerful, viral organism:

> [M]odern death . . . has a life independent of us. It is growing in prestige and dimension. It has a sweep it never had before. We study it objectively. We can predict its appearance, trace its path in the body. . . . The more we learn, the more it grows. Is this some law of physics? Every

> advance in knowledge and technique is matched by a new kind of death, a new strain. (150)

Later, Murray is even more direct. Technology, he says, "creates an appetite for immortality on the one hand. It threatens universal extinction on the other" (285). After discussion of such passages, students can articulate DeLillo's critique: while technology seems to offer talismanic protection against death, it simultaneously spawns terrifying new threats.

I point out that Horkheimer and Adorno called this paradox the "dialectic of Enlightenment," the tendency for Enlightenment rationality and instrumental reason to generate repressive social structures and new forms of mythology. Reframing the paradox in these terms, students can begin to identify another consequence of technological rationality: it spawns new forms of superstition and irrationality. Again, I put students to work locating examples of this dynamic in *White Noise*. The police consult psychics (60); scholars study "American magic and dread" (19); a police officer reports "a body thrown from a UFO" (234), which prompts a host of fresh sightings; when tabloids report "posthumous life in outer space, transmigration of souls, and personalized resurrection through stream-of-consciousness computer techniques," their claims are met with "no sign of skepticism" (144, 145). The resurgence of such irrationality, DeLillo suggests, is inseparable from the dominance of technological rationalism. As individuals increase their reliance on technical systems, they come to view such systems as powerful agents, which they can treat only with something like religious faith. From this perspective, the Enlightenment vision of progressive human emancipation through science begins to look like a collective delusion.

The Postmodern Condition

Once students appreciate the problem of technical mediation, they are ready to explore why DeLillo connects it to various features of the postmodern condition: uncertainty about what is real, difficulty locating origins or foundations, the rise of late capitalism and consumer culture, the decline of the nuclear family, philosophical skepticism and cultural relativism, the rise of cultural studies, and an unchecked proliferation of simulations. It is obviously not possible to discuss all these issues, so I start with one that subsumes many of them: simulation. When prompted, students familiar with Baudrillard recognize that DeLillo's SIMUVAC program involves a "precession of simulacra." During the airborne toxic event, DeLillo emphasizes the absurdity with which SIMUVAC confuses means and ends, real and artificial. One official complains, "we don't have our victims laid out where we'd want them if this was an actual simulation. In other words, we're forced to take our victims as we find them" (139). By examining subsequent deployments of SIMUVAC, students can begin to see its conflation of real and simulated with the life-extending promise of technological rationality—and thus can begin to connect postmodern groundlessness with the technological issues they have already discussed. According to a SIMUVAC executive, the logic of disaster management is, "The more we rehearse disaster, the safer we'll be from the real thing" (205). By the end of the novel, however, disaster-management exercises have become indistinguishable from real events. Only three days after a major chemical evacuation turns out to be a carefully staged drill, "an actual noxious odor" settles over the town but is met with "no sign of official action" (270).

After working through this sequence of examples, I ask students to identify other forms of simulation in the novel. They frequently cite people taking "pictures of taking pictures" of "THE MOST PHOTOGRAPHED BARN IN AMERICA" (13, 12), Sister Hermann Marie simulating her faith for the comfort of unbelievers (317–19), Murray paying prostitutes to feign choking so that he can simulate saving them with the Heimlich maneuver (152), and Willie Mink struggling to distinguish real events from their linguistic representations (306–12). Once a suitable list is formed, students can read such examples through DeLillo's technological frame. Sister Marie's defense of her empty religious practice, for instance, is a virtual restatement of Horkheimer and Adorno's thesis about irrational responses to the modern disenchantment of the world. "As belief shrinks from the world," she argues, "people find it more necessary than ever that *someone* believe" (319). Murray's substitution of paramedical rescue for sex suggests that powerful natural instincts have been supplanted by fantasies of technical prowess. And Mink's pathological confusion of real and representational is inseparable from his absolute commitment to technological salvation. It is this commitment that ultimately unveils the novel's Heideggerian existentialism and thus leads to my final topic.

Death: A Human Condition

Before moving to a final classroom discussion of *White Noise*, I review the previous discussions, underscoring DeLillo's vision of the double bind caused by an increasingly mediated existence. As technological rationality extends life, it inadvertently spawns anxiety about machines, uncertainty about the real, a resurgence of irrationality, and a heightened fear of mortality. This final effect—a dread of death—drives the plot of the novel. Overcome with angst, Babette turns to Willie Mink's revolutionary drug, Dylar, which promises to cure her of her angst. Dylar, in other words, embodies the fundamental promise of technological modernity.

After that brief review, I ask how DeLillo accounts for Dylar's colossal failure. Why is it unsuccessful in alleviating angst? There are a number of passages that shed light on this issue. When Jack asks Babette why Dylar cannot be tested on animals, she replies, "No animal has this condition. This is a human condition" (195). Later, Winnie Richards explains the relation of angst to human experience. She tells Jack:

> I think it's a mistake to lose one's sense of death, even one's fear of death. Isn't death the boundary we need? Doesn't it give a precious texture to life, a sense of definition? You have to ask yourself whether anything you do in this life would have beauty and meaning without the knowledge you carry of a final line, a border or limit. (228–29)

In discussing such passages, students must see both that DeLillo understands anxiety as an unavoidable and healthy (if unpleasant) human emotion and that he specifically invokes the universalist notion of a human condition.

I stress the second point by explaining how the notion of angst figures in the existentialist humanism of Søren Kierkegaard and, later, Heidegger. By such accounts, Heidegger's in particular, angst is not only what separates humans from animals but also what techne—the voracious attempt to rationalize and mediate—incessantly attempts to eradicate. In a technologically advanced culture, death is the final real, the last horizon of technical mastery, the mystery that cannot be rationalized. As Michel Foucault observed, no sooner does modern "bio-power" (the use of disciplines and regulations to extend human life) establish "its dominion . . . over life" than death becomes "power's limit, the moment that escapes it; death becomes the most secret aspect of existence, the most private" (138). By attempting to conquer death, the final frontier of irrationality and mystery, techne has the ironic effect of making death even more terrifying. As Winnie puts it, "If death can be seen as less strange and unreferenced, your sense of self in relation to death will diminish, and so will your fear" (229).

After sketching these ideas about the human condition—a condition that has often justified the project of literary instruction—I ask students what consequences might result from losing our angst. The corollary of the humanist argument, of course, is that if technology succeeded in numbing our fear of death, we would not be fully human. Students have trouble apprehending this point until they consider the figure of Mink. Dylar has reduced him to a nonperson, a "grayish figure" (308), "a composite" of personal memories and mass-mediated ideas (307). His speech is interlaced with incoherent snippets of television dialogue. He is, in short, the essence of white noise. His behavior is governed by external suggestions and messages, because he can no longer distinguish representation from reality. When Jack says, "Hail of bullets," Mink dives to the ground in terror (311). Mink literalizes Jacques Derrida's famous dictum "there is nothing outside of the text" (158). After reviewing Mink's condition, I ask students to diagnose it. What, I ask, has led to his sorry state? Is it his enthusiastic embrace of scientific rationality and its antihumanist premises?

Once the class has arrived at this point, a series of more difficult questions opens up. On the one hand, Mink seems to be the thoroughly postmodern figure—or perhaps the parodic emblem of a misunderstood postmodernism—someone who can no longer separate words from things. His conflation of real and representational implies a critique of postmodern groundlessness. On the other hand, DeLillo himself seems to rely on various descriptions of the postmodern condition for his portrait of contemporary culture. The class might then wrestle with DeLillo's position on postmodernism. Is *White Noise* a postmodern novel or merely a novel about postmodernism? Students can also be asked here to wrestle with DeLillo's vision of modernity. While his critique of technological progress seems to be a rejection of modern values, he cements this critique by invoking the human condition, a concept derived from Enlightenment universalism. If Enlightenment rationality generates insoluble paradoxes, must we reject its assumptions wholesale, or can we hope (in the manner of Habermas) that the project of modernity will eventually see us through? In short, does DeLillo embrace elements of postmodern thinking, as some critics claim, or does he merely depict these ideas in order to satirize them?

These are difficult but important questions. A successful treatment of *White Noise* need not answer them but should make them answerable and provide time for students to address them. But first students must understand the novel's uncompromising critique of the modern ideology of technological emancipation. In my experience, grappling with DeLillo's philosophical framework allows students to gain a perspective from which they can address the far-reaching implications of his work.

White Noise as Wake-Up Call: Teaching DeLillo as Media Skeptic

Kathleen LeBesco

Given the prevailing progress-positive stance of the American public where media technology is concerned, an antidote comes in the form of skeptical critiques of the full-speed-ahead mind-set. I teach in a department of communication arts, where many of our students have decided to pursue a major that allows them to think about electronic media and to learn producing skills in the realms of digital video, sound, and multimedia. Our students clamor for internships in the fray of mass-mediated popular culture; MTV and other major networks are big draws, as are dot-coms and glossy magazines. I encourage my students to become creatively involved with the shaping of the modern media, but first I expose them to a body of critical thought whose authors take aim at the bandwagon pleasures of new media. My hope is that such skepticism will help awaken a new generation of media producers to consider the consequences of media saturation.

The Media Skeptic Tradition

The upper-level course that I teach, The History and Development of Communication Theory, is required for all communication arts majors, and for a number of years it was also open to other majors, for whom it filled the college's core language-and-literature requirement. This course has a long history at my small, private, urban liberal arts college and has changed over time, as many courses do. Since I inherited it in 1999, I have maintained the overall focus on three major periods of media and their attendant social and political transformations: the invention of the phonetic alphabet and writing, which affected ancient Greek civilization; the invention of the printing press and use of vernacular language, which opened the door for the Protestant Reformation; and the development of electronic media (beginning with the telegraph in the mid-1800s), which have begotten today's image-based technologies.

Students first read Plato's well-known allegory of the cave and Socratic dialogue *Phaedrus*. Usually several students have encountered the allegory in previous philosophy or political science courses, but in the context of communication theory it can be seen as critical commentary on limiting one's conception of reality to only those shadows cast by the puppeteers of the electronic media. *Phaedrus*, a challenging text that is nonetheless amusing to students trained to look for Socrates's wit and dry sarcasm, provides an opportunity to consider why one of the great minds of all times was not in favor of writing, a skill that has become a hallmark of intellectual activity in the modern academy. Students grapple with Socrates's reasons for favoring the spoken word over the written—the written word dulls memory, fails to answer questions, is incapable of distinguishing between suitable and unsuitable readers, and so on—as well as with the irony that they know this argument only because it has been preserved in writing by Plato. Contextual material about literacy in ancient Greece is provided by the work of Eric Havelock.

The class moves to an examination of the consequences of Johann Gutenberg's invention of the printing press in Mainz, Germany, around 1450 (see Mumford; Eisenstein; or Graff). While the printing press is thought to have enabled the Reformation, critics of the new technology of the book were not merely clerics haunting the scriptoria of the Catholic Church. Scholars claim that the technology of the press allowed a further consolidation of power among the wealthy (Gass), who had greater access to literacy and more time to read, and among men over women (Spender 161). More common critiques came from the power mongers of the church, who feared the democratizing impulse of a Protestantism that encouraged the faithful to read for themselves and to stop depending on the corrupt intermediaries of the Catholic Church to mediate their relationships with God.

In the last third of the course, students read three full-length works: Neil Postman's *Amusing Ourselves to Death*, Aldous Huxley's *Brave New World*, and Don DeLillo's *White Noise*. Each work concerns itself, in more or less direct ways, with the dangers of a stranglehold of mass media and technologies on the modern citizen. Postman's nonfiction focus on television as a smiling vehicle of cultural death provides a strong backdrop to the two skeptical novels, though their critiques of the relation of the individual to the mechanics of mass production and representation are strikingly different. Postman goes to great lengths to convince readers that the deterioration of the "typographic mind"—characterized by seriousness, content, exposition—is a consequence of the invasion of electronic media and their dumbing down of public discourse.

Literary Skepticism

Huxley's dystopian novel, though written in 1932, presents a world in the thrall of mass production. My students typically find Huxley's vision chilling and are able to draw parallels between the world Huxley warned about and our own, precariously dependent on the whims of corporate media. But Huxley's world seems so odd and futuristic that many students are able to distance from it their experience of media and technology consumption.

It is DeLillo's *White Noise* that leads students to the most complicated and sophisticated understanding of the pleasures and dangers of electronic media technologies. The novel is the last major reading requirement of the semester, and usually two weeks are devoted to its discussion. Students write a paper from eight to ten pages (when they contrast *White Noise* with *Brave New*

World) or from five to seven (when they critique *White Noise* alone). Often they admit to wishing they had been allowed more pages, because of the depth of their analysis. In recent years, I have stopped asking students to write about *Brave New World* but still require them to read it and to participate in class discussions related to it. Huxley's novel has been Cliff's Noted to near death and overinterpreted (often poorly) on the Web, and thus less industrious students tend to rely too heavily, often to the point of plagiarism, on the work of others. Although *White Noise* has received a great amount of critical attention, I find that its relative youth as a novel makes it more of a challenge for students. Their charge is to articulate DeLillo's theory on the relation between communication technologies and human existence. While not restricted from researching other critics' and scholars' approaches to DeLillo, they must interpret the novel in the light of the readings they have completed for the course.

To turn students' attention toward issues of representation, media, communication, and electronic technologies, I usually distribute a reading guide. Its questions are inspired by those listed under "Topics for Discussion and Papers" at the end of White Noise: *Text and Criticism* (517–24), though tailored to a reader interested specifically in communication issues. I encourage students to work through answers as they read the novel, in order to prepare for class discussion and for the eventual writing of their essays. Here are sample questions:

What is the significance of DeLillo's oft-repeated reference to signs that refer to "the Most Photographed Barn in America"? How would a semiotician make sense of the prevalence of these signs?

Examine the place-names (town, city) in *White Noise*. What do they have in common? What might be the purpose of juxtaposing postmodern happenings like the airborne toxic event and Dylarama with places like these?

Consider the discussion between Jack and Heinrich about the weather (22–24). As a media skeptic, how would you interpret this discussion?

What is the significance of the frequent snippets of information, from various media outlets, that punctuate the narrative (e.g., "The TV said: 'Until Florida surgeons attached an artificial flipper' " [29])? What specific kinds of media are these phrases reminiscent of? What about the lists of commercial product names that interrupt (e.g., "MasterCard, Visa, American Express" [100])?

What is brain fade? How is it related to media in the novel? Is it relevant to our real-world information environment?

After running into a colleague off campus who tells Jack that he looks indistinct without his sunglasses and academic gown, Jack heads to the mall (82–84). What is it about his conversation with Eric that compels Jack to shop? What might media have to do with this suddenly activated consumer impulse?

Reflect on Bee's comment, in reference to airplane crash survivors not interviewed by the media, "They went through all that for nothing?" (92). What is the subtext here?

When talking about the properties of coffee, Heinrich says, "Whatever relaxes you is dangerous" (102). How might this statement relate to DeLillo's perspective on electronic media?

When Babette's posture class is caught on public access television, her family is enraptured by her image (104–05). Why are her children so excited? What interpretation might you make about media, embodiment, and reality?

What, literally, is the airborne toxic event (ATE)? What might it represent, on a metaphoric level? In responding, consider its characteristics, the relation between predicted side effects and people's reactions, as well as the change in demeanor (118).

Why is it significant that a railroad accident kicks off the ATE?

Consider the overt purpose of Dylar. How does Dylar relate to other forms of nonpharmaceutical technology discussed in the novel?

When Jack meets Mr. Gray (Willie Mink) in the motel, he recognizes that "[t]he drug [Dylar] not only caused the user to confuse words with the things they referred to; it made him act in a somewhat stylized way" (310). What is DeLillo's message here? Dylar can be read as a metaphor for what? How do we see this confusion made manifest in everyday life?

Why does DeLillo have Willie Mink speak in such an odd manner? How is Mink physically described? What might Mink stand for?

Examine the tripartite ending of the novel. What attitude toward technology infuses the outcome of the scene in which Wilder crosses the highway? How does DeLillo's scene of the family watching the sunset express his stance on technology? And what might the closing commentary on the grocery store mean in terms of technology and consumer culture?

As many of these questions indicate, an overarching theme I expect students to consider is how the characters in the novel view television, radio, film, tabloids, and other media forms. I ask them to compare these overt attitudes with what they feel to be the author's subtext. Does DeLillo treat different media differently, or is his take on all forms the same?

White Noise *and Contemporary Media Skepticism*

The work of Leonard Schlain and of Alexandra Torres is useful in offering students one framework for contemporary media skepticism, though I encourage them to explore others as well. Schlain, a laparoscopic surgeon and communication theorist, contends that the rise in alphabetical literacy created a new reliance on linear left-brain thought, as opposed to the holistic right-brain mode favored by preliterate oral cultures. He sees this shift as concomitant with the departure from reverence toward feminine values and images that enabled the onset of misogyny and patriarchy. Schlain's theory is based on a biologically determinist argument (women are left-brain thinkers and thus dominant when the primary mode of communication is the spoken word; men, right-brain thinkers, prevail when communication entails writing and reading), but it serves as an interesting foil to the argument presented by Torres about *White Noise*. Though unpublished, Torres's dissertation is worth hunting down (e.g., through UMI) by readers interested in a feminist critique of DeLillo's mediated world—something hard to come by in the more visible critical work on *White Noise*.

Torres focuses on the gendered dimension, arguing that television is thought of as a feminine medium because of its associations with consumerism, domesticity, distraction, and endless talk and that television is vilified precisely because of this association (1), a tradition dating back to early associations of men with high culture and women with low (or popular) culture. She claims that

> the "resistance" to television stems from, displaces, and manages the discomfort of white American men having to remake themselves in response to the political, social and cultural reconfigurations of the sex/gender system these upheavals [civil rights movement, Vietnam war, second-wave American feminism, post-Stonewall gay movements] have required. (15)

She situates *White Noise* as a novel "worried about the cultural status and uses of TV" (21), rife with anxieties about the novel's place as storyteller in a contemporary culture marked by TV, film, and electronic media saturation. She maintains that for DeLillo storytelling is a subject-making exercise threatened by the endless talk of television. The onslaught of information produced by electronic media and the secrecy of some of the characters in the novel—namely, Jack's ex-wives—compromise the production of stories. Babette's role in the novel is as much about gender as it is about communication: her

> leadership in helping the family block the flow of information and her embodiment of "proper" femininity are mutually constitutive. When Babette stops playing these roles, when she starts keeping secrets and consuming too much information, a two-fold crisis ensues. (124–25)

Torres recognizes that in *White Noise*, both male and female characters both construct and destroy narrative at various points and that the talk of many characters, regardless of gender, has been molded by media talk (125). But she suggests that male echoing of media is positioned as self-conscious critique, whereas television seems to speak through the women, denying them any narrative construction capabilities of their own. Torres refers to Jack's encounter with Willie Mink, inspired by the cliché of Babette's infidelity, as "a parodic comment on media-inspired masculine violence" but also as "an unfulfillable masculine wish for retribution against the media, and especially against television. For Willie Mink is TV" (156).

This last comment, popularized by critics dating back to Frank Lentricchia, makes sense in the context of Schlain's work, which applauds the recent rise of the right-brain image associated with film, television, and computers—and the parallel return to the veneration of the feminine. If one reads the gendered media dimension of *White Noise* as Torres does, Jack clearly seeks retribution against electronic media because the feminine power of the image threatens his very ability to exist as a fully realized subject.

This example is but one of my methods for linking the novel to a specific strand of contemporary communication theory. Joey Earl Horstman's work compels another connection, to Postman's perspective of media ecology. Horstman, like Torres, depicts DeLillo as understanding that the worldview television offers is antiliterary, "characterized by isolated detachment, political and philosophical and metaphysical cynicism, and a narrow materialism" (vi). Discussing the penultimate scene of sunset viewing, he writes:

> The location of this scene may suggest that Wilder and the supermarket constitute the two ways Jack—or DeLillo—[is] considering going. Wilder, crossing the "modernist highway," points backward, into a past that offers more certainty, more humanity, but, as we have seen, offers just as much tyranny. The supermarket, which creates "an aimless and haunted mood," points to the present, the televisual McWorld that dehumanizes and commodifies everything it touches. Jack's uncertainty about the sunsets (and the uncertainty about how to interpret the scene) reflects DeLillo's own uncertainty about how to form and articulate alternatives to these two options, the only alternatives he can perceive. It is a somber last chapter, and though it doesn't suggest defeat, it also doesn't suggest a way out. . . . (110)

I ask my students to compare this assessment of *White Noise* to their own readings of Postman's *Amusing Ourselves to Death*. They often find the work of Michael Valdez Moses useful in making this comparison, inasmuch as it frames *White Noise* as a novel depicting technology as a threat and a definer of public discourse (63). While students are often sympathetic to Postman's critique of televisual culture, they consistently voice frustration with his lack of coherent solutions or cogent alternatives—a position echoed by Moses, who highlights DeLillo's wariness in considering alternatives to postmodernism, technology, and consumer capitalism (66). This frustration generates discussion about where hope lies in both DeLillo's and Postman's work, if it can be said to exist at all.

The questions listed above help my students develop their own sophisticated interpretations about DeLillo's work as an artifact of communication theory, and I cheer their analysis most heartily when it moves beyond simple answers to my questions. Class time during the DeLillo weeks is dedicated to discussing different answers to these questions and related topics raised by students. I spend some time explaining the difference between text and subtext, as my students are communication arts majors and many have not analyzed a novel since high school. With a sense of that distinction under their belts, they produce thoughtful articulations of the probable communication theory of DeLillo.

Student Interpretations

Students tend to recognize DeLillo as a media skeptic, like Postman, the critic of television. Some of my excerpts from their essays demonstrate the overarching perception of DeLillo as a theorist of communication. They also illuminate levels of agreement or disagreement with what is assumed to be DeLillo's position. Some students see Babette's notion that family television watching deglamorizes the medium as an indicator of DeLillo's belief that the impact of television on society is negative; others argue that DeLillo's fear is exaggerated, and they credit people with the ability to resist mass messages. Still others, like Maggie, see DeLillo as a media skeptic but note that his infatuation with popular culture qualifies that skepticism:

> His opinion on technology in people's lives is that you can't let the technology consume you. DeLillo also believes that you shouldn't worry about the effects of the technology as long as you are aware of the fact that you are being conditioned unconsciously into wanting and consuming.

While seemingly counterintuitive, this interpretation is drawn from Postman's notion that no medium is inherently dangerous if you understand its biases and limitations and from the scene with which DeLillo begins the book's closing chapter. Maggie was part of a class that reached the consensus that innocent Wilder's successful tricycle ride across the dangerous terrain of mass-produced technology (cars) signaled a softening of DeLillo's skepticism. Perhaps, they thought, despite our worries about media technology, Wilder's making it across the expressway unscathed means that we'll be all right after all, that we too will survive our experience of media saturation, but only if we've learned how not to be jaded by the white noise of media.

This perspective is articulated by another student, Jessica J., who compares DeLillo and Huxley as theorists:

> Whereas Huxley's John takes his own life, DeLillo paints a picture of Jack's young stepson, Wilder, cheating death by technology in a literal form—by crossing a multi-lane highway on his tiny tricycle. That the tyke survives annihilation by large technological machines and arrives safely on the other side gives the impression that DeLillo feels as long as consumers of technology keep an attentive view of the stimuli they receive, they will escape death by media forces. . . . DeLillo subscribes to a more optimistic notion of human interaction with technology than Huxley.

When questioned about the issue of Wilder's awareness of the danger during his wild ride, another student, Joanna, offered a useful distinction. Referencing Murray's contention that children are immune to brain fade because of their particular manner of listening and looking, of collecting data (67), she wrote:

> The important difference between viewing like a child and child-like viewing is the influence that is accredited to television. A child, like Steffie and Denise, is highly sensitive to absorbing everything as fact. A child-like approach allows for the viewer to observe the information being presented and to make his/her own conclusions rather than become a component of media ideas.

Other students supported their interpretations of DeLillo as an ambivalent skeptic by pointing out the scene immediately following the trike ride. Jack and his family are able to marvel at the beauty of the sunset produced courtesy of pollution. Though the by-products of technology are reputedly deadly, they are often highly pleasurable to behold. Ashley writes:

> The family eventually gives into media and technology by partaking in the sunset. DeLillo's message is that many people may give in to the media and their effects, but they take it how they want. You can use media productively or you can let media wash over you and control what you do.

Blake paints DeLillo as a questioner of media technologies, though from a different angle:

> Orest's desire to be recognized for sitting in a cage with twenty-seven snakes triggered this question: can we coexist with technology if we can condition ourselves to become one with it so that it won't bite us—that is, take over us? The novel suggests that DeLillo would answer no. Orest couldn't get enough snakes to make his act impressive, and he got bitten anyway. It doesn't take much for us to get bitten; the bite seems to be inevitable in the presence of even a single snake.

Blake's interpretation initially suggests a darker view of DeLillo vis-à-vis media technology. But, to follow through on the metaphor, the much-feared bite actually causes Orest no harm, because the snakes in his cage are not of the poisonous variety. Again, it is possible that for DeLillo media technologies are not as deadly as cultural critics anticipate.

In the final description of the supermarket Michelle sees DeLillo as frustrated by media studies:

> The last paragraph is the perfect ending in response to the effects of media. The shoppers see that there is no point to the organization of the store, no reason for why they do things the way they do. DeLillo's final message in regards to media seems to be that although times have changed and many of us analyze our lives more, including the effects of media on them, in the end we don't care. We still find solace in the thing we know as media. I believe the supermarket in *White Noise* represents the media for the simple reason that no matter what, we keep going back to it because it will essentially give us everything we want.

Michelle praises the lack of a clear-cut message in the novel, admiring how "in the end, we are asked to find our own meanings and come to our own conclusions, traits generally not encouraged by the electronic media."

As much as their interpretations may differ in the details, most students charged with understanding DeLillo as a communication theorist ultimately paint him as a media skeptic in the tradition of Socrates and Postman. When comparing DeLillo to Huxley, Jessica J. writes:

> The general outlook seems to be grim, resulting in two in-depth critiques of not only the powerful effects of media stimuli, but the seemingly innate human need to consume and accept whatever information may be handed out by these forms of media. All in all, [DeLillo and Huxley] maintain a certain level of skepticism and integrity needed to counterbalance the inundating effect of the media, and for this reason they are theorists rather than statistics.

Jessica P. echoes this description of DeLillo as ambivalent theorist: "His theory suggests that technology, in and of itself, is not necessarily an instrument of destruction. . . . that if people learned how to use the new technologies properly, they could be valuable tools." The difficulty comes in recognizing that DeLillo must invoke the disjointed syntax of mass media to make his case in the novel.

> In order to destroy the toxic cloud, DeLillo has his characters use more chemicals, products of technology and science, to eat up the cloud. One could draw a connection to television and to those who would speak out

> against its use while making an appearance on a talk show or news program. It is also similar to Plato's use of the written word to distribute the view he shared with Socrates against the written word.

I leave it up to the students to decide how they feel about this problem faced by media skeptics zealous to spread their critiques but unable to use the dominant communication medium without undermining their position.

The most successful result I can imagine from my use of DeLillo in a long line of media skeptics is that students begin to recognize that communication theory is not bound to the pages of dusty textbooks but thrives in everyday musings and great works of literature alike. When they are able to develop responses to *White Noise* that deconstruct its gendered notions of media, recognize its cogency as a critique of consumer culture spurred on by electronic technologies, or find points of hope for our media-saturated future, they are effectively articulating a media-ecological perspective.

White Noise and the Web

Philipp Schweighauser

In 1992, Lewis J. Perelman predicted in *School's Out* that hyperlearning will eventually replace traditional forms of education: "In the wake of the [hyperlearning] revolution, the technology called 'school' and the social institution commonly thought of as 'education' will be as obsolete and ultimately extinct as the dinosaurs" (50). More than ten years later, we are still far removed from Perelman's vision, and few if any teachers in the humanities regret that. The main problem with Perelman's book lies neither in its economic reductionism (schools are too expensive and therefore out) nor in its technocratic zeal (hyperlearning is at the cutting edge of technological development and therefore in) but in its underlying assumption that traditional forms of education and technology-driven developments in the educational sector exist in an antagonistic relation. In fact, both fervent adherents and opponents of the use of new technologies in teaching tend to make that error. Teachers in the humanities and elsewhere hardly need to decide whether they are for or against the Internet, and for most of us the real challenge lies in integrating e-mail and the World Wide Web with traditional forms of face-to-face teaching. To do this successfully, one needs to think about the potential pedagogic uses of the Internet in order to tap into its resources in ways that truly enhance the quality of teaching and learning.

There are a number of pedagogically effective uses of the Web for teaching Don DeLillo's *White Noise*. I focus here on three functions the Web can serve in the expanded context of traditional classroom teaching (lectures, discussions, seminars, workshops). Taking some of the novel's major themes—media, simulation, commodification, postmodern culture, cultural studies, and ecology—I make a number of suggestions as to how instructors can harness Web resources to enhance their teaching of *White Noise*.

The World Wide Web facilitates access to a variety of different media.

White Noise is very much a novel about the mass media. The short consumer messages interspersed throughout the text testify to a cultural situation in which the images and sounds transmitted by television and radio have become ubiquitous. In *White Noise*, the industrial age has long given way to a new, informational order. Iron City, in which "[t]here is," as both Jack Gladney and his precocious son, Heinrich, emphasize, "no media" (45, 92), represents an anachronism in this media-saturated world. Consequently, it is described as "a large town sunk in confusion, a center of abandonment and broken glass" (85) that expresses "a ghostly longing for something that was far beyond retrieval" (88). DeLillo leaves no doubt that what is beyond retrieval in Iron

City is the industrial age its name alludes to. In the hyperreal world of *White Noise*, the absence of the media makes Iron City quite literally a nonplace, just as the absence of media coverage of the evacuation of Blacksmith's citizens makes that event a nonevent (161–62). As various critics have pointed out, the proliferation of simulacra produced by the mass media has all but obliterated in DeLillo's fictional world an independently existing social reality (Frow; Wilcox; Duvall, "(Super)Marketplace").

The world DeLillo depicts is very much the students' world, even more so than it is the teacher's. Undergraduate students in particular inhabit the virtual worlds of television and cyberspace in greater proportion and with greater frequency than their instructors do (*Nation Online*). While the ease with which they move in this Baudrillardian universe does not necessarily make them sophisticated media analysts, the very media with which students interact on a daily basis can be harnessed to enhance their understanding of DeLillo's novel and some of the broader issues its portrayal of the mass media raises. The Web is a particularly useful tool in this respect because, as the educational expert Rolf Schulmeister points out, one of the main advantages of a multimedial learning environment such as the Web is that it "facilitates simultaneous access to a variety of sources and different types of information (data, texts, images, films)" (9).[1]

Visit4info (www.visit4info.com), for instance, is a sophisticated multimedia Web site that hosts a large searchable database of television, cinema, radio, press, poster, and Internet commercials. The site is particularly strong on television and cinema commercials, which can be viewed in three streaming-video formats. It also provides textual background information about each advertisement, listing the product name, a short plot outline, hyperlinks to the advertiser's product home page and company Web site, and in some cases information about actors appearing in the commercial. *Visit4info* significantly facilitates the work of researchers in the field of cultural studies because it provides them with a ready-made corpus of materials whose collection otherwise would demand a considerable input of time and energy. Moreover, it makes those materials accessible from a single place and in a format (streaming video) that is more convenient to work with than VCR recordings or DVDs. In fact, it facilitates the researcher's task to such a degree that it allows undergraduate students to become researchers. A Web site like *Visit4info*—which advertises itself with phrases like "cool ads" and "hot products"—offers students an excellent opportunity to conduct empirical research on one of the most pervasive manifestations of contemporary consumer culture and to establish links between the findings of this research and the representations of consumer culture and the mass media in DeLillo's novel.

To give a concrete example, students may be asked to browse the database on *Visit4info* (www.visit4info.com/seenad.cfm) and think about how the phrasing of the hyperlink "Links in this product category," which accompanies each commercial, is appropriate for each category. For most of the commercials, *product* is certainly the correct term, but it seems inappropriate for several categories. What, for instance, is the product that is advertised in a public service announcement ("Seat Belts—A Good Habit"), an awareness-raising ad campaign ("Safe Sex"), a sociopolitical campaign ad ("Children's Rights Campaign") or an army recruitment commercial? These and similar questions can be used as a background against which the theme of commodification in *White Noise* can be discussed. In this context, Jack's description of the toxic cloud can serve as a useful entry point for discussing the characteristics of a (fictional?) world in which the mass media play a significant role in the commodification of everything: "In its tremendous size, its dark and bulky menace, its escorting aircraft, the cloud resembled a national promotion for death, a multimillion-dollar campaign backed by radio spots, heavy print and billboard, TV saturation" (157–58). Alternatively, the Web site's commercials for pharmaceutical products may be discussed in conjunction with Babette's belief that "everything is correctible" (191), with the Dylar motif, or with Michael Valdez Moses's assertion that, in the world depicted in *White Noise*, the greatest danger is that "technology may succeed in creating an illusion that it constitutes the only possible manner by which human beings apprehend themselves and their relationship to the world" (71).

Finally, from a pedagogical point of view, both suggestions as to how a Web site like *Visit4info* may be integrated in the teaching of *White Noise* harness "the ability of the computers to become any and all existing media" (Kay 106), and instruction will benefit from how the Web's integration of text, image, and sound enables more sophisticated teaching and learning. Web-based teaching can offer an enhanced learning experience that occurs at different levels of perception and involves several senses (Düx 231).

The World Wide Web offers faster and more convenient access to sources.

While it can be argued that the Web develops its full potential only in a multimedia environment, its provision of a mass of purely textual material adds considerably to its appeal to teachers and learners alike. For information that is not available anywhere else, the benefits of accessing it via the Web are obvious. Much of the textual material available on the Web today and of use to the discerning scholar is, however, also accessible through more conventional means (e.g., archival work). Even so, the main advantage of using the Web lies in greater convenience (unlike libraries, the Web is accessible independent of time and place) and greater speed. As Schulmeister sums up, thanks to the Web, "[t]he study of sources, which is part of the workload of today's students, is rendered more efficient. Time that can be used for more effective studies is saved" (9). I restrict my discussion here to DeLillo-specific textual sources and discuss other types of sources in the following sections.

Curt Gardner's *Don DeLillo's America—A Don DeLillo Page* (perival

.com/delillo/delillo.html) is the principal DeLillo-specific resource. Gardner's metasite not only provides a near-comprehensive, well-organized, regularly updated and annotated list of links to Web sites relating to the author and his work but also includes information that cannot easily be found elsewhere: translated foreign-language interviews, an extensive bibliography of reviews on DeLillo's work, a letter written by DeLillo to a member of an electronic discussion group on *White Noise*, an "oral auto-biography" stitched together from interviews with the author, a calendar of events, and a collection of DeLillo's pronouncements on writing. *Don DeLillo's America* is a true treasure trove and the first place to visit for anyone interested in integrating Web resources in the teaching of DeLillo's work.

A group of three texts available via Gardner's Web site is of special interest. "The Artist Naked in a Cage" is the text of a speech DeLillo gave on behalf of Wei Jingsheng, a Chinese writer and prodemocracy activist who had been jailed for eighteen years and was finally released in November 1997. DeLillo's speech, delivered on 13 May 1997 at an event organized by the NGO Human Rights in China, alternates among three images: a Russian performance artist's impersonation of a dog locked in a cage in the midst of Soho, scenes from Franz Kafka's "A Hunger Artist," and Wei Jingsheng in his prison cell. Taken together, the eleven paragraphs of this short speech pay homage to the courage and determination of a writer in opposition, an artist "so vivid and singular, so unassimilated into the state machine, that the state must find a way to make him disappear" (par. 7). The second text is a pamphlet penned by DeLillo and Paul Auster for the Rushdie Defense Committee USA and published in 1994, five years after the fatwa for Salman Rushdie's assassination was pronounced. Its aim is to raise awareness of the continuing threat to the author's life and to remind the United States and other governments to "exert due pressure to return Salman Rushdie—and all other threatened writers—to the world" (par. 8). The third text in this group was also written in the context of the Rushdie affair. It is an angry reply to John Cardinal O'Connor, who expressed sympathy for the Muslim community's aggravation at *The Satanic Verses* (DeLillo et al.). The group letter is signed by DeLillo and sixteen other Catholic writers and ends with the following sentences: "Mature Catholics do not believe that any dialogue with the non-Christian world can be conducted within a system that prejudges books. Mature Catholics do not believe that a death threat can be met with ambiguity" (par. 4).

DeLillo scholars less familiar with the author's nonfictional writings and interviews will be struck by his unequivocal endorsement of liberal humanist beliefs in the inviolable strength and integrity of the individual, the universal applicability of human rights, and the power of literature to transcend the context(s) of its production. These beliefs are in stark contrast to the postmodern agenda DeLillo's work is most often associated with. Among literary critics there exists a broad, though not uniform, consensus that DeLillo is a paradigmatic postmodern writer. Critics of differing persuasions have (correctly) identified in his work some of the major themes and artistic concerns of literary postmodernism. These include the proliferation of simulacra and an attendant effacement of reference, origin, and context (Kerridge); a preoccupation with consumer culture (Ferraro); a nonrepresentational aesthetics (Kucich); a systemic perspective informed by contemporary social and cultural theory (LeClair); and the evocation of a postmodern sublime (Frow). In DeLillo's work for human-rights causes, however, the real has returned in the form of the bodies of threatened writers, the humanist metanarrative is alive and well, and the cultural relativism Heinrich Gladney practices with such skill has all but disappeared behind surprisingly rash generalizations about "the continuing impact of world Islam on the consciousness of the West" (DeLillo and Auster, par. 1).

A number of critics have addressed these discrepancies and tried to resolve them in one way or another. Frank Lentricchia discusses DeLillo as the "last of the modernists, who takes for his critical object of aesthetic concern the postmodern situation" (Introduction 14); Hal Crowther treats him as "a satirist" who "tries to outrun reality, to stay far enough ahead of it, to look back with a safe lead, but it keeps gaining on him" (332); and Margaret Soltan reads him as a clear-cut liberal humanist. For teaching *White Noise*, it might be more fruitful to highlight the discrepancies and make them work than try to resolve them. Once students have been introduced to some of the aspects that make the novel a work of postmodern fiction, they can be directed to the three texts on Rushdie and Jingsheng and asked to think about how these nonfictional pieces relate to the novel's postmodern concerns. In a second step, a discussion based on the students' findings might address a variety of issues crucial to understanding the novel. These include the implied norms of DeLillo's satire, the related question of whether his portrayal of cultural studies at the College-on-the-Hill is parodic or an exercise in postmodern pastiche in Fredric Jameson's sense, and the novel's placement in a history of ideas that comprises both humanist and postmodern thought. The three texts, all conveniently accessible at *DeLillo's America*, are perfectly suited for this purpose: they are short (the longest runs thirty-two lines) and advance their arguments with the utmost clarity.

The World Wide Web supports self-directed learning.

Most educational experts today agree that self-directed learning is a fundamentally important goal of any pedagogic process. The prominence given to it involves a shift of perspective from the teacher as a source of information and knowledge to the learner as an active participant in the construction of knowledge. The Web both demands and enables forms of self-directed learning:

> Self-directed motivated learning is defined as a process in which the learner becomes active in determining his learning goals, in identifying

> human and material resources for the learning process, in choosing adequate learning strategies and evaluating the results of learning. . . . On the one hand, the new technologies demand independent, active and self-directed learning due to their specific constructional features (interactivity, hypertext structures, feedback, simulation), on the other hand these features support self-directed motivated learning. (Brink 260)

For self-directed learning to be effective, learners must be given the responsibility for selecting and connecting units of information. But to prevent them from being overtaxed and therefore frustrated, teachers should exercise special caution in choosing their initial input. I suggest one possible use of the Web's potential for self-directed learning to enhance students' understanding of the novel's environmental theme and its historical context. The proposed activity can be used on its own or as a preparation for reading an ecocritical article on the novel (e.g., Kerridge).

Students can be assigned to write an essay on the novel's environmental theme that establishes links among a few quotations the teacher has selected from *White Noise* and a few Web sites that have also been selected by the teacher. While the selection of the topic, the quotations, and the Web sites by the teacher ensures that meaningful connections can be established, the students are free to choose how many and which of the units to connect—provided that the links are neither unidirectional nor too obvious. The following three quotations from the novel, for example, profitably address different thematic complexes—the environment and social class, the environment and the media, and the environment and consumer culture:

> I'm not just a college professor. I'm the head of a department. I don't see myself fleeing an airborne toxic event. That's for people who live in mobile homes out in the scrubby parts of the country, where the fish hatcheries are. (117)

> "Japan is pretty good for disaster footage," Alfonse said. "India remains largely untapped. They have tremendous potential with their famines, monsoons, religious strife, train wrecks, boat sinkings, et cetera. But their disasters tend to go unrecorded. Three lines in the newspaper. No film footage, no satellite hookup." (66)

> I unfolded the bag cuffs, released the latch and lifted out the bag. The full stench hit me with shocking force. Was this ours? Did it belong to us? Had we created it? I took the bag out to the garage and emptied it. . . . I found a banana skin with a tampon inside. Was this the dark underside of consumer consciousness? (258–59)

The structural design of the Web sites selected needs to be sufficiently complex, including hyperlinks, hierarchical content structures, and simulations or other interactive elements that allow a learning experience that both requires and enables a significant number of choices on the learner's part. Students will rightly feel cheated if they get the impression that their main task is to discover the one piece of information the teacher meant them to find. Hypertextual structures are particularly suited for self-directed activity and experience: "*Characteristic features of hypertexts or, more generally, hypermedia include the networking and segmentation of information. This structure offers users free choices with regard to the reading sequence and the integration of information into given structures or contexts. At the same time, readers are given responsibility for the selection and linkage of units*" (Nikelski 215; emphasis in original).

The main strength of the first of the four Web sites I propose lies precisely in its hypertextual design. *Welcome to Geography* is a sophisticated site developed by students and staff from a London comprehensive school. It offers a forum for discussing a variety of issues relating to geography and contains a page on the Bhopal disaster, which took place in the same year *White Noise* was published. In the early hours of 3 December 1984, forty tons of the toxic gas methyl isocyanate leaked from Union Carbide's pesticide-manufacturing plant at Bhopal, India, killing at least 3,800 people and permanently injuring thousands of others. The page, authored by Noel Jenkins, juxtaposes two different descriptions of the disaster—one by Union Carbide, the other by a Bhopal victim support group—and asks students to evaluate them by doing further online research (Bhopal Investigation). Jenkins encourages the type of self-directed learning that the hypertextual design of the page makes possible. He stresses the need to evaluate Web resources and provides hyperlinks to important Web sites dealing with the event, including Union Carbide's official site *Bhopal Information Center* (www.bhopal.com) and two activist and survivor Web sites, *The Bhopal Medical Appeal and Sambhavna Trust* (www.bhopal.org) and *International Campaign for Justice in Bhopal* (www.bhopal.net). By providing access to a variety of perspectives on the disaster, Jenkins's page makes use of a crucial advantage of the Web: its potential for the discursive construction of knowledge or, in other words, "a form of discourse that does not have consent but the recognition and use of dissent as its goal" (Fasching 112). Students confronted with this page and the three passages from *White Noise* cited above will notice the cruel irony that links the page to the second quotation, but it is equally possible to establish relations with the other two.

The second Web site I propose is *CNN.com*. Its site-specific search engine allows students to find an article on a recent ecological disaster and engage in a case study on the disaster's representation in the world's largest media outlet. It offers an ideal opportunity for self-directed learning. Its vast store of information forces students to select adequate materials for the learning process, and its hypermedial, nonsequential structure gives them responsibility for establishing connections among different units of information. Moreover, starting from one of the three quotations from *White Noise*, students are free to decide whether they want to engage in the type of media criticism performed by the novel and use *White Noise* to discuss CNN's constructions of the real or tap into CNN as an information source to illustrate the contemporary relevance of the novel's environmental concerns and thus use CNN to discuss the novel. If teachers wish to encourage the former, in most cases more sophisticated approach, they may also point students to an alternative source of information on ecological affairs, such as *Greenpeace* (www.greenpeace.org/international/), and ask them to compare two different accounts of the same ecological event and decide which of the two is more "real." This comparison would provide a good starting point to discuss the novel's repeated suggestion that reality has become a construct generated by the media.

In both cases, students are encouraged to recognize the obvious but important point that reading literature has relevance beyond the classroom. The chief danger of integrating Web sites like *CNN.com* or *Greenpeace* in teaching literature is, of course, that students will lose orientation in their vast informational spaces and end up spending more time following hyperlinks than thinking about the relations obtaining between the fact-generating worlds of media outlets and the fictional world of the literary text. With respect to students' written work, two preventive measures can be taken by the teacher. First, students should be encouraged to ask the teacher if they are unsure whether the findings of their Web research will work for their essay. Second, an in-class discussion of successful and less successful uses of electronic resources should complement the assignment, both before students begin the assignment and as a follow-up based on their essays.

The fourth Web site I suggest is the online edition of the *National Atlas of the United States*, an official project of the United States Department of the Interior. This exceptionally useful site enables users to draw demographic maps of the United States that allow for the simultaneous display of a wide variety of natural and sociocultural parameters of their own choosing (nationalatlas.gov/natlas/natlasstart.asp). The site shows its full potential in conjunction with the first quotation above. With the help of the *National Atlas*, students of *White Noise* may, for instance, correlate locations of toxic release with the distribution of income per capita to find out whether Jack's assertion that toxic pollution affects only the poor is true or not. The site's main pedagogical benefit is its interactivity. Interactive maps enable students to exert control over their object of learning and allow them to experiment at their own pace in an adaptive environment that is at least temporarily freed from evaluation and social sanctions (receiving a low grade, a negative moral judgment). This freedom is crucial to the pedagogical usefulness of all human-computer interactions. Discussing the importance of interactivity in multimedial learning environments, Schulmeister concludes, "For the learning subject, the fact that interaction with a computer or a programme is free of sanctions maybe constitutes the most important aspect" (45).

Several of the pedagogical uses to be made of the Web support a form of learning that resembles the learning researchers routinely engage in. Independent inquiry, the study of sources in different formats, and the discursive construction of knowledge are all facilitated by the Web. One need not join the chorus of those who believe that the new technologies will render traditional classroom teaching obsolete to recognize the potential benefits of integrating the World Wide Web in the teaching of literature. Provided that the teacher is willing to reflect seriously on the opportunities and drawbacks of using the Web as an educational tool, Web-integrated teaching "makes it possible to realize the concept of the (undergraduate) student as a researcher, to shift the balance between reproductive learning and active discovery" (Kuechler 145).

NOTE

[1]All translations from the German are mine.

White Noise and the American Novel

Theron Britt

Don DeLillo's *White Noise* engages a set of issues central to contemporary American literature, but it focuses most clearly on the specific shape of contemporary consumer culture and its impact on the individual. Given this focus, one of the more useful ways to teach this novel is to situate it in the context of the theme of identity in late-nineteenth- and early-twentieth-century American novels. Many of these novels turn on notions of autonomous identity, usually pitting the individual against a constraining society and valorizing to one degree or another that individual as a corrective to social ills. Though it varies considerably from one period to another, or even from one work to another, this theme in selected examples of American realism, naturalism, and modernism[1] nevertheless provides continuity and context for understanding DeLillo's own confrontation in *White Noise* with the threats to individual identity now posed by contemporary consumer culture. Yet instead of merely reproducing the valorization of the individual over society that runs through much of American literary history, *White Noise* engages this abiding theme and works through it in order to express a new, more complex figuration of self to the social.

Late-nineteenth-century realist works such as *The Rise of Silas Lapham* (1885), by William Dean Howells; *Adventures of Huckleberry Finn* (1885), by Mark Twain; and *The Awakening* (1899), by Kate Chopin, are often included in an American novel survey course as examples of realism, and these novels in particular offer a representative realist sample for comparison with DeLillo's notions of identity. Though these three novels take up very different themes, each in its way turns on the realist conception of the individual as an autonomous moral agent and source of value struggling against a corruptive culture. *Silas Lapham* explores American capitalism in a central drama of individual moral choice. That drama stages Silas Lapham as a prototypical American capitalist and self-made man who must face the rampant materialism of his culture and choose between business success and the loss of his personal integrity. Simply put, Lapham's financial rise begets his moral fall; conversely, his eventual moral rise is occasioned by his realization that in the end he cannot be dishonest to save his business. His eventual stand for honesty accompanies his financial fall but also his return to a sort of rural salvation in his roots in Vermont. The choice he makes depicts the victory of internally derived self-regulation over the temptation of social success, of rural values over urban business values, and further makes clear that America's late-nineteenth-century capitalistic selfishness is in part a dangerous perversion of Emersonian self-reliance. Identity in Howells's version of realism, in other words, can be thought of as subject to corruption by the social but ultimately rooted in an intrinsic inner decency.

A much more complicated version of this theme emerges from *Adventures of Huckleberry Finn*. Many readings hinge on Huck's famous decision two-thirds through the novel to go against his society, his conscience, and listen to his heart, his independent and self-reliant inner voice. Faced with the moral dilemma of choosing to be a conforming member of his racist society and turn in his friend Jim, a runaway slave, or helping his friend escape, Huck is aware that a great deal is on the line, not just for Jim but for himself as well. He finally decides to sacrifice himself—in his own mind—and to choose his friend over society's racist rules, declaring as a consequence of his actions, "All right, then, I'll *go* to hell" (201). Quite often this moment is held up as a sort of moral center to the novel, a moment of epiphany in which Huck's resolution illustrates the classic virtues of American self-reliance and independence, and the novel is thus figured as a cautionary story of personal redemption telling us to distrust society and listen to ourselves. In this reading of realist fiction, the fate of the individual is figured in a realm of responsible choice, and as Huck seems to illustrate, the source of agency behind such choice already lies within us, though smothered by social conventions.

The Awakening also stages the rebellion of the individual against the confining strictures of society through Edna Pontellier, who is "beginning to realize her position in the universe as a human being, and to recognize her relations as an individual to the world within and about her" (13). Her relations as an individual are seen through the specific lens of the constraints placed on women by a patriarchal society. Unlike Huck or Lapham, Edna must struggle specifically as a woman trapped in an additional layer of gender-based social restriction that radically reduces her life options to the forms of family, religion, and love. She rebels against them all: against constraints posed by her husband and marriage, against her family obligations, and eventually against the love she once thought might give her life meaning. In the end she makes it clear that "she would give up the unessential," including her life, but she would never "sacrifice herself" to anyone or anything (115), and so she puts her freedom first. Unlike either Huck or Lapham, she ends up turning away from society altogether through her last suicidal swim.

My overly neat presentation of American realist identity through these three novels leaves out a great deal, for the dramas of moral choice in them have a further dimension that qualifies their presentation of identity as the pitting of social restriction against Emersonian self-reliance. Lapham's rise, for instance, is based on his stand for honesty, but Howells is clear that honesty restores Lapham not simply to himself but as well to that larger humanity he shares with all others. Insofar as he lived for himself and his own purposes alone, he falsified his life; and though the choice is his, the moral vision of the novel is also one in which his business includes others. Huck, even more than Lapham, is an ambiguous avatar of self-reliance, especially in the troubling last third of the novel. At the Phelps' farm, Huck is transformed once again, and critics have struggled to make sense of his apparent retreat from his self-reliant stance of chapter 31.[2] In this last section of the novel Huck takes the name of the socially conforming Tom Sawyer and, more telling, accedes to Tom's crazy plan to free Jim; he becomes a compliant tool in a plan that nearly costs Jim not only his freedom but also his life. Huck may in part embody the American drive for personal freedom when he tells us at the end that he intends "to light out for the Territory" because Aunt Sally intends to adopt him and "sivilize" him, but it is often overlooked that Twain is at pains to remind us that when Huck lights out for the territory, he will be but barely "ahead of the rest" (263). It is with this resonant qualifying phrase that we must contextualize his struggle between his inner heart and socialized conscience, for although Huck has at times acted independently—his choice of his black friend over society's racist rules is based on inner motivation—he has not been able completely to free himself from "the rest" who will follow and, more important, who are still within him in the form of the racism of his socially trained conscience. Huck, like Lapham, both exemplifies a strain of American self-reliance and marks a critical distance from it, a tension animating American realism and foreshadowing subsequent refigurations of identity that trouble earlier assertions of self-reliance. Edna Pontellier's ultimate ironic awakening to herself as an autonomous individual is in many ways the most disturbing sign of that troubling countercurrent, which flows through a variety of texts such as Ralph Ellison's *Invisible Man* and Toni Morrison's *Beloved*. These texts, and especially *The Awakening*, mark a critical distance from figures like Huck, who at least has the option to "light out for the Territory." Edna's territory is figured in the text through far-off Mexico, where her lover Robert, a "very foolish boy" (108), thinks they can escape, but she soon sees that Robert's love is a repetition of her husband's and leaves her nowhere to turn, no territory unstructured by the social fact of patriarchy. Perhaps in an ironic nod to constraints she herself must have felt in her own literary tradition, Chopin at one point has Edna sit in a library and "read Emerson until she grew sleepy" (73), a brief reference that not so much invokes the spirit of self-reliance as ironizes its place in a woman's experience.

Near the turn of the century this tension between an autonomous individualism and the shaping power of the social is more dramatically exploited by American naturalist writers such as Frank Norris, Theodore Dreiser, Jack London, and Stephen Crane, who tend to constrain the apparently autonomous agent bequeathed by realism within a determining horizon of social, economic, and natural forces. More explicitly than the realists, these writers often took the limits to autonomy as a major theme. Perhaps oversimplifying their literary forebearers, they reacted against notions of self-reliance, offering instead ragged depictions of individuals who are deprived of autonomy, who face the prospect that personal moral choice no longer matters in an amoral society or godless universe.

In part because of the accelerating industrialization of American society at the end of the nineteenth century, the agrarian social structures of Lapham's rural Vermont were giving way to the forces of cities, railroads, big business, and an ever-growing consumer culture. All these forces contribute to a revision of the (qualified) individualism of the realists, for the marketplace in naturalist writing has more to do with one's fate than does personal choice, and consequently moral dilemmas fade in importance in a universe dominated not by conscious choice but by socialized habits or unconscious desires. So the naturalist writers focused on scenes of coercion rather than on dramas of personal moral choice. In their narratives the willing self as a responsible agent is merely a pleasant or sometimes harmful fiction; in this new narrative horizon, Huck's socially trained conscience becomes an amoral and impersonal determinant. Dreiser's *Sister Carrie* (1900) shows how impersonal energies engulf individual intentions, how people act directly in response to a sequence of impulses and temptations. Norris follows social Darwinism and sees instinctual impulses behind human behavior; he believes that man's innate animality is a force stronger than his will. London represents the individual as largely at the mercy of an amoral society; though natural forces do not always overpower the individual, survival is determined by factors that, in the final instance, always are out of one's control, and the group, not the individual, is what survives.

Crane portrays a fundamentally godless and hence indifferent universe, yet individuals must learn to accept dependence not on God but on one another. In his often anthologized short story "The Open Boat" (1897), he recounts a struggle for survival of four men lost at sea who must band together against a fate brought about "when, willy-nilly, the firm fails, the army loses, the ship goes down" (57)—that is, when the failure of a collective enterprise lands the individual in a situation beyond the individual's control. In this story the strongest and in some ways most decent of the men does not survive, leading the narrator to surmise that "nature does not regard [every man] as important, and that she feels she would not maim the universe by disposing of him" (71). We see people as unable to control their fate, but also in a new position of responsibility: the men "felt that they could then be interpreters" and in fact *must* by default be left in charge of making sense of the world (77).

The existential conclusion of the correspondent from Crane's "The Open Boat"—that people are alone in a godless and hence amoral universe—anticipates and overlaps with the many and varied strains of subsequent modernist writing. Crane can thus serve as a balancing figure who helps show how the place of the individual in American modernist narrative crucially shifts from the naturalist's vision of the individual as a victim of amoral forces—natural, economic, or instinctive—to a vision in which the meaninglessness of the universe forces people to be, as never before, a source of value. Of the many examples of this modernist reworking of individualism, Ernest Hemingway's *The Sun Also Rises* (1926) has been one of the most often taught. It has remained in the classroom over many years, perhaps because it initially served as a prime example of modernist aesthetics; more recently it also has functioned as a touchstone by which to engage the unconscious or at least unreflective racism and sexism of its era. Many would agree that for better or worse Hemingway set the tone for a generation of writers, and in *The Sun Also Rises* he gives voice to the alienation felt by a lost generation but, more to the point for my argument, also to a so-called heroic response to modernist alienation on behalf of the individual.

This individualism is best noted in Hemingway's narrator, Jake Barnes, who has been literally emasculated in World War I and—unsurprisingly in the aftermath of a senseless and brutal war—struggles in a morally tainted, decadent world of disillusioned and damaged postwar expatriates. All aimlessly drifting around Europe, these people are as emasculated symbolically as he is physically. In this debased social context the main theme of the novel is the familiar American one of the individual who, like Lapham or Huck, tries to live a good life while resisting the corrosive influence of the loss of values and subsequent alienation.

The central characters are Jake, Robert Cohen, and Lady Brett Ashley. Because his culture has produced an overwhelming surfeit of senseless death and destruction, Jake searches among his cultural ruins for a way to salvage some meaning and value in his life. This search in postwar Paris engages with an even deeper level of social corruption than the one Huck encountered, and his estrangement from society goes far beyond Huck's, since Jake rejects its conscience. He is disgusted by the hypocrisy and triviality of his society and reports the existential isolation and drift that Crane's correspondent articulated. Yet unlike either Twain or Crane, Hemingway seems to embrace an Emersonian vision of self-reliance (yet one devoid of transcendence): from the outset he valorizes Jake's personal experience over Robert's dependence on book learning, Jake's tough-minded self-analysis and self-awareness over Brett's half-knowing evasions.

Although few of the characters in *The Sun Also Rises* can be directly linked to Emersonian individualism, they are usually classified into three groups that illustrate the need for an inward turn: the wounded, the pretenders, and the dignified Spaniards. The first two groups take up residence in Paris and are the main focus of the first half of the novel. Hemingway uses the wounded, such as Jake and Brett, to show just how disillusionment came to those closely involved with World War I. The pretenders, such as Robert, are there for contrast to the disillusioned; they are the people who still buy into the romanticism of a previous generation or who simply fake and posture in their everyday lives. The fishing trip into the Spanish countryside and the Spanish characters introduced in the last third of the novel offer an alternative to the failure of Jake's society to generate a viable system of values (168). On the trip, Jake experiences nature and the simple virtues of friendship. The image of Spain as an alternative society is furthered through the young Spanish bullfighter Pedro Romero, whose honesty and courage in the face of death assert a heroic value to Jake's self-awareness, internal strength, and dignity in the face of great personal suffering.

In Hemingway's novel, a tough-minded individualism generates both meaning and value independent of a society lacking in both. One must look inward, Hemingway shows us, because the traditional measures of religion, reason, or even love have produced nothing but death, destruction, or emptiness. He was influential perhaps in part because his point of view centered in a seemingly heroic individualism that offered an alternative to the vacuum in values following World War I. There is a great temporal distance between Hemingway and DeLillo, and much can and should be said for intervening literary developments, but for pedagogical purposes the corrupt society and corresponding inward turn shown by *The Sun Also Rises* help illustrate how and why the central role of the individual has come through at least one strain of literary modernism as both a solution and a problem for contemporary writers.

This quintessential American theme of the self struggling in society has persisted into the period of *White Noise*, but in our new social environment, often characterized as postmodern, we find an unprecedented sense of threat from society to the self that Hemingway and many other American writers have turned to as a refuge or source of value. Like those of the naturalists and modernists before him, DeLillo's world is "full of abandoned meanings" (184) and characters set adrift, yet the dehumanizing forces for disillusionment DeLillo finds in contemporary American culture have escalated since Hemingway. For DeLillo, the very nature of the individual is in question and can no longer be assumed as a source of value; the individual is better conceived in the postmodern period as a subject who is a site of contestation for various social codes. It is as if in contemporary American society Huck's "conscience" is on the brink of total triumph. At a level not seen before in realism, naturalism, or modernism, the perceived social threat to the autonomy of the individual is figured in *White Noise* not just as constraining the self but as something closer to annihilating the self.

Frank Lentricchia helped open this path of inquiry when he claimed that DeLillo's work moves readers "to the view that the shape and fate of their culture [dictates] the shape and fate of the self" ("Don DeLillo's Primal Scenes" 413). John Frow, among others, continued this line of reasoning by linking the novel's presentation of culture to a malleable sense of self-identity but focused primarily on the "Baudrillardian melancholy" of the loss of a stable cultural referent; for Frow, simulacra and simulation govern the novel's presentation of a world in which "identity is simulated in the play of difference and repetition," largely as a result of "the deadly serious principles of a capitalist society" that commodify the individual and thus set us all adrift in a world lacking a stable ground point (423, 425). John Duvall deepens this analysis of social malaise, deftly using Fredric Jameson and Jean Baudrillard as touchstones, in a detailed and extremely useful reading of the novel's unmasking of "American proto-fascism" and its meditation on "the effects of mediations that pose as the immediate," especially the space of the shopping mall and television, in American capitalistic culture ("[Super]Marketplace" 128). These and other readings usefully map Baudrillard's ideas of simulacra and simulation in the novel's presentation of cultural indeterminacy as a function of late capitalism. That is, they allude to the economic underpinnings of the cultural effects found in the novel but negotiate a type of post-Marxist interpretive strategy that allows for analysis of American culture as a semi-autonomous function of the economy. In the main, they explore the particular mechanisms of contemporary American mass media that *White Noise* presents in order to foreground the ways in which DeLillo shows us the loss of depth and apparent groundlessness of postmodern American culture.

While these readings remain valuable for what they illuminate about the novel's presentation of the forces animating American social life, they tend to concentrate on what Lentricchia called the "shape and fate of the culture" and give less thought to relating that culture to his balancing term, the "shape and fate of the self." Though most readings show DeLillo as critical of American culture, they leave out the mechanism, implied or explicit, by which he in fact critiques the culture of the simulacra. At this point a naive-sounding question is in order: If we are simply socially constructed, what could possibly exceed that construction and both motivate a critique and serve as a point of comparison? Here literary history provides a useful contrast: Howells had a nostalgic rural retreat and implied moral center he could invoke as counterweight to a corrupt business culture; Twain's Huck showed the inner strength of his heart, if qualified, as a retort to socially sanctified racism; and Crane and Hemingway retained the individual as the only source of value left in a meaningless universe and absurd and amoral society.

For DeLillo the solution of his precursor modernists has become his problem, for he questions any implied ground in the individual asserted by them; he questions both the nature and stability of the individual. For him and for his readers the troubling question has become how the individual, if socially constructed, can be a source from which to critique the culture of which it is a part. In other words, given the postmodern undermining of absolutes and loss of norms, especially the norm of the self-reliant individual, how can any work situated in such a horizon generate a ground from which to offer a critique?

Hemingway's individualistic heroism is no longer an answer for DeLillo, since the world of *White Noise* depicts the contemporary individual living in and subjectively experiencing both self and surrounding world as an indeterminate white noise—an even hum—in which significant epistemological and ethical differences melt into a numbing sameness. Nor is this merely a literary problem: DeLillo shows in great tragicomic detail how a variety of social forces for indeterminacy—the postmodern upshot of the meaninglessness chronicled by Crane and Hemingway—traverse the contemporary American home and cultural space and contribute to a historically new and, it must be stressed, deeply disturbing subjective sense of individuality. This sense is neither liberating nor heroic; it is more like that of the schizophrenic—not the joyous schizophrenic of Deleuze and Guattari but the obscene and drifting schizophrenic of Baudrillard and Jameson.

In stark contrast to Hemingway's Jake Barnes, Jack Gladney is a proof text for this schizophrenic self. He is mired in a subjective experience of blurred boundaries. As the narrative tracks his ominous confrontation with his multiple "American environments" (9) in his desperation to combat his "feeble presentation of self" (17), he edges ever closer to Jameson's notion of the schizophrenic. As for the clinically schizophrenic, Jack's experience of family life, of work, and of the American world of shopping malls and fast-food franchises consists of isolated, disconnected, discontinuous signifiers that fail to link up into a coherent sequence. If his life were a story, it would be plotless, random. This discontinuity poses a threat to his identity, since, like the schizophrenic, he increasingly has less sense of self in any older, normative way; he lacks, as Jameson notes, a sense of continuity in time, the persistence of the "I" and "me" over time ("Postmodernism" 119). Baudrillard's description of the schizophrenic further illustrates Jack's abiding fear, for like the schizophrenic, Jack "can no longer produce the limits of his own being, can no longer play [or] stage himself, can no longer produce himself as mirror. He is now only a pure screen, a switching center for all the networks of influence" ("Ecstasy" 133).

As a "switching center" for multiple and perhaps inconsistent social codes, Jack suffers a sort of late-twentieth-century meaning disorder, an inability to make cohere the categories that have organized his identity and his world. Thus it is no surprise that throughout the novel he reports a growing fear of his approaching death. The chemical released by the airborne toxic event,

Nyodene D, may lead to his physical death (though even here there is no certainty, since its effects will take thirty years to manifest themselves); but, more important, his sense of identity is dying, for he reports his mind as increasingly fragile, fragmentary, and—like the schizophrenic's—indistinct. On an outing to a hardware store, for example (ironically enough to buy rope), he bumps into his academic colleague Eric Massingale, who acts slyly surprised to see Jack off campus without his usual camouflage of dark robe and glasses. Massingale is moved to describe him as "a big, harmless, aging, indistinct sort of guy." This obvious slight to Jack's sense of himself as a distinct being puts him "in the mood to shop," but the things he shops for are not in themselves what he desires (83). Rather, he's clear that he "[shops] for its own sake," that the shopping itself seems to be the point, for it is not the use values of the things he and his family buy that matter—we don't learn what it is they actually purchase—but the codes these things convey (84). In immediate response to the assault of being an "indistinct sort of guy," an assault not just on what he is or his socioeconomic status but on his very existence as a person, Jack finds momentary solace in an epic shopping binge that unites him with his family, letting him be, finally, "one of them, shopping, at last." Tellingly, though, after the shopping binge they drive home "in silence" and go to their "respective rooms, wishing to be alone" (84).

More telling of what a thoroughly socially constructed being he is, shopping unites Jack with himself, again only momentarily, for he feels that "these sums in fact came back to me in the form of existential credit" (84). He is able while shopping to see himself literally in "some reflecting surface" (83) of chrome, glass, or TV monitor. He also sees himself in a more profound subjective sense; as he shops he narrates that "I filled myself out, found new aspects of myself, located a person I'd forgotten existed" (84). Shopping at the mall is paralleled by shopping at the supermarket, for there too he revels in "the sheer plenitude those crowded bags suggested" and glories in "the sense of replenishment we felt, the sense of well-being, the security and contentment these products brought to some snug home in our souls—it seemed we had achieved a fullness of being that is not known to people who need less" (20). For a brief moment, shopping and his purchases reassure him of the "fullness of being" of his existence, a reassurance he also gets from a trip to the ATM machine when he realizes that "something of deep personal value, but not money . . . [has] been authenticated and confirmed" (46). As his friend Murray says of the supermarket, "This place recharges us spiritually" (37), as if a person were a bank account. However, it is a short respite before he returns to "the vast loneliness and dissatisfaction of consumers who have lost their group identity" (50), since no income level, purchase, or ATM transaction can reverse Jack's middle-aged slide out of the core market segment of a media-defined collective identity. Given his shrinking place in the marketing scheme, Jack is waking up to a "vast loneliness," to "brain fade" (67), to a sort of schizophrenic drifting in a world of information overload, abandoned meanings, and abandoned identities that, like the latest California lifestyle, end up being dumped into the trash compactor with the rest of life's dreck.

Unlike Jake Barnes but like the clinical schizophrenic, Jack finds nothing heroic in his confrontation with death and remains unable to link up the disparate bits of his experience into a meaningful whole, a personal identity. Instead he is, as the SIMUVAC worker tells him, merely the sum total of his socially coded data (141) in a world of discontinuous material signifiers where remarks—his, anyone's—exist "in a state of permanent flotation" and "[n]o one thing [is] either more or less plausible than any other thing" (129). This indeterminate social space is the point at which multiplicity melts into sameness, where more choice, more information, more facts resolve into an even hum of equally plausible, hence meaningless, white noise. The boundary problems Jack is experiencing lead not to the modernist alienation Jake feels relative to his lost generation but to a more profound malaise, the postmodern "end of skepticism" (27). Characteristic of the postmodernism that this novel shows layered in multiple American environments, the end of skepticism is not just for semiliterate tabloid readers; it applies to the narrator and nearly every character in the novel—because a skeptic must have a reliable point of origin against which a proposition or idea can be tested. That point of origin, previously found at the core of Jake or more ambiguously in Huck, has either vanished or become radically ambiguous.

Positing the end of skepticism is a way of speaking about the pervasive indeterminacy of Jack's experiences and is figured in many ways, perhaps most tellingly by the absence of reliable and hence reassuring figures of authority. During the airborne toxic event the fear that "those in positions of authority will long since have fled, leaving us in charge of our own chaos" (120) seems as disturbing to Jack as the toxic cloud itself. Like the narrator at the end of Crane's "The Open Boat," who finds himself in charge of interpretation, Jack must himself set the limits and controls that God or reason once provided. Yet unlike Crane's narrator, Jack seems frightened by this inward turn, since he struggles in a far more chaotic social environment and lacks the resources to impose order.

But DeLillo does not leave us with only a diagnosis of the dehumanizing effects of American culture. He also points to a cure, for if the problem is the "brain fade" or incremental loss of distinct identity induced by the white noise of American culture, the solution is neither a return to a simpler time of rural values, which worked for Silas Lapham (lost values effectively ironized by the nostalgic rural aura of the Most Photographed Barn in America), nor an escape to a "Territory" beyond the reach of social restriction: there is no cultural space not touched by the bombardment of consumerism, no retreat into the self as a heroic fortress. Rather, the path of resistance to simulation in *White Noise* begins by evoking in the sections "Waves and Radiation" and "The Airborne Toxic Event" the dominant force of society in the construction of identity. In these sections the novel does not merely chronicle the pervasive effects of the social real but also figures them as deadly to the self. That is, it posits underneath social construction a resistant human need for individual autonomy and, more to the point, a way to achieve it. Because the novel poses Jack's "feeble presentation of self" as a problem, it necessarily implies an alternative against which his drifting self may be measured. Against the manipulations of the multiple American environments that traverse contemporary American life, *White Noise* offers an insistent counterargument that explores both the desirability of and the limited yet still viable possibilities for a mode of subject formation that would resist brain fade.

The particular path taken to resist a socially produced schizophrenic subject position is made clearest in Jack's encounter with the nun, Sister Hermann Marie, after he shoots, is shot by, and then saves his wife's seducer, Willie Mink. While the nun bandages his wound, they have an exchange centered on belief, a scene that recalls an earlier discussion with Murray on believing in life after death as a cure for Jack's fear of death. Murray tells him, "Millions of people have believed for thousands of years. Throw in with them." Jack calls this advice "a convenient fantasy, the worst kind of self-delusion," asking finally, "But don't I have to believe? Don't I have to feel in my heart that there is something, genuinely, beyond this life, out there, looming, in the dark?" (286). To this rhetorical query about the necessity for sincerity of belief, Jack's conversation with Sister Hermann Marie offers an oblique answer by calling for a sort of second order of belief.

Jack at first finds her quaint, but when he discovers she does not herself believe in God, the angels, heaven, and hell, he is more than surprised. But she tells him, "Hell is when no one believes," and what she is trying to teach him is a basic lesson in both cultural and personal survival. Of her mission in the world she says,

> Our pretense is a dedication. Someone must appear to believe. Our lives are no less serious than if we professed real faith, real belief. As belief shrinks from the world, people find it more necessary than ever that *someone* believe. Wild-eyed men in caves. Nuns in black. Monks who do not speak. We are left to believe. Fools, children. Those who have abandoned belief must still believe in us. They are sure that they are right not to believe but they know belief must not fade completely. . . . There must always be believers. . . . There is no truth without fools. (319)

Her pretense of belief is based in the need for a cultural and personal sense of identity that is not simply an effect of marketing. Her pretense, she tells Jack, is not for nothing; it is "For the world, dumb head" (319). Though she reveals a scorn for a classic metaphysics of "[t]he devil, the angels, heaven, hell," she has not rejected the human purpose of metaphysics. In this sense she is indeed a postmodern moral agent, fulfilling through her dedication her religious function as part of the "tiny minority" who "believe things no one else takes seriously" in order to give the rest of us a marker (318), a fixed point against which we can define ourselves and thus resist the schizophrenic drift of contemporary American (and by now global) consumer culture. It is not the content but the fact of her belief that matters. She ends their conversation with a "storm of words" in German, the meaning of which Jack cannot, of course, decipher, but neither he nor the reader needs to know their literal meaning, for the meaning is in the structure, a rhythm that reminds Jack of a litany, a hymn, or a catechism and that he finds "beautiful" (320). Like a catechism, a call and response, her belief sets up a point of origin necessary not for Jack's soul but for his self-definition. Her pretense of belief is enough, perhaps, in the welter of consumer society to give a basis for his autonomous identity that white noise seems about to dissolve. At the same time her pretense ironically presents that identity as necessarily imbricated in social relations.

In this way DeLillo's postmodern take on the American theme of the self struggling in society takes to a new level the problem illustrated in part by Silas Lapham, Huck Finn, and Jake Barnes. DeLillo's new postmodern iteration of the American assertion of autonomous identity retains a remnant of realism's and modernism's inward turn, in the form of a posited basic human desire or need for a stable autonomous identity. Why else does Jack Gladney protest against his culture's brain fade? But beyond that ground in human desire, the creation of identity—contrary to the positions staked out by previous realist, naturalist, or modernist writers—is not well accomplished by ignoring society and looking inward to some intrinsic truth. It is better mediated through socially defined oppositions: there is no truth without fools, no self without other.

Because the American culture of white noise has flattened previously stable oppositions into a numbing sameness, making it ever more difficult to differentiate one thing and eventually one self from another, the familiar American struggle for autonomy now requires more than merely turning down the sound of culture and gazing inward to one's heart; it requires an arbitrary moment outside white noise, a cultural polestar, a stable marker, a belief by which self-identity may function. Unlike the world of the realists, naturalists, or even modernists, the world of *White Noise* is one in which contemporary American consumer culture has almost erased that marker. As Sister Hermann Marie warns us, "You will lose your believers" (319). Since we have lost the grand narratives that once sustained us, the "great old beliefs" (318), we clearly lack the cultural resources required to go back to an older and more stable society. If Hemingway suggested that we simply turn inward for sustenance, DeLillo suggests that we follow a more circuitous route.

White Noise maintains a link with our literary past by positing an underlying human need for autonomous identity, to that extent endorsing a limited sort of postmodern humanism. But it goes beyond the answers of the literary past when it complicates this turn by framing this need in its necessarily social fulfillment. In the end the novel suggests not only that our postmodern cultural moment is deadly to the individual but also that we must resist the full sweep of postmodern indeterminacy. We can resist by exploring various social mechanisms of belief as solutions to the brain fade that besets us. Of course, the distressing option remains that we acquiesce to Huck's conscience, to brain fade, and ultimately to death, finding ourselves like the confused elderly shoppers at the novel's conclusion, "sweet-tempered people taken to the edge" of schizophrenic drift (326).

NOTES

[1]These literary periodizations are pedagogically useful yet of course inevitably fluid and always open to contestation.

[2]An excellent staging of the critical discussion of the problematic ending and of its relation to issues of race in the novel can be found in the essays in the section "The Controversy over the Ending" of Graff and Phelan's critical edition (279–334).

White Noise, Postmodernism, and Postmodernity

John N. Duvall

Teaching *White Noise* in an undergraduate survey course of American literature since 1865 means that DeLillo's novel will bear much of the burden of representing postmodernism. In a fifteen-week semester, if one devotes five weeks to realism and naturalism and another five weeks to modernism, then only the final five weeks remain to consider the contemporary period. (This five-week model is probably a best-case scenario for post-1950s literature, a period underrepresented in most anthologies, which devote the bulk of their space to earlier, more canonical texts.) The pressure on *White Noise* to be representative only increases when one acknowledges that many contemporary texts have little to do with postmodernism.

To be more concrete, consider briefly how a survey might turn from modernism to the contemporary. If the modernist portion of the course has used T. S. Eliot's *The Waste Land* (1922) as a kind of touchstone, then any number of novels, from Ernest Hemingway's *The Sun Also Rises* (1926) and F. Scott Fitzgerald's *The Great Gatsby* (1925) to Nella Larsen's *Passing* (1929) and William Faulkner's *Light in August* (1932), allow one to develop issues of modernist alienation through the thematics of the wasteland. Whether the survey's examination of the Harlem Renaissance includes Larsen's novel or Zora Neale Hurston's *Their Eyes Were Watching God* (1937), a logical turn into the contemporary might be Toni Morrison's *The Bluest Eye* (1970). Morrison's novel allows students to make links between Pecola Breedlove's alienation and that of such characters as Faulkner's Joe Christmas, Hemingway's Jake Barnes, Willa Cather's Jim Burden, or Tennessee Williams's Blanche DuBois. Like its modernist predecessors, *The Bluest Eye* sifts through the metaphoric wasteland in search of authentic identity, specifically authentic racial identity. Quite simply, the quest for authenticity in Morrison's early novel resonates more with modernism than postmodernism. As the example of *The Bluest Eye* helps clarify, contemporary literature by ethnic and minority writers, especially when it yearns for authenticity, often cannot embrace wholeheartedly postmodern theories of indeterminate and fragmented identity. This is not, of course, to say that authors such as Ishmael Reed, Maxine Hong Kingston, Amy Tan, and Morrison herself have not figured in discussions of postmodernism. But as bell hooks argues in "Postmodern Blackness," postmodernism's questioning of identity can be more problematic for minority writers to the extent that they remain committed to constructing usable racial or ethnic identity (28).

The burden on *White Noise* to represent the postmodern difference is further complicated by the plethora of ways that postmodernism has been defined and periodized. There are in effect three distinct versions of postmodernism—the philosophical, the cultural, and the aesthetic. While the time frame of the last two can be reconciled to some extent, it does not square with that of philosophical postmodernism. Jürgen Habermas's philosophical modernity, for example, begins with Descartes's belief in the self-sufficiency of reason and continues through Kant and the Enlightenment; Habermas's postmodernism begins with Nietzsche's attack on reason. As a result of Habermas's periodizing, many important forms of modernist aesthetics—surrealism, Dadaism, mythic intuitionism—temporally fall within his postmodernism. That Jean François Lyotard locates the beginning of modernity with Nietzsche only shows how easily the terms of the philosophical debate can create confusion. Instructors looking for a useful overview that touches on all three aspects of the postmodern (the philosophical, the cultural, and the aesthetic) should turn to David Harvey's *The Condition of Postmodernity*, particularly chapters 1, "Modernism and Modernity," and 2, "Postmodernism."

Since there is little consensus on what constitutes either cultural or aesthetic postmodernism, one might find a better representative than *White Noise* to illustrate a particular version of postmodern poetics. For example, if one turns to Linda Hutcheon's influential definition of postmodern fiction as "historiographic metafiction" (*Poetics* 105–23), *White Noise* will not serve nearly so well as E. L. Doctorow's *The Book of Daniel* (1971) or Robert Coover's *The Public Burning* (1977). Historiographic metafiction blends the reflexivity of metafiction with a postmodern sense of the fictionality of all historical interpretation. Since *White Noise* is neither metafictional nor overtly concerned with the problem of representing the past, in Hutcheon's terms, DeLillo's novel would seem to fall outside this conception of postmodernism.[1]

If *White Noise* does not fully exemplify Hutcheon's sense of postmodern fiction, why might it nevertheless be taught as representative of the postmodern? An analogy may be useful to begin answering this question: DeLillo stands to postmodernism as Fitzgerald stands to modernism. James Joyce and Faulkner both are better representatives of an experimental, high-modernist narrative form, but Fitzgerald always embraced modernity as the matter of his fiction—from the products of modernization (the automobile, the telephone, jazz recordings) to the rise of psychoanalysis. Similarly, one can point to a number of high postmodernists, such as Thomas Pynchon, Donald Barthelme, and Kathy Acker, who write with a more ludic style and feature more ontological disruptions in their work than DeLillo does, yet DeLillo always more concretely claims American postmodernity as his subject matter. His treatment of such issues as media culture, advertising, and celebrity shows us an America where conspicuous consumption is no longer a privilege of the wealthy (as in *Gatsby*) but rather has become the social labor of the middle class.

The way, then, that *White Noise* relates to the postmodern may be less as an exemplar of postmodernism than as a meditation on postmodernity—what it feels like to live in the age of media saturation. Such a meditation, seen from the perspective of twenty years after the novel's publication, must increasingly be placed in historical context. It is difficult to imagine teaching a modernist text without providing students some background on the rise of psychoanalysis and the effects of industrial and technological modernization; it is just as important to give students a sense of the urgency that characterized discussions of postmodernism in the early 1980s. This was the moment that the translations of a number of French theorists of postmodernism first appeared, notably Jean Baudrillard's *Simulations* and *In the Shadow of the Silent Majorities* (both in 1983) and Lyotard's *The Postmodern Condition* (1979). Moreover, the Marxist critic Fredric Jameson's important study *Postmodernism; or, The Cultural Logic of Late Capitalism* (1991), which engaged all this new French theory, had its beginnings in a widely read essay with the same title that he published in 1984 ("Cultural Logic").

If there is a version of postmodernism with which *White Noise* deeply resonates, it is Jameson's view of the totalizing reach of multinational capitalism. For Jameson the possibility of an oppositional aesthetic—a postmodernism—to comment critically on postmodernity has been erased by late-twentieth-century multinational capitalism. In a world of ubiquitous media and advertising, all new aesthetic production almost instantly is implicated in some form of commodity production. This commodification of aesthetics has profound effects on the nature of representation, identity, and meaning itself. Because *White Noise* depicts a contemporary America in which the image has lost much of its capacity to ground a critique of the order of things, DeLillo's novel works on a number of levels to help instructors designate the postmodern difference.

Postmodern Representation and Simulation

Students are always amused by Jack Gladney and Murray Siskind's visit to the Most Photographed Barn in America in chapter 3, particularly Murray's reading of the situation where all the tourists are busily snapping pictures of the barn.[2] Although intrigued by Murray's claim that "[o]nce you've seen the signs about the barn, it's impossible to see the barn" (12), students often lack a vocabulary to make sense of the apparent illogic of the claim that none of the tourists can see the very barn they are photographing.

Since *White Noise* so directly and frequently thematizes the role of simulation in contemporary America, a useful way to help students think about this concept is to introduce them to the work of Baudrillard, the French sociologist and theorist of consumer culture.[3] In chapter 7 of his *Jean Baudrillard: Selected Writings*, Mark Poster has excerpted a brief section of the essay "The Precession of Simulacra" that neatly introduces the notion of the hyperreal—a reality that feels unreal because it is generated by a model (166–84). If the older presumption is that first there is a reality that can be represented or mapped, hyperreality occurs when the model (more often than not a corporate one) produces the physical space one inhabits. In this regard, Baudrillard's claim that "Disneyland is presented as imaginary in order to make us believe that the rest [of America] is real, when in fact all of Los Angeles and the America surrounding it are no longer real, but of the order of the hyperreal and of simulation" (*Simulations* 25) can be a useful jumping-off point for class discussion. Focusing on this point allows students to articulate their own experience with themed spaces, which then helps them see how Baudrillard's sense of America applies to *White Noise*. If you teach, as I do, primarily middle-class students, then to begin such a discussion just ask them about the restaurants where they have eaten. Students will reveal their familiarity with national chains that exist on every strip throughout America, restaurants that promise the roadhouse experience, the Italian experience, the Australian experience, or the Western experience. It is of course a short step to ask them about their knowledge of commercials that advertise those restaurants.

One of the best examples to help students understand the difference between modern and postmodern representation and what is at stake in the scene of the Most Photographed Barn is the origin of the Universal Studios theme park in Orlando, Florida. Aware that a number of people who visited Disneyland in California also liked to tour movie back lots in order to see where many famous films were made, Universal Studios decided that it could profit with a similar symbiotic relation with Disney World in Florida. They therefore opened a theme park in Orlando, complete with back lots. Coming to Florida now means that one does not miss a significant feature of the California experience, since in either locale one can see a working film and television studio. The difference may not be immediately discernible to the eye of the tourist, but the ontological relation has shifted in Orlando, where the back lots have assumed a different order of imitation: there is no intrinsic history to the Florida studios that might make them a site of tourism. Clearly, the model (tourism) preceded their physical reality, and whatever filmmaking activity now occurs there provides only an ancillary economic benefit to this space's (hyper)real economic purpose, which is to bring in tourists. Once students have the model of the Universal Studios theme park to contextualize DeLillo's depiction of hyperreal tourism as an activity in which the historicity and materiality of one's destination matter less than one's consumption of an experience that serves as a collective suspension of disbelief, they are better prepared to process not only Murray's analysis of the Most Photographed Barn but also the way that *White Noise* imagines simulation touching nearly all walks of contemporary American life.

Class discussion can easily follow up on the issues raised by the Most Photographed Barn, because Jack frequently encounters simulation—a band playing "live Muzak" (84), an old Moorish movie theater that has been converted to a mosque (89). Perhaps the two most significant subsequent representations of hyperreality are SIMUVAC and the nuns of Germantown. In each instance,

DeLillo creates a parodic purchase on what it feels like to live in the present. SIMUVAC, a state-funded agency created to simulate evacuations for emergency preparedness, uses the actual evacuation of Blacksmith resulting from a chemical spill "to rehearse the simulation." The technician to whom Jack speaks is oblivious to the ways in which his work for SIMUVAC completely confuses the real and the model:

> The insertion curve isn't as smooth as we would like. There's a probability excess. Plus which we don't have our victims laid out where we'd want them if this was an actual simulation. In other words we're forced to take our victims as we find them. We didn't get a jump on computer traffic. Suddenly it just spilled out, three-dimensionally, all over the landscape. You have to make allowances for the fact that everything we see tonight is real. There's a lot of polishing we still have to do. But that's what this exercise is all about. (139)

The technician is clearly disappointed that the real event is an inferior representation of his work, which is to model the real. By exaggerating the hyperreality of this scene, DeLillo exposes the Disney-like condition of American postmodernity. Even religious faith becomes a form of simulation. When Jack's plan to kill Willie Mink goes wrong and they both end up wounded, Jack drives them to a Catholic hospital. At the hospital he converses with a nun, Sister Hermann Marie. Assuming she is a true believer in church doctrine, he is shocked to learn that the nun's faith is a simulation. He concludes that her dedication is a pretense, but she explains that it is just the opposite: "Our pretense is a dedication. Someone must appear to believe. Our lives are no less serious than if we professed real faith, real belief. As belief shrinks from the world, people find it more necessary than ever that *someone* believe" (319).

Postmodern Identity

Simulation, which problematizes notions of origin and authenticity, carries over into the depiction of identity in *White Noise*. One way to help students articulate the postmodern difference is to assign a short essay (600–900 words), due the second or third day of discussion on the novel. The assignment might read:

> Since reading T. S. Eliot, we have seen numerous instances of alienated characters, from Jake Barnes to Pecola Breedlove. Alienation largely has defined the twentieth-century portion of our course. Is Jack Gladney alienated in the same way that these earlier characters are? Is he unhappy with who or what he is? You may also consider other characters,

such as Babette, Murray, and Willie Mink. Are they alienated? Is there any authentic identity that the characters in DeLillo's novel presume they should or might have? How do they imagine themselves?

As the first-person narrator and central character, Jack draws the attention of most students. They recognize that in this largely episodic novel he, although worried about death, is not unhappy with who he is. Occasionally a student may try to link Jack's attempt to tap into some primitive authentic male rage when he discovers Babette's affair with Willie Mink with Jake Barnes's quest for authentic masculinity, but this argument breaks down: the path of male rage is motivated more by Murray's suggestion than by Jack's obsession, and once Jack is shot, he simply forgets about his revenge plot.

A point to seize on from this writing exercise in subsequent classroom discussion is that, although Jack may be alienated, he is by and large content with his alienation. The same may be said for Babette. Husband and wife fear death, but watching television and shopping are always options that can defer thoughts of personal mortality. Paradoxically, the media culture and advertising that surround them are continually nostalgic for origin and authenticity, but for individuals subject to such representations, notions of origin and authentic identity seem to have disappeared. A scene focusing on identity that dovetails nicely with the Most Photographed Barn in America occurs at the end of chapter 4, when Jack reflects on his status as the world's leading Hitler scholar. He complains of Babette's desire to have the family watch television together on Friday nights and comments on his practice of atoning for this distasteful activity by "read[ing] deeply in Hitler well into the night" (16). In a modernist novel, such a move might signal a desire to get in touch with one's authentic identity, but in DeLillo's postmodern representation Jack's very scholarly identity is revealed as simply another moment of the hyperreal, in which the model of scholarly names generates the real. At the urging of the college chancellor, Jack invents an extra initial to become in his professional identity J. A. K. Gladney, a name suggesting the English and Germanic philologists of the early part of the twentieth century.[4] Like the barn, which owes its aura or fame entirely to the pictures people take of it, Jack's status as the leading Hitler scholar depends on the repetition of his name in scholarly circles. Yet, unable to read and speak German, he clearly lacks a key credential to be a Hitler scholar let alone a star in the field. Even his acknowledgment that he is "the false character that follows the name around" (17) is not sufficient to generate alienation, because, far from seeking a more authentic identity to replace his specious professional identity, he begins a surreptitious crash course in German to maintain that identity in the face of an international Hitler conference that the college will host. If one wishes to use *The Great Gatsby* rather than *The Sun Also Rises* as the example of white male modernism, one can approach the difference between modern and postmodern identity by comparing Gatsby's dissimulation to Jack's simulation: Gatsby renames himself and buys elaborate props in order to pretend to be something that he is not—the heir of a wealthy family—while Jack renames himself and uses such props as his dark glasses and academic robes in order to simulate something that he in fact is, an internationally known Hitler scholar.

Students who turn to Murray in their papers usually can see that he is even less alienated than Jack. It is clear from his interpretation of the aura of the Most Photographed Barn that he actively celebrates the loss of authenticity that would make a modernist alienated. Murray consistently urges his students and Jack to submit to the total flow of desire that media culture produces.[5] Such a position typifies all his colleagues in the Department of American Environments. Over lunch with Murray and his colleagues, Jack admits his guilty pleasure at watching a television show depicting natural disaster. The department chair proclaims that, given the "brain fade" caused by the excess of psychic data, "If a thing happens on television, we have every right to find it fascinating, whatever it is" (66). When Jack responds that he is not sure how to feel about that claim, the consensus from the American Envrionments Department faculty is to feel bad: "We all feel bad. But we can enjoy it on that level" (67). In other words, feel alienated, but enjoy your alienation.

Because Murray is a postmodern cultural semiotician, his presence in the novel makes it easier to speak about postmodernity. Yet his relation to postmodern identity is complicated. Although he celebrates the flow of desire and the fragmentation of identity in media culture, he himself remains largely aloof from the very popular culture that he studies and teaches; in other words, he may immerse himself in popular culture, but he does not identify himself with any of it. His apparently comic attempt to maintain an ironic critical distance on media culture serves as his cover in his professional and personal lives as he plots to found Elvis studies and to seduce Babette. His interpretations, therefore, ironically suggest a measure of paranoid control: his teaching urges others to submit to the flow of media culture while he tries to hold his identity together in order to be a coherent interpreter of the signs of culture that reveal that coherent identity is no longer possible.

The character that most clearly suggests the disintegration of identity is Willie Mink. Like the Most Photographed Barn, Willie is both a source of humor and a cipher to undergraduates. They tend to read him through his addiction to Dylar, the drug created to suppress the fear of death, and its key side effect that causes him to take literally anything suggested by the images of language. Everything Murray currently is, Willie once was. As the designer of Dylar, Willie was a plotter, a professional with the goal of mastery and power, as well as a seducer of women. Through Murray and Willie, one can introduce students to the two major tropes that have been used to name what succeeds modernist alienation: paranoia and schizophrenia. Murray in his will to power and control represents the paranoid; Willie in his total inability to distinguish reality from its linguistic mediation suggests a cultural schizophrenia. For a sophisticated account of how paranoia relates to various theories of schizophrenia from Jameson to Gilles Deleuze and Félix Guattari, see chapter 1 of Patrick O'Donnell's *Latent Destinies*, a study acutely aware of the reciprocal relation between paranoia and schizophrenia. For O'Donnell, cultural paranoia is an effect of living in an age in which the ever-increasing fragmentation of identity seems matched only by the ability of capital to market consumer goods and services to those who are subject to such fragmentation. In short, the more schizophrenic identity becomes the norm, the more possibilities for paranoia circulate within culture, a condition exemplified by the mirroring relationship between Murray and Willie, one suggesting that to be the former is to be well on the way to becoming the latter.

Media Culture

Because a survey of American literature since 1865 may touch base with *The Education of Henry Adams*, *White Noise* helps measure the cultural change from the beginning to the end of the twentieth century. Given the state of the dissemination of information through the print media at the beginning of the twentieth century, it was still possible through heroic effort to approach Henry Adams's goal of grasping what constituted current human knowledge. With the growth and development of the electronic media and the explosion of information generated by the advent of personal computers, Adams's goal for his education is now scarcely imaginable.

The television is always on in the Gladney household, and yet its presence is so subliminal that it can enter unnoticed into various family discussions. The frequent non sequiturs in the novel where "the television said," however, are only a part of the general circulation of misinformation in that home. While looking at how *White Noise* represents the role of television, the instructor may wish to introduce another of Baudrillard's theses, namely, the notion of the implosion of meaning in the media. Developing the implications of Marshall McLuhan's famous formulation that "the medium is the message," Baudrillard posits something beyond the neutralization of content that this position implies: "there is not only the implosion of the message in the medium; in the same movement there is the implosion of the medium into the real" (*In the Shadow* 101). If the binary oppositions of content/media and media/real are erased, then no amount of circulated information can create a critical purchase on human experience. In Baudrillard's model, television is no longer a meaningful mediation of reality but that which instantiates the effect of the real. This reversal points us once again to the notion of simulation, in which the modeling of the real is itself perceived as reality.

The people evacuated from Blacksmith as a result of the airborne toxic event feel deflated when their collective terror fails to register on network news. Although they directly experienced terror, their ability to process that experience hinges on its televised representation. Because television is supposed to show these people what is important and newsworthy, their experience ceases to be real when it is not covered. *White Noise* parodies this unconscious relation to the consumption of television images by having characters repeatedly articulate what normally would remain unspoken, as when one man rages, "What exactly has to happen before they stick microphones in our faces and hound us to the doorsteps of our homes, camping out on our lawns, creating the usual media circus?" He does not literally desire an increase in the pain and suffering of the evacuees, the adding of media exploitation to their confusion and homelessness; what he seeks is the comfort of a validation. In a world where television is so ubiquitous that, instead of mediating the real, it constitutes the real, these people have been denied completion, the ability to watch themselves shout at the cameramen, "Leave us alone, we've been through enough, get out of here with your vile instruments of intrusion" (162).[6]

The preceding example leads to a paradox that is worth pointing out in teaching *White Noise* in a postmodern context. Although this novel depicts a world that captures Jameson's sense of the nearly ubiquitous reach of multinational capitalism, DeLillo writes with a parodic spirit that Jameson explicitly sees as disqualified in postmodernism. For Jameson, the possibilities of parody died with modernism and its distinctive private styles; now there is so much fragmentation throughout social life that the notion of a linguistic norm that could be parodied has disappeared. As Jameson sees it, postmodernism is no longer capable of achieving the critical distance necessary for parody and ends up recombining previously articulated styles (*Postmodernism* 16–17). Similarly, Jameson sees little vocation for the contemporary novel, and in passing a teacher might note that at the College-on-the-Hill, popular culture has completely won the day. Professors study cereal boxes, and there are seminars in movie car crashes, but no one reads a novel.

Yet DeLillo writes novels, and although *White Noise* is not exactly an instance of historiographic metafiction, it does resonate with Hutcheon's belief that postmodern parody still has a role to play in creating a critical purchase on the present. It may be that DeLillo helps create a linguistic norm through the very things that he satirizes—television viewing and advertising. From the opening page, with its catalog of consumer goods and brand names, to the trios of similar brand-named products that recur throughout the novel, such as "The Airport Marriott, the Downtown Travelodge, the Sheraton Inn and Conference Center" (15), "MasterCard, Visa, American Express" (100), "Krylon, Rust-Oleum, Red Devil" (159), *White Noise* plays on consumerism, the last shared language perhaps of First World culture. The culminating moment of media culture's role in constructing the consumer's unconscious occurs when Jack listens as his dreaming daughter speaks in "a language not quite of this world" syllables "that seemed to have a ritual meaning": Toyota Celica. Jack experiences the brand name as "a moment of splendid transcendence," an indication of just how desperate he is to find some spiritual grounding in his life. Yet the brand name is not "a verbal spell or ecstatic chant," only the voice of the TV repeated in "substatic regions too deep to probe" (154–55). Such parodic instances of brand names erupting either from the mouth of his child or in Jack's own narration are not signifiers of any transcendent meaning but instead underscore once again how the novel makes visible the ways in which Americans and their acts of consumption are unconsciously scripted by advertising.

While I have emphasized a postmodern context for teaching *White Noise*, I urge anyone preparing to teach this novel for the first time to read Cornel Bonca's cautionary remarks about the limitations of teaching the novel simply as an instance of "applied" Baudrillard or Jameson (456–58). Yet whatever other pedagogical ends *White Noise* can serve (as the other essays in this volume admirably illustrate), its treatment of issues of representation, identity, and media demarcate in the undergraduate survey a shift from the alienation of early-twentieth-century literature to the sometimes paranoid, sometimes schizophrenic feel of late-twentieth-century American consumer culture, a feel that persists in our postmillennial moment.

NOTES

[1]In some ways *White Noise* is the historiographic metafictional novel manqué. At moments when one might expect the narrator to comment overtly on resonances between his experiences in the present and the Nazi past (such as perhaps reading as an ironic repetition of concentration camp victims the refugees who are forced by a poisonous cloud from Blacksmith and who are funneled to the former Boy Scout camp), Jack Gladney is strangely silent. Although he is a scholar of Hitler, Jack seems oblivious to both the historical implications and hermeneutic possibilities of his subject.

[2]A detailed reading of the centrality of this scene can be found in Lentricchia ("Tales" 88–91).

[3]Much thoughtful work has been done on *White Noise* and its relation to the theories of Baudrillard. Frow, Messmer, and Wilcox all provide an overview that will help the instructor prepare background material on Baudrillard. A fuller critical treatment of simulation can be found in Kellner (76–83).

[4]Scholars from this period appearing in such journals as *PMLA* and *JEGP* (*Journal of English and Germanic Philology*) frequently used two- and three-letter initials with a last name to identify themselves—as if to say that their scholarship was more important than their personal identity. J. A. K. Gladney reverses this claim by turning the older convention into an affectation.

[5]See for example Murray's summary of his lecture on movie car crashes on how to look past the violence (217–19) and his advising Jack in chapter 37 to become a killer rather than a dier.

[6]For a fuller explication of the way this scene and other moments of television consumption suggest that all forms of the electronic media come to be experienced counterintuitively as unmediated, see my essay "The (Super)Marketplace of Images."

White Noise, Materialism, and the American Literature Survey

Ted Billy

Almost from its inception, American literature has shown tendencies of being a subversive art form. We can attribute this, in part, to the disparity between the rhetoric of democratic ideals promoted by the founding fathers and the capitalistic-materialistic fabric of American culture. From Ralph Waldo Emerson and Henry David Thoreau to Lorraine Hansberry and Sylvia Plath, many American authors have waged a rear-guard attack against the materialistic excesses of our society. I have often structured my American literature survey courses to reflect this antimaterialistic strain, and when I teach the contemporary American literature course or the Great American Writers survey (which spans all eras), I like to close with Don DeLillo's *White Noise*. In this novel, DeLillo not only adds his voice to the antimaterialistic chorus but also fashions a narrative that sums up the whole subversive strain. Thus I find *White Noise* particularly useful when situated in the context of literary works that subvert the prevailing American materialistic ideology of the last two centuries. In this long span of time, American writers have dramatized the perversion of the American dream of success by materialistic values. *White Noise* succeeds especially well because it is perhaps the most humorous and scathing of these indictments to date.

In American literature, the antimaterialistic tradition both begins with and interrogates the gospel of industriousness in Benjamin Franklin's *Autobiography*. In Franklin's insistence that the appearance of industry is preferable to industry itself, students can begin to understand the emphasis on busyness in the Protestant work ethic. Emerson and Thoreau take issue with Franklin's emphasis on externalizing one's personal identity. Emerson aptly sums up this perspective in his aphorism that "Things are in the saddle, / And ride mankind" (435). (I like to teach Franklin's *Autobiography* and Thoreau's *Walden* in tandem early in the semester to establish the materialistic/spiritual dichotomy of American culture, a schizoid complex that is perfectly represented in contemporary form in *White Noise*.) Herman Melville's *The Confidence-Man* takes the inquisitive impulse of capitalistic America to task by exposing commercial transactions as swindles of the imagination. Every commodity in Melville's nihilistic antinovel is the object of a confidence trick. Henry James's *The American* contributes to this tradition in a different way, making Christopher Newman a capitalistic hero and yet dramatizing his materialistic myopia in the narrow-minded way he attempts to acquire European culture and, eventually, a European wife. A multimillionaire, he envisions the process of cultivating himself as a matter of seeing hundreds of famous churches and cathedrals and visiting large numbers of museums and art galleries. Mark Twain's *A*

Connecticut Yankee in King Arthur's Court also makes a dubious hero of its protagonist, Hank, a Yankee whose overactive ingenuity only succeeds in perpetrating a slaughter of apocalyptic proportions. What seems like a satire on chivalry and feudalism on the surface is actually a critique of capitalism and materialism. Kate Chopin's *The Awakening* is a feminist chronicle of one woman's rebellion against her imprisonment in a circumscribed world of materialistic comfort provided by her often absent husband. Although Edna is well provided for, her rebellion is largely prompted by the recognition that she exists mainly as the prize piece of furniture in her husband's house.

White Noise's twentieth-century antecedents include Edith Wharton's *The House of Mirth*, which extends the metaphor of woman as commodity in a scathing indictment of the New York leisure class. Lily Bart rises in nobility as she descends the social ladder from privileged luxury to pathetic penury. Theodore Dreiser's *The Financier* dramatizes how an individual's life can become totally consumed by pecuniary urges. In this early-twentieth-century novel, Frank Cowperwood perfectly embodies the acquisitive obsession that DeLillo mocks at the end of the century. Sinclair Lewis's *Babbitt* situates its antimaterialistic critique in middle-class middle America. George Babbitt's Zenith is a capitalistic city of God whose towering office buildings disguise the spiritual poverty of its inhabitants. Like Lily Bart, Babbitt eventually rises in the reader's estimation when he joins his son to rebel against the crass conformity of his herd-minded clan. Of course, F. Scott Fitzgerald's *The Great Gatsby* stands as the prime exemplar of cautionary tales concerning the seductive allure of the materialistic aspect of the American dream of success. Gatsby, the platonic creation of young Jimmy Gatz, personifies the glitz and glitter that have come to be associated with the cult of the famous in the twentieth century. At bottom, of course, he remains a "poor son-of-a-bitch" (183). Tennessee Williams's *A Streetcar Named Desire*, in contrast, frames the theme as a conflict between a fading aristocrat who holds on to cultural values (Blanche DuBois) and a blue-collar worker who aspires to higher status (Stanley Kowalski). Ultimately, in the play's climactic confrontation, the fragile Blanche succumbs to the materialistic ape. Lorraine Hansberry's *A Raisin in the Sun* is another play dealing with the conflict of spiritual and materialistic desires, and we sympathize with the Younger family's quest to gain a better life. Yet, at the end, the Youngers unite to reaffirm their essential dignity by turning down the chance to regain their lost money. Saul Bellow's *Henderson the Rain King* resembles James's *The American* in that its protagonist is also a multimillionaire who feels the need to improve himself and goes to drastic lengths to do so. Only when Eugene Henderson is in the heart of Africa and removed from his financial fortune does he learn to care about others and to transcend his self-preoccupation. Sylvia Plath's *The Bell Jar* follows in the tradition of Chopin, Wharton, and Hansberry by portraying the confining stereotype of woman as a clotheshorse, a fashion plate, and a trophy wife. Esther Greenwood's revolt against this stereotype takes her to an insane asylum, but

Plath proves her point that, for too long, American society has relegated women to the status of handmaidens to male ambition. A truly talented woman in mid-twentieth-century America had nowhere to go in a culture fixated on materialistic values.

All these major texts offer an abundance of themes to explore, of course, but they do lend themselves well to a unified focus on antimaterialism in an American literature survey. I first became aware of this focus in the 1980s, when I taught many of these works in the course Great American Writers at the University of Delaware and noticed how frequently they addressed the externalization of personal identity in American culture. In its treatment of the commodification of American society, *White Noise* is the perfect capstone text for such a course. It both reaches back to the transcendentalists' attack on corpse-cold materialism and points forward to the extremely technological world we inhabit at the present moment. In its dramatization of the difficulties of keeping a blended family cohesive, the novel echoes many of the concerns expressed in important feminist texts. It demonstrates that the contemporary world can offer us everything we need to survive and perhaps even thrive, but it cannot give us what we need to truly live: spiritual nourishment. Like Kafka's hunger artist, we are starving for something that seems unattainable in our commodified culture.

Another way to contextualize *White Noise* for students is to have them view the novel from the perspective of Thorstein Veblen's *The Theory of the Leisure Class*, because conspicuous consumption, as Veblen prophesied at the end of the nineteenth century, has become the hallmark of success in America. He argued that people accumulate material things primarily to gratify themselves and build their reputations by impressing their neighbors with their worth. In a sense, Veblen is the diagnostician of the keeping-up-with-the-Joneses syndrome. So long as individuals see their materialistic lot as inferior to the community standard of living, he said, they will experience "chronic dissatisfaction"; even when they attain that standard, they will experience a "restless straining" to widen the gulf between themselves and it (20). Conspicuous leisure, in Veblen's view, implies the nonproductive consumption of time in activities that have little to no useful purpose (e.g., fox hunting). In DeLillo's novel, tourists who take pictures of the Most Photographed Barn in America flaunt their conspicuous leisure. A concomitant of conspicuous consumption and leisure, in Veblen's view, is the conspicuous waste of the leisure class that aims to externalize its personal success. Conspicuous waste includes not simply lavish houses and frivolous social pursuits but also fashionable, nonfunctional clothing and the prestige of useless learning. Jack Gladney's habitual wearing of his dark glasses and academic gown on campus and his specialty in Hitler studies are examples. Elegant attire, for Veblen, is the insignia of conspicuous leisure, and the scholar's robe makes Jack ill suited for anything but lecturing. (Here one should remind students that *scholarship*, etymologically, implies leisure-time activity.) Moreover, by placing property and privilege ahead of all other human values, Veblen affirms, the leisure class actually impoverishes American culture.

It is a useful classroom exercise to have students list examples of conspicuous consumption, leisure, and waste in *White Noise*. Some students may not at first view these materialistic excesses as negative. But a reminder of the Thoreauvian maxim "simplify, simplify" (91) will generate a healthy discussion on what we really need and what we think we need to thrive in today's society. A good way to begin such a discussion is to call attention to the opening chapter, in which DeLillo introduces his antimaterialistic theme with the convoy of college students bearing numerous possessions into their dormitories. Surely most American college students recall how they spent a hot day in August lugging belongings (evocative word!) into a claustrophobic living space. But self-definition through an excessive amount of material goods applies to just about everyone in the novel. Before the final pages (where spirituality makes an important cameo appearance), the closest DeLillo's characters come to the sacred is when they make ritualistic trips to the supermarket, America's secular cathedral. Consuming is their attempt to fill an inner void. They equate an overloaded grocery cart with personal fulfillment. Malls also serve as a mecca for social interaction because genuine interpersonal communication is discouraged in a commodified culture.

DeLillo does provide alternative modes of spirituality in the novel but deftly erodes their significance, as when he devotes an early chapter to the simulacrum of the Most Photographed Barn in America and then relegates the barn to a one-sentence paragraph of insignificance during the "Airborne Toxic Event" chapter. What once passed for an object of hermeneutic contemplation becomes trivialized as the Gladneys flee the prospect of physical contamination. The same is true of the malls and supermarkets in the novel: they unite the isolated monads that assume the status of human beings, but they can also be disorienting, especially to older shoppers who become lost in a mall (e.g., the Treadwells [59–60]) or are bewildered by the rearrangement of supermarket shelves: "They scrutinize the small print on packages, wary of a second level of betrayal" (326). Indeed, "The world is full of abandoned meanings" (184), as Jack observes. But meanings, once abandoned, lose all validity in a world of consumer consciousness.

The infantile Wilder embodies the concept of life as a series of fleeting gratifications. In one especially hilarious scene, the Gladneys eat in their car like voracious, prehistoric cave dwellers:

> We decided to eat in the car. . . . We wanted to eat, not look around at other people. We wanted to fill our stomachs and get it over with. We didn't need light and space. . . . We were content to eat facing in the same direction, looking only inches past our hands. . . . We ate fully dressed, in hats and heavy coats, without speaking. . . . I chewed and ate, looking only inches past my hands. (231–32)

Most students will remember times when extreme hunger compelled them to masticate mindlessly in a car, but DeLillo here is dramatizing the solipsistic nature of the urge to fill the void. Almost always in the novel, spiritual hunger is subordinated to the compulsion of physical gratification.

Perhaps more so than any other novel, *White Noise* dramatizes the late-twentieth-century preoccupation with externalizing personal identity in America. Here the central focus of Erving Goffman's highly influential study *The Presentation of Self in Everyday Life* will give students an illuminating angle of vision. Goffman maintained that all social interaction is performative, with each person an actor who attempts to create a strong impression according to the audience and situation (17). (If some students resist this notion, ask them to consider the roles traditionally played by students and teachers in the classroom.) Goffman contends that we gain a sense of identity through our interactions with others. (This is why Jack becomes so disturbed when his colleague Massingale appears unimpressed by him when they meet in the hardware store in their street clothes.) Goffman also emphasized the projection of a front, a fixed, idealized façade that persists throughout all a person's encounters with others. Jack takes up his chancellor's advice "to do something about my name and appearance if I wanted to be taken seriously" as a Hitler innovator: "The chancellor warned against . . . my tendency to make a feeble presentation of self. He strongly suggested that I gain weight. He wanted me to 'grow out' into Hitler" (16–17). Hence, instead of doing something useful in enhancing his knowledge of his area of expertise, such as learning German, Jack bulks up and adds an extra initial to his name. But he feels hollow inside: "I am the false character that follows the name around" (17). Here it is useful to ask students what they do in their own lives to manufacture a stronger presentation of self.

Throughout *White Noise*, appearance is a primary standard of measurement for personal success. In modern America, DeLillo demonstrates, only the extrinsic self can have value, and it increases in worth (or cash value) according to the number of things it can control. Acquisitive desires have replaced inquisitive instincts. In a materialistic culture, the intrinsic self atrophies at the expense of the extrinsic self. Small wonder that the American ego has become a commodified entity.

The Gladneys, living totally on the surface, project their self-images through materialistic means. They believe that they must radiate accomplishments and glow with narcissistic pride. In this context, Christopher Lasch's *The Culture of Narcissism* can be a useful lens for students to view the solipsistic personalities of the Gladneys. Lasch maintains that "[t]he modern propaganda of commodities and the good life has sanctioned impulse gratification and made it unnecessary for the id to apologize for its wishes or disguise their grandiose proportions. But this same propaganda has made failure and loss insupportable" (56). Accepting and adopting Goffman's notion of social relations as role-playing, he maintains that the "performing self" constructs a reality "out of materials furnished by advertising and mass culture" (166). In the late twentieth century, success manuals stressed "winning images" over performance: "Nothing succeeds like the appearance of success" (116). He anticipates what DeLillo dramatizes throughout *White Noise*, that "the propaganda of consumption . . . addresses itself to the spiritual desolation of modern life and proposes consumption as the cure" (138).

In Lasch's view, modern capitalism "subordinates possession itself to appearance and measures exchange value as a commodity's capacity to confer prestige—the illusion of prosperity and well-being" (137). Moreover, advertising is an institution that does not so much promote specific products as manufacture its own product: perpetually unsatisfied consumers whose "unappeasable appetite" makes consumption a way of life—"Consumption promises to fill the aching void" (138). Murray Siskind contends that the path to self-augmentation lies in the proper gestures and expressions to project one's identity. Yet DeLillo shows that augmenting the extrinsic self and externalizing personal prestige result only in alienating depersonalization.

Murray, "a visiting lecturer on living icons" (10), serves as a guru of pop culture and an apologist for consumerism. He views television as having a myth-making function as a "primal force in the American home": "The medium practically overflows with sacred formulas if we can remember how to respond innocently" (51). Revering the world of "[w]aves and radiation," he finds car crashes significant as expressions of the spirit of American optimism and sneaks into Denise's room to do an archaeological study of children's artifacts. More important, he believes that food labels contain psychic data that reveal vital information when decoded: "All the letters and numbers are here, all the colors of the spectrum, all the voices and sounds, all the code words and ceremonial phrases. It is just a question of deciphering, rearranging, peeling off the layers of unspeakability" (38). Yet DeLillo undermines this rhapsodic apotheosis of the signs and wonders of the technological age when Murray absurdly argues that Jack should repress his fear of death by being a killer rather than a dier. In opposition to Murray's glorification of the material, Winnie Richards implicitly affirms the spiritual when she advises Jack to see death as a necessary boundary to life. For Winnie, the real texture of human existence depends not on one's accumulation of commodities but on one's awareness of the precious brevity of life. Winnie tries to convince Jack that he cannot overcome his preoccupation with mortality as long as he continues to identify with the externals of existence. But hers is a solitary voice crying in the wilderness of consumerism.

Among the subtlest of DeLillo's indictments of capitalism comes in the form of the pervasive and pernicious role played by the television set in the Gladney household. Almost a major character in the novel, television functions to indoctrinate Jack and Babette's children to the supposed necessity of luxuries. For example, during the airborne toxic event, Jack seems startled when he hears his daughter talk in her sleep: "She was only repeating some TV voice.

Toyota Corolla, Toyota Celica, Toyota Cressida" (155). He sees something transcendent in this unnerving moment, but in this context I usually introduce students to some relevant passages from Neil Postman's compelling dissection of television, *Amusing Ourselves to Death*. Postman argues, and *White Noise* graphically demonstrates, that television does not shape our culture; it is our culture:

> Television has become, so to speak, the background radiation of the social and intellectual universe, the all-but-imperceptible residue of the electronic big bang of a century past, so familiar and so thoroughly integrated with American culture that we no longer hear its faint hissing in the background or see the flickering gray light. This, in turn, means that its epistemology goes largely unnoticed. And the peek-a-boo world it has constructed around us no longer seems even strange. (79)

Given that part 1 of *White Noise* is entitled "Waves and Radiation" and that television (in its bread-and-circuses function) has become the Delphic oracle of our epistemology, the inhabitants of Blacksmith are understandably crushed that the airborne toxic event is not covered by the national media; their plight is therefore meaningless (162). Similarly, the Most Photographed Barn in America has importance not because of what it is but because of the many pictures taken of it.

Jack Gladney is DeLillo's prime example in the novel of the deleterious consequences of materialistic preoccupation and spiritual poverty, and I often ask students to spend some time discussing his strengths and weaknesses as a character. In doing so, they often inadvertently paint a portrait of themselves as unquestioning consumers. In his self-absorption and delusions of grandeur, Jack embodies the narcissism that Lasch condemns. He sees his students as extensions of their parents' tuition money and concentrates on projecting an impressive façade. Yet his self-image has validity only as a consciously created illusion. By concentrating on projecting himself onto the external world, he has internally atrophied, becoming "hollow at the core," to use Joseph Conrad's description of Mister Kurtz (58).

It is useful to ask students to explain Jack's manic spending spree at the shopping mall immediately after his ego deflation by Massingale, who remarks that Jack looks "harmless" and "indistinct" without his academic robe and dark glasses (83). Some students may not realize how this casual comment shocks Jack into a crisis of self-confidence, which spurs him to hope that his lavish buying will reinforce his self-image: "I began to grow in value and self-regard. . . . The more money I spent, the less important it seemed. I was bigger than these sums. . . . These sums in fact came back to me in the form of existential credit" (84). Despite the euphoria of this purchasing orgy, Jack's unity with his family is only temporary: on returning home, the Gladneys withdraw to separate rooms as isolated monads.

Later in the novel, following his contamination, Jack begins to throw out many of his belongings. It is a good idea to ask students to discuss the implications of this action. If some students have had the misfortune of losing a parent, they may be able to shed light on the painful process of giving up the personal effects of the departed. Ironically, after his several binges of divestment, Jack realizes that ownership is a delusion fostered by those who wish to free themselves of the burden of mortality. Blaming his possessions rather than himself, he remains materialistically attached to life. For Jack (and DeLillo), we are what we eat and what we discard. The bottom of the garbage can reveals "the dark underside of consumer consciousness" (259):

> The full stench hit me with shocking force. Was this ours? Had we created it? . . . Is garbage so private? Does it glow at the core with personal heat, with signs of one's deepest nature, clues to secret yearnings, humiliating flaws? What habits, fetishes, addictions, inclinations? What solitary acts, behavioral ruts? (258–59)

It is important to remind students that one of the working titles for the novel was "The American Book of the Dead," which underscores that *White Noise* is a critique of the deadening effects of materialism and consumerism. *The Great Liberation upon Hearing in the Intermediate State*, more commonly called *The Tibetan Book of the Dead* (see Evans-Wentz and Dawa-Samdup), stresses liberation from the attachment to earthly things as a means of gaining enlightenment and avoiding the cycle of rebirth and suffering: "Tibetans try to see death for what it is. It is the end of attachment to things. This simple truth is hard to fathom. But once we stop denying death, we can proceed calmly to die" (White Noise 38). (In the comically simultaneous lectures on Hitler and Elvis delivered by Jack and Murray, Murray states that Elvis "began to study the *Bardo Thödol*, commonly known as *The Tibetan Book of the Dead*. This is a guide to dying and being reborn" [72]). Jack, never transcending his attachment to worldly goods, envies Wilder, to whom pleasures do not seem to cling: "He is selfish without being grasping, selfish in a totally unbounded and natural way. There's something wonderful about the way he drops one thing, grabs for another" (209). Even when faced with the prospect of death, Jack cannot bear to let go.

One benefit of teaching *White Noise* is that the serious topic of death is tempered by an overall comical context. Thus, discussions of how American culture compartmentalizes and represses old age and death do not tend to be maudlin. Throughout the novel DeLillo argues that materialistic craving springs from the desire to evade the inevitability of death. Similarly, Lasch argues that "the campaign against old age" is "the most characteristic expression of the times" (351):

> This irrational terror of old age and death is closely associated with the emergence of the narcissistic personality as the dominant type of personality structure in contemporary society. Because the narcissist has so

> few inner resources, he looks to others to validate his sense of self. He needs to be admired for his beauty, charm, celebrity, or power—attributes that usually fade with time. (356)

One of the most comical instances of this phenomenon occurs in chapter 33 when Jack instinctively clutches a copy of *Mein Kampf* to his chest after mistaking the distant figure of his father-in-law for a Bergmanesque emissary of death.

As Lasch contends, and as DeLillo's novel demonstrates, the prospect of old age and death inspires apprehension "in a society that has deprived itself of religion" (354). Jack's acquisitive ego cannot tolerate the idea of the temporality of all earthly things. Throughout much of the novel, life for him is a matter of accumulation, not casting off. This behavior changes when he becomes exposed to Nyodene D. and is "tentatively scheduled" to die (202). At this point he becomes like many of the elderly throughout the novel, who are periodically disoriented by cavernous shopping malls, rearranged supermarket aisles, and altered television schedules. Ultimately, the tabloids in the closing scenes of the novel cannot minister to a consciousness that is, in William Butler Yeats's phrase, "sick with desire / And fastened to a dying animal" (96).

I believe that the closing reference to the tabloids at the checkout counters of the supermarket serves as a synecdoche for *White Noise* itself. Some students, asked to consider the implications of that image, may suggest that DeLillo implies that Americans are checking out of life while clutching on to the superfluous. If it is a challenge to teach *White Noise* in an American literature survey course so that students view the narrative as more than a comic meditation on one very dysfunctional blended family, the challenge of teaching the ending of the novel is greater: to have students internalize DeLillo's message so that they fundamentally change in relation to our society. The novel functions in a manner similar to T. S. Eliot's portrayal of J. Alfred Prufrock, the poster boy for diffidence and uncertainty in the early twentieth century. Along with many other canonical works of American literature, *White Noise* shows how the single-minded pursuit of materialistic success can lead to the loss of inner vitality, making the intangible self a void. Our students face the daunting task of maintaining their intrinsic identities in a world where only the extrinsic seems valued. DeLillo's novel reinforces the urgency of this task.

TEACHING *WHITE NOISE* IN THE CONTEXT OF OTHER DELILLO NOVELS

Plot Summary: Motives and Narrative Mechanics in *Underworld* and *White Noise*

Michael Bérubé

It is commonly argued, and not exclusively by sports fans, that competitive sports provide a refuge of clarity and simplicity in a bewilderingly complex and ambiguous world. If it is an effort to keep track of who did what to whom and why in Passchendaele in 1917 or Shrewsbury in 1402, it is a relief to recall more straightforward matters like the Jets' 16–7 victory over the Colts in Super Bowl III, Tiger Woods's 15-stroke victory in the 2000 US Open, or Billie Jean King's straight-sets routing of Bobby Riggs in 1973. In sports the outcomes are indelible and indisputable, whereas in life we journey, in our middling way, through a dark wood, never learning how the big story begins or ends. When Bobby Thomson hits that one-strike pitch off Ralph Branca for a three-run home run on 3 October 1951, for example, the Giants win the pennant, the Giants win the pennant, the Giants win the pennant—and the outcome is not challenged in court, the Dodgers do not ask for a statewide recount, the Supreme Court does not step in and award the game to Brooklyn by creatively reading the equal protection clause of the Fourteenth Amendment. Sure, occasionally you get your figure-skating controversies and your inscrutable gymnastics scores, but the "objective" sports—the ones involving goals, runs, touchdowns, baskets, meters, and seconds—are thoroughly decisive: someone wins, someone loses, end of story.

Unfortunately for fans of clarity, though happily for fans of competitive sports, this argument—like Don DeLillo's *Underworld* itself—is full of garbage.

While it is tempting to compare DeLillo's Giants-Dodgers narrative with his US-USSR narrative (indeed, the temptation can hardly be refused, since the novel is structurally predicated on the intertwining of the two narratives), it is, I believe, a serious mistake to think of the sports contest as a simpler, less mediated version of Us versus Them. Instead, I suggest that we regard both narratives as examples of and meditations on the function(s) of narrative in general, and I argue that *Underworld*'s narrative strategies and temptations can lead us to a useful rereading of *White Noise*'s well-worn hypotheses about the nature of plots. Classroom discussions of plot in *White Noise*, I've found, tend to degenerate into point-and-counterpoint debates between students who agree with Jack Gladney that all plots move deathward and those who insist, citing Murray Jay Siskind, that to plot is to live. Though these debates are sometimes fun or illuminating, more often (in my experience) they are predictable, and, what's worse, they tend to invite students to eschew specificity in favor of ambitious remarks about the nature of consciousness and the unknowability of the universe. Over the past few years, during which I've taught *Underworld* three times in survey courses and *White Noise* three times in survey courses and in honors seminars (never teaching both novels in the same course), I've discovered that it's possible to use the various plots of *Underworld* to illuminate *White Noise* even when students haven't read the former. I explain to students that *Underworld* begins with two shots heard 'round the world, ask them to compare sports narratives with geopolitical narratives, insist that they give specific examples of different kinds of narratives, and then tease out the implications of those differences by suggesting that *Underworld* is centrally concerned with the question of motive whereas *White Noise* is remarkably indifferent to it.

The argument runs like this. My first point about sports narrative is elementary enough, though it has some far-reaching consequences: a large part of the appeal of sports, quite apart from the sheer athleticism and visual stylin' that make up the bulk of most highlight reels, plays of the week, and professional leagues' advertising campaigns, is the appeal of narrative itself. The Giants-Dodgers play-off is a remarkable story involving a nail-biting tied game broken open in the eighth inning by one team, followed by an improbable four-run rally by the other in the bottom of the ninth. But there are innumerable elaborations on this story, some of which involve the minutiae of this one game (the Giants' boneheaded baserunning error in the second inning, for instance) and others that involve the history of the sport (and the rivalry among the three New York teams in the postwar era). Understanding the game entails understanding the narratives in which it participates, the tangents and contexts and backstories and extrapolations that often make sports narrative more seductive for the qualities of the narrative than for the qualities of the sports.

One of the things that make sports narrative compelling is precisely the uncertainty about who shoulda won and who wuz robbed. Ask any basketball fan about the final seconds of the US-USSR gold-medal game in the 1972 Olympics. Or ask any Buffalo Sabres fan about game 6 of the 1999 Stanley Cup finals, in which Brett Hull scored an exceptionally dubious goal in triple overtime to lift the Dallas Stars over the Sabres—a goal so disputable it compelled the NHL to modify its crease rules. Or ask any Oakland Raiders fan about the New England Patriots quarterback Tom Brady's late-fourth-quarter fumble in the 2001 NFL play-offs, a play that arguably should have ended the game and the Patriots' season but was reviewed and ruled an incomplete pass, thus propelling the Patriots into overtime and eventually to the Super Bowl. Or ask any Dodgers fan about the allegations that the 1951 Giants embarked on an ambitious and highly illegal program of sign stealing that not only hoisted them into a tie in the pennant race but also was responsible for Thomson's homer (though, as the Giants' partisans will tell you, Thomson still had to hit the ball even if he knew what pitch was coming). Any serious sports fan knows that the game, whatever game it might be, is plagued—or perhaps enhanced—by shady practices, questionable rulings, and ambiguous outcomes that defy explanation and infuriate fans everywhere. And although this aspect of class discussion tends to be boy-heavy, I've found that young women are increasingly sports-literate (thanks to ESPN and Title 9) and can easily cite the judging scandal that led to the awarding of gold medals to Canada's Jamie Salé and David Pelletier in the 2002 Olympic figure-skating competition or (for those with longer memories) the epochal Mary Decker–Zola Budd collision in the 3,000-meter final at the 1984 Olympics.

The Giants sign-stealing controversy, interestingly, flared again almost fifty years after the play-off, when Joshua Harris Prager published an article on the 1951 pennant race in the *Wall Street Journal* (an article that did not fail to mention *Underworld*). Although it's uncommon for a question of justice and fairness in sports to appear fifty years later in a major daily newspaper, the point remains that competitive sports generate thousands of such questions, which are central to thousands of narratives of sport. In *Underworld*, the juxtaposition of Thomson's homer and the Soviet Union's second nuclear test serves many purposes, not least of them that it invites readers to situate both events in the larger contexts and narratives that (we hope) make sense of them. Just as Thomson and Branca thread their way through the book, so too does the arms race, leading us to narratives about downwinders, plutonium experiments, physics packages, mutually assured destruction, Lenny Bruce on the Cuban missile crisis, Marvin Lundy's half brother Avram Lubarsky's apartment in Gorki, the career of J. Edgar Hoover, and the emergence of the national security apparatus. From the events of 3 October 1951, questions of justice proliferate like so many multiply targetable nuclear warheads. To take one obvious example, Simeon Biggs, aka Big Sims, argues that Branca became part of a Thomson-Branca dog-and-pony show because of his race: "You can survive and endure and prosper if they let you. But you have to be white before they let you" (98). Biggs puts both hands on baseball's third rail, the sport's long history of racism, contrasting Branca with the California Angels pitcher Donnie Moore, who in 1986 gave up the home run to Dave Henderson that eventually led to the Angels' American League play-off loss to the Boston Red Sox after the Angels had led the series 3–1 and led the fifth game 5–2 in the ninth (with two outs and two strikes, at that). Moore, Biggs reminds us, did not survive the ninth-inning play-off comeback; three years later, he killed his wife and himself, and Biggs insists that because of his race, "Donnie Moore was not allowed to outlive his failure. The fans gave him every grief and there weren't any skits at the baseball dinners" (98). It's an interesting argument, but any baseball fan would object that it overlooks the career of the most famous goat of 1986, Bill Buckner, whose horrid misplay of Mookie Wilson's squibber down the line gave the Mets a bizarre 6–5 ten-inning win in game 6 of the World Series. Buckner is white and was not spared because of his whiteness: Boston fans turned on him and forced him into seclusion. On this count, Biggs seems to be unequivocally wrong. And yet, who would deny that the Red Sox were one of the most thoroughly racist franchises in the game? Who could confidently say that race was not a factor in Moore's life after the 1986 playoff? Are the many texts and contexts of the cold war any harder or easier to parse than these endless narratives of luck, fate, race, and retribution?

In the novel's final section, "Das Capital," at the Kazakh test site (where, in a sense, the novel began—there and at the Polo Grounds), our protagonist, Nick Shay, turns to Viktor Maltsev, the representative of a post-Soviet company ("Tchaika") that offers nuclear incineration of hazardous waste, and asks, "Viktor, does anyone remember why we were doing all this?" "Yes, for contest," Viktor responds. "You won, we lost. You have to tell me how it feels. Big winner" (793).

At least two things are going on in this exchange: first, the irony of hearing Nick called a "big winner" long after we've learned that he defines himself in terms of loss (the Dodgers, his father, George Manza) and even spent $34,500 to buy a baseball as a reminder of loss; second, the reduction of the cold war to a "contest" without any motive other than to produce a winner and a loser. There's nothing here about democracy or the worker's paradise, nothing about market and command economies, nothing about NATO and the Warsaw Pact, Czechoslovakia or Chile, Pershings or SS-18s, capitalist lackeys or evil empires. Just winners and losers, as in the play-offs; one side goes on, to spin its narrative another day, and one side goes home.

Contrast this scene, then, with Brian Glassic's response to Big Sims's Moore argument:

> ". . . well I'm sorry but how do we distinguish Donnie Moore from all the other ball games and all the other shootings?"
>
> "The point is not what we notice or what we remember but what

> happened," Sims said, "to the parties involved. We're talking about who lived and who died."
>
> "But not why," Classic said. "Because if we analyze the reasons honestly and thoroughly instead of shallow and facile and what else?"
>
> "Unhistorical," I said.
>
> "Then we realize that there were probably a dozen reasons why the guy started shooting and most of them we'll never know or understand." (99)

Glassic complicates Big Sims's comparison of Branca and Moore by foregrounding precisely the thing Viktor refused to engage in his two-word summary of the superpower conflict that structured the latter half of the twentieth century: the question of motive. This question, finally, is the real distinction between sports and the rest of our lives: though sports may present complex questions about justice that are also complex questions about narrative, sports offer their fans a form of narrative that is evacuated of motive. No one asks Michael Jordan, "Why were you trying to hit that buzzer beater?" No one grills Tom Brady about why he was trying to unload the ball. No one wonders why the Giants were trying to beat the Dodgers, regardless of whether they were stealing signs. It is for contest, that's all.

Juxtaposing the narratives of baseball and of the cold war, then, *Underworld* insists on the importance of motive. DeLillo, like Thomas Pynchon (with whom he is often compared), makes much of the multivalence of the term *plot*, spinning paranoid tales around the word's more sinister connotations, from "diabolical scheme" to "area of cemetery land." But what's striking about *Underworld* is that, unlike postmodern paranoid fictions in which all plotting is sinister and probably related to someone's eventual demise, this novel shows us time and again how difficult it is, outside the world of sports, to live in a story without a plot, a narrative without a motive.

Accordingly, I suggest that we can use *Underworld* to illuminate *White Noise*'s ruminations about the relation of plot to death. One might, for instance, provide students with an excerpt from the Glassic-Biggs exchange and ask—if indeed Glassic is right and there are a dozen reasons for any event, most of which we'll never know or understand—why we should bother trying to discern motive. Why read for plot at all? In the past I've asked students to write an essay analyzing one string of events in *Underworld*; in the future, applying the same logic to *White Noise*, I might assign an essay in which students read the novel by way of two of the twentieth century's most influential English-speaking theorists of narrative, E. M. Forster (*Aspects*) and Frank Kermode. For Forster, of course, there can be no plot without causality: " 'The king died and then the queen died' is a story," he writes in *Aspects of the Novel*. " 'The king died and then the queen died of grief' is a plot" (86). Kermode's *The Sense of an Ending*, a brilliant, elusive book devoted in part to explaining the longer Western narrative tropes underlying the many varieties of modernist experimentalism, argues that plotting is indispensable to human beings living outside a religious dispensation that explains to them the purpose of their living, from genesis to revelations. Kermode's argument is practically transcribed in *White Noise* through Murray, a former sports reporter (no accident there) who not only provides the novel with a kind of running commentary on its forays into American popular and commerical culture but also rationally and bloodlessly convinces Jack to kill Willie Mink:

> We start our lives in chaos, in babble. As we surge up into the world, we try to devise a shape, a plan. There is dignity in this. Your whole life is a plot, a scheme, a diagram. It is a failed scheme but that's not the point. To plot is to affirm life, to seek shape and control. (291–92)

Yet as Kermode points out, the plot that affirms life may well spring from our fear of death:

> Men, like poets, rush "into the middest," *in medias res*, when they are born; they also die *in mediis rebus*, and to make sense of their span they need fictive concords with origins and ends, such as give meaning to lives and to poems. The End they imagine will reflect their irreducibly intermediary preoccupations. They fear it, and as far as we can see have always done so; the End is a figure for their own deaths. (7)

The first half of this passage sounds like Murray, perhaps, but the second half recalls Jack's discussion of plots at the outset of the novel, when he tells his students, "All plots tend to move deathward. This is the nature of plots. Political plots, terrorist plots, lovers' plots, narrative plots, plots that are part of children's games. We edge nearer death every time we plot." DeLillo follows this rather obvious announcement of one of the novel's major preoccupations by having Jack disclaim any insight into what he has just said: "Is this true? Why did I say it? What does it mean?" (26).

I have always read these questions as being somewhat disingenuous, though I confess I have not been able to decide whether the disingenuousness is Jack's or DeLillo's. Surely DeLillo knows what he is about when he peppers a novel with discussions about the functions of plotting, so it seems a bit heavy-handed to have a character offer one such discussion and then puzzle over it. As for Jack, perhaps his need to disavow responsibility for an argument about plotting arises from a disingenuousness born of fear: if motive lies at the center of plot, how better to obscure one's relation to plots (and thus, perhaps, to death) than to claim not to know why one tells one's class about the relation of plots to death?

Still, though I am not fond of this passage, I think that *Underworld* can help pry it open. First, let us imagine that Jack sincerely does not understand his motives for saying that all plots move deathward. We might then be inclined to remember that Jack apparently does not understand his own motives for studying Hitler or for founding Hitler studies, and tends to speak about his career in the most shallowly professionalist terms available. He has carved out an academic niche, he has established a new field and a scholarly reputation of some sort, but, tellingly, we never get a sense of the intellectual substance of this field or of Jack's work in it. From here we can move to the more general observation that the major characters and events in *White Noise* seem to be without motive. We can secure this point in part by looking at the minor characters who do have clear motives, like Orest Mercator, who is "training to break the world endurance record for sitting in a cage full of poisonous snakes" (182) and who bends his entire being to this goal: "He inhaled food according to aerodynamic principles. Pressure differences, intake velocities. . . . He was creating an imperial self out of some tabloid aspiration" (265, 268). Motives in *White Noise* tend to be the stuff of tabloid aspiration and are inevitably trivialized, even when they involve terrorist plots of the kind we have lately become all too familiar with, as in the tabloid item Babette reads to an audience of blind people: "Members of an air-crash cult will hijack a jumbo jet and crash it into the White House in an act of blind devotion to their mysterious and reclusive leader, known only as Uncle Bob" (146). By contrast, the novel's central event, the release of the chemical Nyodene D in the "airborne toxic event" (107), is utterly motiveless. If we compare *White Noise*'s airborne toxic event with the 1984 toxic leak at the Union Carbide chemical plant in Bhopal, India (which occurred about a month before the book's publication and which DeLillo is often credited with having eerily anticipated), the motivelessness and the agentlessness of the event should seem all the more remarkable—not because Union Carbide intended to poison thousands of residents but because *White Noise* contains so little treatment of the causes of the event. There's not a word about the train that derailed, the chemical company that was transporting Nyodene D, or the large-scale socioeconomic forces behind chemical spills and other industrial disasters. In *White Noise*, the airborne toxic event is presented as just another one of "[t]he networks, the circuits, the streams, the harmonies" (46) that fill the air, like the hum of consumers in the mall or the ubiquitous and intangible webs of information that define Jack's life at Autumn Harvest Farms and at the ATM.

The salient exceptions to the rule are, of course, Babette's plan to have sex with Willie Mink in exchange for Dylar, which she undertakes in a desperate and doomed attempt to alleviate her fear of death, and then Jack's plan to kill Mink and take his Dylar. These are plots in Forster's sense, and it is clear that the second plot follows causally from the first. But it's fitting that both plots go so terribly awry, since Dylar itself seems to be a dud. It causes Mink to confuse words with things, thus affording us some speculations on the relation between language and what Heidegger called Being-toward-death (this is one facet of the novel's affinities with existentialism): it suggests, however comically, that we must be willing to accept the inevitability of death if we are to understand the functions of language. But since the drug does not succeed in counteracting its users' fear of death, both Babette's and Jack's plots to obtain Dylar seem pointless and futile. The revenge plot that drives Jack to kill Mink for having sex with his wife also fizzles, even though—or because?—Jack obsessively repeats versions of his plan to himself some eight times in chapter 39. Interestingly, had the revenge plan worked, it would have confirmed both Murray's thesis and Jack's: it would have imposed order on chaos and it would have moved deathward. Does Jack's failed plot, then, suggest that he had it right the first time, when speaking to his students—or perhaps later, when he thought, in that elegiac moment amid the plots and headstones in Blacksmith Village's "Old Burying Ground," "May the days be aimless. Let the seasons drift. Do not advance the action according to a plan" (98)? Very possibly, in which case we should turn from Jack's personal idiosyncracies to the question of the novel's narrative structure: is it possible that Jack inhabits a narrative that has no plan, an aimless novel in which motives are either pernicious or preposterous things?

The final sentences of *White Noise* faintly echo James Joyce's immortal short story "The Dead," though in Joyce the snow is general all over Ireland and here the confusion is general all over the supermarket. As often happens in *White Noise* (think of the joy Jack experiences at the mall or at the ATM), it is extremely hard to determine whether we are to take this ending "seriously" or "ironically" or by means of meta-ironic sentences containing lots of "scare quotes." Is this a real ending, an invocation to all the living and the dead (as in Joyce) or to the tabloid cults of the famous and the dead? Perhaps, perhaps not. But even if the ending is "real," one of the problems with *White Noise* is that it offers too many endings. When Wilder crosses the highway (322–24), we can see this minor miracle as a summation of the novel's treatment of death and language, since Wilder cannot speak and is the only character in the novel who does not fear death. When Jack encounters the German nun (316–20), who speaks like a cross between Jean Baudrillard and Jackie Mason, we can read the scene as a summation of the novel's concern with simulacra and simulation. The rearrangement of the supermarket shelves likewise seems to tie up one of the novel's narrative threads, the relation between subjectivity and shopping. But other aspects of the novel are left hanging: Jack continues to avoid Dr. Chakravarty of Autumn Harvest Farms, knowing that he has death inside him and that it's "just a question of whether or not I can outlive it" (150). And, of course, "[t]he men in Mylex suits are still in the area, yellow-snouted, gathering their terrible data" (325). Too many endings—and no sense of closure.

The reason for this state of affairs, I think, is that, unlike *Underworld*, *White Noise* is nearly motiveless. In other words, the novel doesn't conclude conclusively precisely because the motives in the novel are so uncertain or unascertainable, found only in waves, codes, circuits, streams, simulations—and ridiculous, tabloid-quality plots. I cannot even say that *White Noise* is antiplot; rather, I claim that the novel affects a studied ambivalence toward plotting, so much so that it is difficult to say whether the novel is plotted. No doubt this ambivalence accounts for some degree of the novel's oft-remarked tonelessness, as well as for our nagging inability to say with any certainty whether DeLillo has written an existentialist critique or a postmodern celebration of consumer capitalism's reification of human desires. *Underworld* complicates and magnifies the question of motive by narrating itself backward and by contrasting the motivelessness of sports with the macromotivations of superpower conflict and the micromotivations of ordinary men and women. *White Noise*, however, presents a form of narrative that somehow manages neither to eschew nor to embrace the consolations of plot. Reading DeLillo backward from *Underworld* to *White Noise* in *Underworld*ian fashion, I find this indifference to plot considerably more vexing than I did when I first read *White Noise* twenty years ago. Perhaps I am more sympathetic, after reading *Underworld*, to the traditional view that, as Kermode phrases it, "tracts of time unpunctuated by meaning derived from the end are not to be borne" (162), even as I continue, as a reader trained in the modernist narratives of the twentieth century, to "discard the fictions that are too fully explanatory, too consoling" (161). Or perhaps I am more vexed (though still vastly impressed) by *White Noise* because I am rereading it not backward from *Underworld* but forward from my first reading, now twenty years closer to my own death—in which case I surmise that the rereading of novels is as necessary as the making of plots for those of us who want to compose a narrative of our life, a narrative that comprehends our own partial plots and motives as intensifications of rather than compensations for the unavoidable fact that we cannot know the manner or the meaning of our ends.

Inventing Hope: The Question of Belief in *White Noise* and *Mao II*

Mark A. Eaton

> Out of some persistent sense of large-scale ruin, we keep inventing hope.
>
> —Don DeLillo, *White Noise*

"When the Old God leaves the world," one character muses in Don DeLillo's *Mao II*, "what happens to all the unexpended faith?" (7). The question of what has happened to faith since the proverbial death of God is a pivotal one in DeLillo's novels, especially in *White Noise* and *Mao II*, which are both preoccupied with, among other things, the question of belief. And "the question of belief" is just the right phrase, too, for belief in DeLillo's fiction is always attenuated by doubt in a kind of cognitive dialectic. Whether his characters are challenging a positivist belief in the reality of the natural world or trying to hold on to their belief in some supernatural realm, belief in anything seems precarious at best, provisional or untenable at worst. Although DeLillo arguably underestimates the persistence of belief in the Old God, his novels accurately enumerate the various dispensations that actually proliferated rather than disappeared in the late twentieth century. What happened to some of the unexpended faith, in other words, is that it got redirected into new forms of religiosity or else displaced, as it were, onto otherwise secular apprehensions of reality. In *White Noise* and *Mao II*, for instance, the range of belief systems includes not only evangelical Christianity but also Eastern religions like Islam and Buddhism, as well as "a flood of unorthodox spiritualities" frequently grouped under the rubric of New Age religions (McClure 142). DeLillo's fine-tuned fictional worlds often disclose a "sense of transcendence that lies just beyond" the most mundane aspects of everyday life, what the author himself once called "a kind of radiance in dailiness." "Sometimes this radiance can be almost frightening," he remarks. "Other times it can be almost holy or sacred" ("Outsider" 63). By describing the many permutations of unexpended faith in his novels, the author takes an inventory of the current religious scene. By infusing his fictional worlds with radiance and intimations of transcendence, he reveals the interpenetration of the sacred and profane in contemporary culture. Above all, DeLillo captures something essential yet paradoxical about belief: where there is belief, there is likely to be some measure, however small, of doubt.

Doubt is as old as faith, of course, yet the nature of doubt has changed since the advent of modernity. Once viewed as the opposite of belief and punishable by death, unbelief has become in the modern era a well-nigh inescapable aspect of belief itself. As the philosopher Charles Taylor eloquently writes, a uniquely modern melancholy of unbelief arises

> in a world where the guarantee of meaning has gone, where all the traditional sources, theological, metaphysical, historical, can be cast in doubt. It therefore has a new shape: not the sense of rejection and exile from an unchallengeable cosmos of significance, but rather the intimation of what may be a definitive emptiness, the final dawning of the end of the last illusion of significance. It hurts, one might say, in a new way. (39–40)

Painful as it may be to contemplate, the notion that there's nothing more than what we can see here and now has emerged as a distinct possibility. In the modern context, agnosticism became a viable if not the dominant intellectual position, and the notion of transcendence in turn lost credibility. "As Christianity came under pressure from Enlightenment rationality," Andrew Delbanco argues similarly, "the idea of transcendence . . . detached itself from any coherent symbology," leaving many people with a "lurking suspicion that all our getting and spending amounts to nothing more than fidgeting while we wait for death" (5, 3).

Certainly "many people appear to have become completely indifferent to religious and philosophical questions" (M. Taylor 4), yet even with the ascendancy of science, "there has been no wholesale rejection of the possibility of belief" (Roof 48). On the contrary, faith remains absolutely central to many people's lives and is clearly on the rise throughout much of the world. There is no question that the so-called secularization thesis—the view that Enlightenment rationalism would ultimately supersede religion altogether—has been decisively challenged by historians of religion, who point especially to the spread of evangelical Christianity as evidence for the resilience and vitality of belief despite the challenges of modernity (P. Berger, *Desecularization*; Jenkins).

DeLillo's novels grapple with big questions like the existence of God, the meaning of life, what happens after death, and so on. His interest in such questions, one suspects, has more than a little to do with his Catholic upbringing. With its heavy emphasis on eschatology, Catholicism is an obvious subtext to Jack Gladney's obsession with death and the afterlife. "I think there is a sense of last things in my work that probably comes from a Catholic childhood," DeLillo admits. "For a Catholic, nothing is too important to discuss or think about, because he's raised with the idea that he will die any minute now and that if he doesn't live his life in a certain way this death is simply an introduction to an eternity of pain" (Passaro). DeLillo's characters tend to struggle on their own with such questions, however, without the benefit of older certainties, much less catechisms. Far from being lapsed Catholics, they seem entirely cut off from any religious traditions, yet they still want to believe that there is more to life than waiting around for death. This desire helps explain what makes DeLillo's characters susceptible to charismatic leaders and cults. As John Duvall points out, "DeLillo has long been fascinated with crowds and people's collective urge to be part of something larger than themselves, to surrender to a power that would explain the felt alienation of their lives and . . . protect them from a recognition of their own mortality" (*Don DeLillo's* Underworld 15). DeLillo clearly understands our human need for some higher purpose in life, some reason to hope for a better future, at a time when the world offers plenty of reasons to despair. His characters desperately cling to belief as a means of "inventing hope" in the midst of the seeming chaos and confusion of modern life (147). His novels highlight some of the bizarre but surely understandable strategies people use to create meaning or, as Delbanco aptly puts it, "to hold back the melancholy suspicion that we live in a world without meaning" (3).

In the world today the dialectic between belief and unbelief has, if anything, intensified. The last fifty years have seen a profound reshaping of religion, although not a weakening or turning away from belief, as many secular liberals assumed. One critic speaks of a fundamental shift "from a world in which beliefs held believers to one in which believers hold beliefs" (Roof 42). This formulation captures the move away from traditional forms of religion toward a more eclectic spirituality. But an equally significant shift has occurred, I argue, in the very nature of belief. Doubt has curiously emerged as an aspect of faith, such that believers are attuned to the resonance of unbelief, while nonbelievers in turn "combine skepticism with varying degrees of faith, or openness to faith" (48). As doubt and skepticism have become much less stigmatized, and even as outright atheism has become something of a default position among intellectuals and the unchurched in America, so too has belief itself been altered—shaded, we might say—by the dominant ideology of pluralism.

This is the world our students have inherited, for better or worse, and DeLillo poses the question of belief in such a way that they may well recognize some of their disparate faith traditions, or perhaps their struggles with faith. *White Noise*, especially, maps out the contours of "a new religious America," to borrow Diana Eck's phrase, which is characterized by an unprecedented range of spiritual options. And "nowhere," Eck observes, "is the sheer range of religious faith as wide as it is today in the United States" (4–5). Wholly secular approaches to DeLillo's novels tend to miss his point about the diffusion of unexpended faith into all sorts of religious and metaphysical systems. His novels provide a kind of case study in how religious belief not only persists but indeed has expanded in our supposedly secular postmodern era. By approaching these novels from the perspective of religious studies, we can gain a much fuller understanding of the vicissitudes of belief in Don DeLillo's America.

I've taught *White Noise* at two different institutions: one with close ties to the United Methodist Church, the other with no denominational ties but a clear commitment to Christian higher education. Increasingly at many institutions—not just religiously affiliated ones—students identify themselves as conservative and evangelical. Yet even these students have experienced a subtle but unmistakable transformation of their faith under the pressure of pluralism. DeLillo's religious eclecticism, the anything-goes ethos of his novels, rings true to the experiences of Christian students who may feel marginalized or silenced even though they espouse what is, after all, the nation's majority faith. In the more secular world of the larger academy, they've learned to mimic if not fully endorse a virtuous tolerance for other faith traditions. Yet it's worth remembering that many students are believers, often quite devout believers. Since these days they come from all kinds of religious backgrounds as well as from distinctly nonreligious ones, *White Noise* mirrors the pluralistic world they inhabit. The novel thus presents a wonderful opportunity to address the question of belief in our classrooms, thereby responding to rather than completely ignoring the reality of our students' spiritual lives.

In order to better understand DeLillo's analysis of belief in *White Noise* and *Mao II*, students first need to consider the changing nature of belief in these postmodern times. I take the time to rehearse widely available data on beliefs and church attendance in the United States, since the statistics are eye-opening enough to be discussed at some length. Polls continue to show a high percentage of people who profess to believe in God. The *New York Times* reported in 1997 that 96% of Americans say they believe in God; 90% think there is a heaven; and 87% consider themselves Christians (Mizruchi ix). While only 40% of adults say they attend religious services regularly, 69% say they belong to a church or synagogue, and 90% claim that they pray to God or some higher being (Gallup and Lindsey 2–3). At the very least, these figures suggest that the population of the United States is much more religious than one might think. But they may paint a misleading picture of the current state of religion, by exaggerating the orthodoxy of belief and by occluding the prevailing secularity of American culture. Students need a little guidance in making sense of statistics from the *Times* and Gallup polls, so I point them to a number of influential recent studies that help contextualize the facts. Since most students have little or no background in recent religious history, these studies equip them to understand not only DeLillo's representation of religion in his novels but also how their own religious practices and beliefs fit into the overall religious picture in America. Resourceful students will look up some of these books on their own, so I provide a short bibliography, but I also simply cull a few selected quotations from these works and put them on a class handout. My purpose in reading passages from relevant works in religious studies is to demonstrate that whatever the polls say about widespread belief in God, the ways in which people think of their belief relative to other beliefs and to the larger culture are evolving. "Many people remain convinced of God's existence," Robert Wuthnow has observed, "but realize increasingly that the reality of their world is secular" (10). Belief in God doesn't necessarily result in regular church attendance, because today "a wider range of people express religious beliefs that move outside Christian orthodoxy" (C. Taylor 107). Belief is thus detached from traditional religious communities, as are spiritual disciplines like prayer. According to Wade Clark Roof, "the current religious situation in the United States is characterized not so much by a loss of faith as a qualitative shift from unquestioned belief to a more open, questing mood" (9). "Inherited forms of religion persist and still influence people," he insists, but the heterogeneity of religious practices signals "a shift in the center of religious energy" (7).

Since the 1960s and 1970s, many baby boomers sought alternatives to what they disparagingly called organized religion, often by rejecting their parents' churches in favor of a more personalized spirituality. Ironically, in doing so they conformed to a patently consumerist approach to faith, as the authors of one study, *Shopping for Faith: American Religion in the New Millennium*, suggest: "Today's diverse religious landscape . . . can be compared to a busy marketplace where competition thrives and seekers shop" (Cimino and Lattin 5). In this competitive, free-market environment, the traditional Christian denominations such as Methodist and Episcopalian have been contracting, whereas newer types of churches, many of them associated with Pentecostalism, are flourishing. Indeed, "evangelical Christianity is the fastest-growing form of religious life" in the United States today (C. Taylor 38). Yet Islam and Buddhism have also grown considerably, to the point where Muslims now equal Presbyterians (Mizruchi ix). So while most Americans identify themselves as Christian, religious diversity is a sign of the times.

With his finger on the spiritual pulse of contemporary American culture, DeLillo brilliantly delineates "the increasingly complex hybridity of religious forms" (Mizruchi ix). Much of the two or more weeks I spend on DeLillo is devoted to unpacking the religious images and themes in *White Noise*, his most extensive treatment of the question of belief. The amazing diversity of beliefs in *White Noise* is worth noting at the outset, since it illustrates the sheer range of options available in the current religious climate. DeLillo typically indulges in hyperbole to make his point, but the varieties of religious experience are everywhere evident in the novel. The waxing and waning of traditional, mainline denominations; the proliferation of New Age spiritualities; the emergence of a kind of apocalyptic environmentalism; the rise of religious fundamentalisms; the popularization of quasi-religious practices like yoga; even the more insidious and sometimes deadly practices of cults—all these phenomena and more fall under DeLillo's purview. "These new spiritualities, like the more traditional forms," John McClure has written, "are often inflected with the rhetoric and values of consumer capitalism, but they tend, at the same time, to appeal to people dissatisfied with secular strategies of fulfillment" (142). The first important lesson to draw from *White Noise* is that there are seemingly as many beliefs as there are believers, and that consumerism, if not a religion in itself, infects virtually all religions.

The influence of consumerism is easy to demonstrate by reading aloud, or by having students read aloud, a few key passages in the novel. At one point, for instance, the cynical professor Murray Siskind advises Jack Gladney to sample the variety of religions and "[p]ick one you like." "Read up on reincarnation, transmigration, hyperspace, the resurrection of the dead and so on," urges Murray. "Some gorgeous systems have evolved from these beliefs." Knowing that Murray is a nonpracticing Jew and a pop culture professor in the American Environments Department, Jack demands to know, "Do you believe in any of these things?" Murray simply dodges the question: "Millions of people have believed for thousands of years" (286). Not one to practice what he preaches, the closest Murray himself comes to a religious experience is at a tourist site known as the Most Photographed Barn in America: "Being here is a kind of spiritual surrender," he tells Jack. "A religious experience in a way, like all tourism" (12). Murray clearly stands in for the professoriat as a whole in DeLillo's satire of academic life, and at the time *White Noise* was published, Murray's dilettantism could easily have been used to advantage by neoconservatives in the culture wars. DeLillo's portrait of petty academics is amusingly accurate, but I find that the exquisite irony of his satire is often lost on undergraduates. For my purposes, the whole cast of ridiculous college professors is important mainly for what it reveals about belief in the academy, which is often invested in knowledge per se. Another professor in the novel, the New York transplant Alfonse Stompanato, stays on the cutting edge of intellectual trends by making popular culture his only religion: "When he talked about popular culture, he exercised the closed logic of a religious zealot, one who kills for his beliefs" (65). I have more to say below about how DeLillo's later novel *Mao II* explores the dangers of religious fundamentalism, but for now let me suggest only that the specter of fundamentalist zeal arises whenever anyone latches on to a particular religion and embraces it so exclusively, so wholeheartedly as to become irrational or worse: one who kills for his beliefs. The United States does not, of course, corner the market on religious fundamentalism, but we do have our fair share of fundamentalists. DeLillo is surely onto something when he hints that the fickleness and superficiality of Americans when it comes to their beliefs ultimately mean less than how far Americans are willing to go to defend them.

Most characters in *White Noise* are almost comically innocuous in their beliefs. They are primarily seekers, exemplifying a new paradigm of finding religious experiences not in traditional churches but in various world religions or even in quasi religions. Wuthnow writes: "a profound change in our spiritual practices has indeed taken place during the last half century," in which a "traditional spirituality of inhabiting sacred places has given way to a new spirituality of seeking" (3). Following Murray's advice to sample the world's religions and "pick one you like," many characters in *White Noise* are engaged in a freewheeling quest for spiritual guidance. Jack's ex-wife Janet lives on an ashram in Montana and goes by the name Mother Devi; Tweedy Browner, Bee's mother, is described as having "a sense of Protestant disrepair about her" (86). The phrase "Protestant disrepair," tossed off here with DeLillo's usual aplomb, in fact indexes an important development in church history: the shrinking of mainline denominations amid an increasingly commercialized field of religious institutions. In his book *Selling God* (1994), R. Laurence Moore writes that the "sheer diversity" of religions means that churches now "have to sell" themselves, "not only in the competitive church market but also in a general market of other cultural commodities" (10–11). In the same vein, Donald E. Miller points out that "so-called mainline denominations are clearly losing their market share. In the past several decades denominations such as the Methodists, Presbyterians, and Episcopalians have lost between 20 and 40 percent of their members" (4). Thus Tweedy Browner, a baby boomer herself, abandons Protestantism for a cultlike rural commune, while Jack's colleague Murray Siskind and Jack's other sometime spouses exemplify the eclecticism of people who view the whole array of world religions as a kind of spiritual playground.

Jack's first and fourth wife, Babette, embodies this same therapeutic approach of searching for self-fulfillment through lifestyle changes, exercise programs, and even psychopharamacology. Her role in the Blacksmith community is that of self-help guru; she gives lectures at a local Congregational church on yoga, Sufi dervishes, and correct posture. Her grab-bag approach to self-fulfillment illustrates the anything-goes attitude of New Age adherents: "Nothing is foreign, nothing too remote to apply." Perhaps the best example students have for this kind of arrogant appropriation of exotic religious practices is the pop star Madonna. Babette's disciples still flock to her classes, listening with rapt attention as she goes on and on about "yoga, kendo, trance-walking," and so on. For his part, Jack marvels "at their acceptance and trust, the sweetness of their belief. Nothing is too doubtful to be of use to them. . . . It is the end of skepticism" (27). Unmoored from its traditional grounding in a coherent religious framework, belief goes soft. There is a nostalgic quality to such sentimental belief, as if by disavowing any incredulity one might make up for the loss of certainty that made traditional belief systems impervious to doubt.

A similar lack of skepticism is seen in Babette's unquestioning acceptance of tabloids, and it is worth exploring DeLillo's critique of tabloid journalism in some detail for the ways in which an age-old belief in paranormal phenomena has been displaced into the realm of kitsch. Sitting in a makeshift shelter after the airborne toxic event with "a small and brightly colored stack of supermarket tabloids" (142), Babette relates one preposterous tale after another to a group of people who seem to have no problem believing "documented cases of life after death," the "transmigration of souls," or even "personalized resurrection through stream-of-consciousness computer techniques" (144).

The discourse of the tabloids—hyperbolic, surreal, eschatological—doesn't seem over-the-top; instead it is accepted with a sort of "passive belief . . . [as] a set of statements no less real than our daily quota of observable household fact" (144–45). To be sure, DeLillo mocks how easily Babette and her listeners swallow these outrageous tales, but he also forces us to ponder their extraordinary appeal to some twenty million readers per week. We can relate to the scene in which Jack, standing in the checkout line at the local supermarket, is ineluctably drawn to the glossy covers with their sensationalistic headlines: "Everything we need that is not food or love is here in the tabloid racks. The tales of the supernatural and the extraterrestrial. The miracle vitamins, the cures for cancer, the remedies for obesity. The cults of the famous and the dead" (326). Indeed, the author once told an interviewer that the tabloids "ask profoundly important questions about death, the afterlife, God . . . in an almost Pop Art atmosphere" (qtd. in Osteen 179).

DeLillo's critique of American culture is deliberately embedded in that culture: he realizes his own susceptibility to cooptation, his own fascination with the very cultural forces he deplores. The last time I taught *White Noise*, I brought in a stack of tabloids and split students into groups to cut out the most outlandish stories they could find. Each group reported its results in a lively exchange of clippings, with stories ranging from the merely bizarre to the deliberately shocking. In its undisguised sensationalism and blatant prevarication, tabloid journalism sheds light on the fringes of faith in America today. Belief in alien abductions or metempsychosis is easy to ridicule, but the popularity of these publications may give students pause the next time they pass through the checkout lines at the supermarket. This exercise helps drive home DeLillo's point about the end of skepticism in our culture, a corollary to the plasticity of belief.

If tabloids are a relatively easy target, they prepare students for a much more difficult task: to acknowledge how thoroughly implicated we are as Americans in the ideology of consumerism, which has become so naturalized as to be taken utterly for granted. The effects of consumerism on religion are pronounced in *White Noise*, and students need to be jarred out of their complacency and comfort zones to appreciate fully the author's critique. Since the suburban world of DeLillo's novel is suffused with advertising jingles, screaming headlines, and TV sound bites—the white noise of American mass culture—it will no doubt be familiar to them. The trick is to get them to empathize with the deep spiritual hunger that DeLillo's characters feel, a hunger that cannot be fed simply by acquiring more things.

Jack emerges as a spiritual seeker who finds moments of transcendence not in traditional religion but in shopping: the grocery store provides him with a "sense of well-being," even a "fullness of being" (20); when a cash machine confirms his bank balance, "[w]aves of relief and gratitude" flow through him (46). "The system had blessed my life," he says emphatically. "I felt its support and approval" (46). In a shopping spree at the Mid-Village Mall, he says, "I filled myself out, found new aspects of myself, located a person I'd forgotten existed" (84). Shopping may assuage his basic desire simply to buy stuff, and we can all identify with the emotional uplift of a shopping spree, but shopping is no panacea for deeper anxieties about marriage, profession, and imminent death.

With no connection whatever to a viable tradition or a community of faith, Jack latches on to whatever shards of spiritual significance he can find, whether in quotidian consumer goods or man-made disasters. He likens the thick, black, billowy cloud, euphemistically dubbed by experts an airborne toxic event, to the Romantic sublime: "Our fear was accompanied by a sense of awe that bordered on the religious" (127). He finds spiritual intimations in the most mundane—or in this case the most spectacular—events of the day. And because nearly everything in the novel is open to interpretation (I have in mind here the hilarious discussion about whether rain is real or merely a figment of our imagination [22–24]), DeLillo simultaneously captures the epistemological crisis at the heart of our postmodern condition and "a sense of something extraordinary hovering just beyond our touch and just beyond our vision" (DeLillo, "Outsider" 63). Given the post-Enlightenment disenchantment of the world, we might say that Jack's world is re-enchanted, such that a bag of groceries offers a sense of well-being (20); a family dinner gives off "extrasensory flashes and floating nuances of being" (34); his daughter's "ecstatic chant" of a car name, Toyota Celica, strikes him "with the impact of a moment of splendid transcendence" (155); and, finally, simply watching his children sleep makes him feel "selfless and spiritually large" (155).

DeLillo clearly engages in what McClure calls "a post-secular project of resacralization" (144), but the author's take on the transcendent is by no means unambiguous. In a bizarre scene near the end of *White Noise*, for instance, the youngest child, Wilder, performs what amounts to a miracle by riding his tricycle across an expressway in rush-hour traffic and emerging unscathed at the other end. It's not at all clear what to make of this miracle; indeed, DeLillo goes out of his way to emphasize its utter incomprehensibility: "The women could only look, empty-mouthed"; "The drivers could not quite comprehend"; "What did it mean, this little rotary blur?" (322, 323). On the one hand, the scene is deliberately cinematic, the suburban equivalent of Sergei Eisenstein's famous Odessa steps sequence in *Battleship Potemkin* (1925), or rather an ironic update of countless chase scenes in which the hero improbably dodges adversaries, bullets, and oncoming vehicles with nary a scratch. The bystanders who watch Wilder set out across the freeway can only hope "for the scene to reverse, the boy to pedal backwards . . . like a cartoon figure on morning TV." On the other hand, DeLillo's language lightly applies a religious frame of reference for Wilder's wild ride—he is "mystically charged" (322), as if guardian angels are escorting him to safety. The suburban landscape is paradoxically both secularized and imbued with spiritual significance, the transcendent, a sense of the miraculous.

DeLillo's analysis of belief and doubt in *White Noise* culminates in another bizarre scene in the penultimate chapter, when Jack, bleeding profusely from a bullet wound, seeks help in "a three-story building that might have been a Pentecostal church, a day-care center, world headquarters for some movement of regimented youth" (315). Instead, it "appeared to be a clinic" run by Catholic nuns (316). What follows is a curious philosophical discussion about belief, the upshot of which, as Jack is astounded to learn, is that the nuns themselves don't believe in heaven. When Jack protests that nuns, of all people, have to keep the faith, one sister knowingly observes that "nonbelievers need the believers. They are desperate to have someone believe." "As belief shrinks from the world," she claims, "people find it more necessary than ever that *someone* believe. . . . Those who have abandoned belief must still believe in us" (318, 319). Jack's unbelief, in other words, is belied by his certainty that someone else believes. This paradox is a variation on the dialectic of belief and unbelief I started with. If even the most devout believers find themselves entertaining serious doubt, the converse is also true: nonbelievers need to believe that there are believers. Ultimately, Jack solves the problem by resolving to believe everything: "White noise everywhere. . . . I believed everything" (310). In *American Magic and Dread*, Mark Osteen astutely glosses this scene:

> DeLillo is suggesting that the impulse to believe, a faith in the bare potential for sacredness or transcendence, will always endure. Tabloids, TV, supermarkets, toxic clouds—like it or not, these are the sites where spirits live and the shapes that spirits take. (188)

The author picks up and develops this important insight about the persistence of belief in *Mao II* (1991), a political thriller that opens at a large gathering of Moonies in a football stadium. *Mao II* is a wonderful novel to pair with *White Noise*, because it elaborates on the earlier book's analysis of belief and deepens its treatment of cults and other mass religious movements, thus touching on the contentious politics of belief: the damage belief sometimes causes in people's lives, as well as the violence it often engenders in many parts of the world. If time does not permit reading the entire novel, *Mao II* can easily be excerpted; the opening section of the novel, titled "At Yankee Stadium," is only sixteen pages and works well as a short set piece about religious cults; the last section, "Beirut," is also relevant, because it speaks to the spectacular rise in Islamic fundamentalism over the last several decades.

Cults are on the periphery of *White Noise*, but in *Mao II* they take center stage, and DeLillo shows us why crowd psychology plays such a crucial role in them and that belief can still be virulent in our otherwise cynical, noncommittal age. "Here they come," the novel begins, "marching into American sunlight" (3). A mass wedding is staged at Yankee Stadium, where 6,500 couples are to be married by the Reverend Moon, "a man of chunky build who saw Jesus on a mountainside . . . and now he is here, in American light, come to lead them to the end of human history" (6). Moon is the master of ceremonies, the charismatic leader of a cult:

> The blessed couples move their lips in unison, matching the echo of his amplified voice. There is stark awareness in their faces, a near pain of rapt adoration. He is Lord of the Second Advent. . . . His voice leads them out past love and joy, past the beauty of their mission, out past miracles and surrendered self. . . . He leads them out past religion and history. (15)

Belief becomes so all-consuming that it compels followers to give up their personal desires, their families, their very identities. The main character, Karen Janney, is marrying a man named Kim Jo Pak, whom she has only recently met. Her parents, Rodge and Maureen, watch anxiously from the stands, peering through a pair of binoculars and trying in vain to spot their estranged daughter. Looking out on the sea of faces, Rodge muses, "They are a nation . . . founded on the principle of easy belief. A unit fueled by credulousness" (7). In one of DeLillo's trademark narrative devices, the point of view shifts freely between the parents and Karen, or rather the limited omniscient narrator is focalized now through Rodge and now through what the narrator calls Karen's "mindstream" (8). This dizzying shift in perspective forces students to consider the scene from the viewpoints of parents and participants alike. DeLillo's humor and irony are evident in the self-pity of the parents, whose only daughter has joined a cult, marrying without their consent a Korean or Japanese guy—"He's either Korean or Japanese. Rodge didn't get it straight"—they've never met who knows only "about eight words of English" (4–5). From Karen's perspective, what most disturbs her parents is simply the "intensity" of her belief: "This is what frightens them. We really believe. They bring us up to believe but when we show them true belief they call out psychiatrists and police" (8).

Mass religious cults like the Moonies do tend to prey on the most vulnerable people in our society and draw them in through the promise of spiritual certainty and a sense of belonging to some larger purpose. Though Karen is middle-class and seems fairly well adjusted, she gets caught up in the movement enough to marry a complete stranger, and then she leads a group of disciples around the country to collect money for the church. She is the kind of character who cannot live without the security of an "absolute being" who provides, in her view, "a way out of weakness and confusion" (163). In DeLillo's novel *The Names* (1982), one character chides his wife: "You need things to be committed to. You need belief" (128). Karen is described as someone who also needs to believe in something or someone, not the Old God in this case but in Reverend Moon: "She believed deeply in Master and still thought of herself as a seeker, ready to receive what was vast and true."

Like so many of her fellow seekers, she has not been fulfilled by traditional religious institutions: "She began to think she was inadequate to the strict plain shapes of churchly faith" (78). DeLillo's seekers are engaged in an almost haphazard spiritual journey that leads them away from organized religion into less traditional, albeit highly organized, faiths. Even if they don't find exactly what they're looking for, they latch on to fads or cults in obsessive and self-destructive ways. Even if they do not wholly believe in the religions they follow, their commitment, once made, is wholehearted.

Belief is a problem for many of DeLillo's characters, who are "driven by homeless spiritual impulses and mesmerized by new religious movements" (McClure 142). Those highly skeptical of God talk still sympathize with the human impulse to believe. They ridicule Karen's personal belief in the Reverend Moon as a deity—"Karen thinks God is here. Like walkin' and talkin' " (69)—yet they admit to feeling dissatisfied with their disbelief or lack of faith. "I don't like not believing," the photojournalist Brita says at one point. "I'm not at peace with it. I take comfort when others believe. . . . I need these people to believe for me. I cling to believers. Many, everywhere. Without them, the planet goes cold" (69). I can think of no better illustration of this coldness than a poignant scene near the end of DeLillo's *Underworld*. Another nun, Sister Edgar, experiences a crisis of faith when a young homeless girl she had been trying to help is brutally raped and murdered. She had seen in the girl "a radiant grace" and "even a source of personal hope, a goad to the old rugged faith" (811), but after Esmeralda is killed, Sister Edgar is well on her way to loss of faith. "She says a desperate prayer," but then:

> She believes she is falling into crisis, beginning to think it is possible that all creation is a spurt of blank matter that chances to make an emerald here, a dead start there, with random waste between. The serenity of immense design is missing from her life, authorship and moral form. . . . It is not a question of disbelief. There is another kind of belief, a second force, insecure, untrusting, a faith that is spring-fed by the things we fear in the night, and she thinks she is succumbing. (817)

The things we fear in the night: this is DeLillo's shorthand for the dark forces of inhumanity and violence at work in our world. These dark forces certainly call into question the belief in a benevolent God. When such religious belief is finally abandoned, DeLillo astutely realizes, it doesn't always get replaced with unbelief; rather what replaces belief is another form of belief. Adopted as a defense against all the evil in the world, such a faith is committed not so much to the nonexistence of God as to the essential depravity of human beings. One becomes fearful, untrusting, paranoid, and utterly pessimistic. Without question people do inhumane things; the evidence is on every front page. Instead of succumbing to evil and giving up hope, why not try to keep a modicum of faith in human beings—in our capacity for civility, empathy, and love? Sister Edgar's loss of faith in the face of an ever-present evil is a familiar story—more familiar now, I suspect, than stories about people who maintain, against all odds, their belief in human goodness or in God. For some reason, we are drawn to endless reiterations of the crisis-of-faith story, which somehow seems more compelling and more truthful, because who, after all, could continue to believe in the face of such horrors as are daily witnessed all over the world? But whether his characters sustain or lose faith, DeLillo represents the dialectic between belief and unbelief as a signal feature of deep spiritual malaise.

That malaise has worsened during the first years of this century, and for good reason. I end with a coda of sorts on the dangers of misdirected belief—or, more precisely, on the danger of allowing one's belief to motivate violent acts. There are certain passages in *Mao II* that seem astonishingly prescient in the wake of September 11, 2001. The novel contains, for instance, a running debate about the architecturally iconic World Trade Center towers. At one point Brita complains about the sheer size of the buildings with the comment "the size is deadly" (40). Later she comes across a painting "showing the World Trade Center at precisely the same angle she saw it from her window and in the same dark spirit . . . two black latex slabs that consumed available space" (165). Meanwhile, in a development unconnected to these musings on the Twin Towers, there are rumblings of a jihad in the Middle East. In the final section of the book, Brita is on assignment in Beirut covering a terrorist organization. The leader, a young militant named Rasheed, explains to her that Muslims resent a "Western presence" in the Middle East because it is "a threat to self-respect." "Terror makes the new future possible," Rasheed sneers. "We do history in the morning and change it after lunch" (235). *Mao II* imagines a bleak future in which people either live outside history, as Karen does ("He leads them out past religion and history" [15]), or make up history as they go along, as Rasheed threatens to do ("He is saying we make and change history minute by minute" [235]). These are the extremes, perhaps, of what happens when belief is perverted to serve corrupt ends.

The cover of *Underworld* features a photograph of the World Trade Center, which, like the painting Karen Janney describes, shows the Twin Towers in a "dark spirit" as massive concrete "slabs" reaching up to the clouds. After 9-11, of course, that cover photograph took on added significance. In the foreground, a church facade is visible through dense fog; the cross is perched right between those two giant skyscrapers that no longer exist. In the wake of the most vicious terrorist attack on United States soil, this picture struck me as an uncanny gloss on how religion can be an astonishingly destructive force as well as an undeniable force for good. Looking closely at the photograph, I suddenly noticed a bird soaring off to one side of the Twin Towers. I like to think of that bird as a dove. The last word of *Underworld* is, in fact, "Peace" (818), a word that resonates more deeply now than it did when the book was first published. DeLillo tellingly chose to end his magnum opus about the cold war and its aftermath on a hopeful note, and I take heart by this gesture to remind my students that, despite the seemingly insurmountable problems of our world today, we may hear the still small voice of hope if we listen closely beneath all the white noise. I urge students to examine their beliefs and behavior, as well as the kinds of religious institutions they may or may not be affiliated with, in relation to ongoing changes in the nature of belief itself. Finally, I encourage them to think about how they can make a positive impact on the world we live in: to grapple with the toughest issues of our times and try to change things for the better. I hope my approach to these novels, instead of challenging or undermining my students' beliefs, contributes to a deeper understanding of what is truly at stake in the question of belief.

Loyalty to Reality: *White Noise*, *Great Jones Street*, and *The Names*

Margaret Soltan

We are a nation of three-minute celebrity, so one hesitates to designate Don DeLillo, or anyone else, America's preeminent contemporary novelist. But the durable respect and attention he has earned from readers, critics, and fellow novelists here and abroad, coupled with the general sense that the themes he isolates in his work consistently reflect the deepest currents in our social and moral life, have persuaded many observers that DeLillo is in fact *the* novelist of our time. The grainy image of the Twin Towers on the cover of *Underworld* (1997) and DeLillo's descriptions of their unsettling physical and spiritual power in *Players* (1977) convey precisely the sensitive, anticipatory instinct that Matthew Arnold had in mind when, in his essay "The Function of Criticism at the Present Time," he wrote that "genuine creation" emerges only when "a gifted nature [comes] into possession of a current of true and living ideas" (825).

DeLillo is above all a novelist of ideas, in the tradition of high modernists such as James Joyce, Thomas Mann, André Gide, William Faulkner, and Malcolm Lowry, all writers with whom he has identified himself. One useful way to begin talking about *White Noise*, in fact, is through the prism of those modernist precursors and their preoccupations. Although stylistically more accessible than these writers, DeLillo shares with them a persistent anxiety about the waning of a sense of reality among people living in a complex and traumatizing world. Virtually all his novels represent, among other things, desperate searches for authentic verbal, emotional, and spiritual expressivity amid a simulacral environment that is at once numbing and clamorous. DeLillo makes clear this "loyalty to reality" (the phrase is Czeslaw Milosz's [xv]) in various interviews. He has said:

> In contemporary writing in general, there's a strong sense that the world of Beckett and Kafka has redescended on America, because characters seem to live in a theoretical environment rather than a real one. I haven't felt that I'm part of that. I've always had a grounding in the real world. ("Outsider" 62)

He both describes this theoretical world in his novels and searches for legitimate and plausible ways to transcend it in favor of social and spiritual reality.

Teaching the novels of DeLillo demands, therefore, the recognition and clarification of his major propositions about contemporary reality, ideas most purely expressed in his difficult and dark novel *The Names* (1982) and in the less difficult but equally dark *Great Jones Street* (1973). I propose here a classroom approach to *White Noise* that involves focusing on the basic content of DeLillo's apparent moral philosophy by reading the novel alongside excerpts from these two other DeLillo novels.

Pedagogically, it is not as easy as it might seem to present DeLillo's fundamental ideas in the context of a reading of *White Noise*. The very sources of that novel's enormous popularity in and beyond the classroom—its coy ironies, fatuous conversations, and outrageous comic set pieces punctuated by catastrophes that eventually resolve into farce—can also produce an intellectual complacency, if you will, about one's understanding of the novel's ambitions. A novel that opens with an entertaining description of American college students unpacking their massive number of consumer goods at the beginning of an academic term is almost too smoothly assimilable by American college students, who may believe they have grasped the intent of the novel when they have only, as it were, learned how to laugh at it.

My approach to teaching *White Noise* would assign chapter 11 in *Great Jones Street* (esp. pp. 83–93) and chapter 12 (pp. 273–309) in *The Names*. These chapters and passages distill the essential elements, the abiding concerns, of DeLillo's expressed philosophical thought in a way that *White Noise*, a novel told from the disengaged and rather clueless perspective of Jack Gladney, cannot.

DeLillo's dominant theme, sounded throughout his novels and certainly stressed in *White Noise*, is sound. He explores the possibility of breaking through the clamor and hum of empty ambient noise in our daily lives so that meaning and truth can become audible. As Cornel Bonca notes in an essay about language in *White Noise*, DeLillo believes that the truth of our shared vulnerability to death and our accompanying sense of empathy for one another as mortal beings lies "hidden though immanent" in the welter of sound in the modern world. Given this shared vulnerability, our most important ethical posture in the world is that of listening (460). A week's worth of lecture and discussion might be profitably devoted to the various types and values of sound (loud noise, white noise, music, human speech, crying, shrieking, etc.) that DeLillo includes in his novels and to the characters (Bucky Wunderlick, Bill Gray, Sister Edgar, Owen Brademas) who radically silence themselves in an effort to hear the reality of human suffering under that layer of sound. "What's all the noise about in DeLillo? Why and how do various characters attempt to transcend it?" have been for me excellent opening questions for classroom discussion of *White Noise*.

Just as DeLillo is no Franz Kafka or Samuel Beckett, so he is no John Cage, submerging us in the techno- and psychobabble our world proliferates, because, after all, there's no escaping it. He's not trying to make us love or find beautiful the incessant sonic inanity that accompanies our existence, in the way that Murray Siskind tries to make Jack Gladney love it. DeLillo's own composer character, Bucky Wunderlick in *Great Jones Street*, rejects his strung-out girlfriend's approach to postmodern sound pollution when she tells him, "[I]f everything's getting ugly, the only thing you can do is try to teach yourself it's beautiful, it's beautiful" (90). Bucky understands that acquiescence in this culture means either deadly passivity or violent aggressiveness, and his entire story in the novel is the effort to overcome blaring nihilistic mundanity through temporary retreat to monastic silence. As Bonca suggests, when DeLillo's characters

> finally stop listening to language as denotation and listen to it as utterance instead—when at last language "evades the responsibilities of content"—what is immanent in language emerges, and the novel's powerful affirmation of language becomes possible. (476)

Affluent, postmodern Americans such as the Gladneys, who float in a lightly swaying hammock-world where soft lulling words and tones—white noise—prevail, are lotus-eaters: hopeless, opiated, struck dumb, or pointlessly loquacious amid the welter. Their circular and clueless speech may be funny, but it's also their own pathetic contribution to aural idiocy, for these people are after all blatantly inadequate to the tasks of moral autonomy, world understanding, and self-consciousness. At times it seems that everything life presents to them, from a crying child to the death of a colleague to a sunset, stuns and silences them, or evokes from them comically stupid commentary.

In teaching the novel, instructors should push students beyond their laughter at, say, Murray and Jack's infantile, distracted chatter in the supermarket about the sudden death of one of their colleagues (169) and toward the spiritually intense authorial sensibility behind these lines. As a writer, DeLillo is rather like Kafka, as Walter Benjamin describes him: "Even if Kafka did not pray—and this we do not know—he still possessed in the highest degree what Malebranche called 'the natural prayer of the soul': attentiveness" (*Illuminations* 134). In *The Names*, James Axton diagnoses his problem as a "failure to concentrate, to occupy a serious center" (317). Death, DeLillo clearly suggests, should occasion more than stumbling, distracted, irrelevant remarks; but in the brain-fade environment of postmodern America, Murray and Jack are too distracted to confront it. Indeed, if American culture knew what to do with death, Babette Gladney wouldn't be ruining her life and the life of her family by chasing down Dylar, the bogus wonder drug that promises release from death fear. When, in *Great Jones Street*, Wunderlick's girlfriend suddenly dies in his apartment, his first instinct is to search not for a coroner or a hospital but for a nun, "someone who believed in the sacredness of dying and the veneration of the dead" (93). His particular dream is of a German nun—who indeed materializes, not in *Great Jones Street* but in *White Noise*.

Instructors might clarify DeLillo's intent in *White Noise* to take life and death seriously, to be actively attentive to them and to rediscover sources—aural hints—of sacred truths, by considering three nuns in DeLillo's work: the nun whom Wunderlick urgently wants when Opel dies; the nun who attends to the wounded Jack at the end of *White Noise* and articulates a new, postmodern form of religiosity to him, in which the language of the Catholic church is phatic rather than referential ("Her eyes showed a terrible delight in my incomprehension. . . . She spoke faster, more expressively. Blood vessels flared in her eyes and face. I began to detect a cadence, a measured beat. She was reciting something, I decided" [320]); and Sister Edgar in *Underworld*. (Nuns become more and more important as DeLillo's work proceeds, from one merely alluded to in *Great Jones Street* to the theological nurse in *White Noise* to the crucial character of Sister Edgar.) A useful writing assignment might be to compare the scenes in which these nuns appear and to discuss their function and significance in each novel.

DeLillo's serious characters (he features many comic, nonserious ones) want to be adequate to life and death; they want to overcome the matter-of-fact lassitude that so many characters in *White Noise* express. We might ask students to consider the differences between the straightforward amusement Oscar Wilde conveys in the patter between Gwendolyn and Cecily in *The Importance of Being Earnest* (it might be useful to have students read aloud from and compare the two sorts of dialogues) and the much more fraught exchanges between characters in DeLillo's work, exchanges that resemble Joe Orton's writing (author of *What the Butler Saw*) more than Wilde's. Instructors might point out that DeLillo has written a play, *The Day Room* (1986), seemingly influenced by Orton.

The conversations in *White Noise* are comic in part because they are totally derivative. Characters are able only to echo the clichés and formulations of the therapeutic, consumption-oriented culture (epitomized by the *Oprah Winfrey Show*) that defines them. Themselves constructions of media, these characters produce highly mediated utterance. This utterance is farcical, because farce emerges when, as Henri Bergson among others have noted, human beings are made to seem mechanical or in some way less than fully human. But beneath this humorous surface lies a grim idea about what DeLillo, in *The Names*, calls the "self-referring world" (297). A glimpse of the human as suddenly robotic underlies the Bergsonian notion of farce, but in DeLillo's world people begin to suspect that robotism is all they have left, that their comfortable, high-functioning, high-tech, postmodern world is doing their living for them. *White Noise* overflows with scenes of characters being bested or undone or closely tutored by controlling technology, as in the toxic event, Heinrich's biochemical philosophy of life, or Jack's interaction with a bank machine. (Students might be asked to describe, in a writing assignment, some of their own weird interactions with technology.) Only at the end of the novel does Jack confess that he is "afraid of the imaging block. Afraid of its magnetic fields, its computerized nuclear pulse. Afraid of what it knows about me." As *White Noise* fades out, he finds clarity, announcing, "I am taking no calls" (325). He is beginning, as his novel concludes, the process of overcoming white noise—he is starting to shut out the sound of the postmodern world.

While the sound of quiet white noise dominates Jack's novel, the sounds of Wunderlick's immensely successful and staggeringly loud rock music dominate *Great Jones Street*. But both characters can be seen as grappling with forms of false and destructive noise, with the debasement of language into meaningless verbosity (both novels feature long, vapid monologues from frenetic characters), and with ways of escape from noise and hyperactivity ("The artist," says Wunderlick, "sits still, finally, because the materials he deals with begin to shape his life, instead of being shaped, and in stillness he seeks a form of self-defense . . ." [126]). Throughout chapter 11 of *Great Jones Street*, Wunderlick struggles with the same themes and crises that Jack does: he is actively searching for authenticity (there's a short essay on beautiful, authentic strawberries at the beginning of the chapter) and selflessness ("I'd like to lose interest in myself," Jack says to Murray in *White Noise*. "Is there any chance of that happening?" "None," replies Murray [152]) in a simulacral and self-absorbed culture. Both novels feature frozen characters, like Opel and Mink, who have become suicidal victims—virtual machines—of opiated culture. Both feature main characters who speculate that, as Wunderlick says, "Maybe what I want is less" (87). That is, the heroes of both novels sense that the glamour and promise of affluent consumer culture, in which material goods make an effort to provide what spiritual goods once did, so that pills like Dylar attempt end runs around the difficult business of what Martin Heidegger called "being toward death" (Lilla 27), are dangerous frauds. Both heroes, finally, struggle against what Murray calls "brain fade" (67) and toward a new clarity of utterance in which one can "reach beyond the sounds to whatever it was they designated," as Wunderlick says (92). These parallels between *White Noise* and a far more sober novel can help isolate the serious intent behind the parodic lightness.

Passivity and evasion are the great sins for DeLillo; his novels articulate a moral imperative involving the willingness to go up against a numbing and coddling world in order to discover authentic being. In *Great Jones Street* and *White Noise* the essential narrative movement is therefore from a sort of existential bad faith in which one avoids confrontation with reality, luxuriating in the false seductive rhetoric of postmodernity, toward an incipient good faith in which one no longer averts one's eyes from death and from the true nature of human life.

DeLillo has made clear in interviews that this strenuous moral imperative applies to any serious reader of his work:

> Making things difficult for the reader is less an attack on the reader than it is on the age and its facile knowledge-market. The writer is driven by his conviction that some truths aren't arrived at so easily, that life is still full of mystery, that it might be better for you, Dear Reader, if you went back to the Living section of your newspaper, because this is the dying section and you don't really want to be here. (*Interviews*)

In this remark he touches on a number of themes crucial to his worldview: that the self-referring world of images and advertisements automatically issues facile knowledge; that because, as he says elsewhere, the novel has a "set of balances and rhythms . . . that we can't experience in real life," it can "rescue history from confusion"; that, nonetheless, for all of art's efforts, life is and remains mysterious; that we will never truly pierce that mystery but will at best, if we are very attentive, hear emanations of its underlying truths; and that to pick up a DeLillo novel is to turn to "the dying section," not the living section (*Interviews* [interview with Mehren]). Like all serious artists, he will draw our attention to final things, to a life shaped by retrospective, even morbid, thoughts about itself. But these same truths, as Andre Comte-Sponville writes, "can also make us live—that is what classics and classicists called beauty" (61).

DeLillo's metaphysics emerges most strikingly in *The Names*, a novel full of sounds as well as places to which most Americans cannot, or will not, respond. In part because the focus of this novel is so intensely on American bad faith, it is an excellent one with which to conclude classroom discussion of DeLillo's ideas. The book is divided into chapters that name places—"The Island," "The Mountain," "The Desert," "The Prairie"—and these arid locations act as symbolic backdrops for the story: the effort of one American to overcome his evasion of the tragic reality of human life. James Axton's very name suggests the exertion required to break out of the self-referring world.

As in his other novels, DeLillo here essentially narrates a set of ascending steps toward transcendent knowledge. He can be thought of as a more generous, less sardonic Flannery O'Connor, affording his heroes greater spiritual clarity and accomplishment than she ever gave hers. Bill Gray in *Mao II*, Bucky Wunderlick in *Great Jones Street*, and James Axton in *The Names* are brilliant and perceptive characters, able to feel the degeneration of the postmodern world into malign silence or idiotic noise and also able to withdraw from that world in search of the true, lost articulation of humanity. Their adventures are a series of illuminating encounters with false rhetoric and with illegitimate attempts to regain expressive purity. As soon as they recognize and reject false rhetoric, they are able to move closer toward the true. In Wunderlick we see most explicitly the paring down of the radical rejectionist, but all of these characters undergo strenuous deprivation for the sake of epiphanic disclosure. (This plot trajectory is identical to that of DeLillo's most important mentor, Joyce, in *A Portrait of the Artist as a Young Man*. Intellectual and spiritual clarity come about in that novel after a series of similar repudiations.)

What is it that DeLillo indicates these characters need to learn? First, they must understand why, as Wunderlick says, living defensively is the central theme of our age. They must clarify the basis of their own—always temporary—defensive withdrawal from the world. For Wunderlick and for Gray in *Mao II*, brilliant writing is blocked because they feel horrifyingly appropriated by a violent and deaf audience. Both pull back. But both, having grasped that what most terrifies them is the sense of having lost their individuality, their autonomy, in the artist-murdering chaos of the crowd, return to the world morally enlightened and endowed with a kind of courage.

It is to Axton, the main character and narrator of *The Names*, that DeLillo gives the most inflected, self-conscious moral knowledge. An expatriate American living in Greece, Axton begins the novel in a condition of willed ignorance (he doesn't know, or doesn't want to know, that he works for the CIA) and of active evasion—evasion of his personal misery as well as of the Acropolis and all it stands for. He makes a sharp initial distinction between his preferred modern Athens, "imperfect, blaring" (noise again), and the daunting "beauty, dignity, order, proportion" of "that somber rock," where "so much converges" (3). By the end of the novel, though, he is climbing the hill to the Parthenon and realizing that "it was not a thing to study but to feel. It wasn't aloof, rational, timeless, pure. . . . It wasn't a relic species of dead Greece, but part of the living city below it." The noise of the Parthenon is the exhilarating and deeply reassuring sound of human conversation among the many foreign tourists at the site. It is also, even more important, a noise from the past: Axton hears a "human feeling" in the stones themselves: "I found a cry for pity . . . [an] open cry, this voice we know as our own" (330).

This epiphany is akin to the moment in *Mao II* that Gray recalls as he's dying. Decades before, he was sitting in a taxi to the airport in order to catch a flight for which he would be very early. The cabbie, hearing Gray complain about his tendency to arrive too early for events, says to him, "I was born under the old tutelage, the earlier the better." Gray tells himself he must remember this (and he does—it is one of his final thoughts), for it is "the uninventable poetry, inside the pain, of what people say" (216). The poetry peculiar to each separate human being, uninventable by others, and issuing from the sorrow of a particular life is what the British social theorist Gillian Rose called "the rhetoric of virtue, virtue alive to the negative, [which is] discernable in the pathos of syntax, where eternity shines through violence, where transcendence percolates immanence" (146). We are drawn to this profoundly individual and vulnerable rhetoric, for it discloses truly and beautifully the complex reality of our wounded being. Thus the American critic Wayne Koestenbaum says this about why we love artists like Maria Callas: "[T]he steel and wobble [in her voice] announced a predicament; we loved the mistakes because they seemed autobiographical, because without mediation or guile they wrote a naked heart's wound" (137).

The next stage in DeLillo's spiritual progress, then, is compassion. Selflessly attentive to the pathos of other people's syntax (conveyed to us by writers like Gray, who record it for us), we refine, through a lifetime of aesthetic and social experience, an attitude of kindness; we learn that cruelty, in a formulation made famous by the philosopher Richard Rorty, "is the worst thing we do" (130). Our art must convey not melodramatic and self-indulgent emotionality but, rather, that combination of control and passion typical of DeLillo,

Joyce, Callas, and all other truly great artists. We must retain objectivity and distance in regard to this pain, or we will be able neither to see it nor think about it.

Having begun to experience the compassion for the suffering of others and oneself that Wunderlick feels when he is drawn, for instance, to a deformed child who lives in his building on Great Jones Street, and having begun to register one's implication in a world of power and knowledge, one can, DeLillo suggests, aim for the highest step in this spiritual progress: a return of the soul to the city, where one can now begin truly to act on behalf of justice. Rose describes this progress in terms of the act of mourning:

> Mourning draws on transcendent but representable justice, which makes the suffering of immediate experience visible and speakable. When completed, mourning returns the soul to the city, with renewed and reinvigorated participation, ready to take on the difficulities and injustices of the existing city. The mourner returns to negotiate and challenge the changing inner and outer boundaries of the soul and the city; she returns to their perennial anxiety. . . . [One must bring] a soul . . . to wail at the walls. (36)

Most of the characters in *The Names* inhabit the abstract, evasive realms of the air or underground. If they are businesspeople, they fly about doing their obscure multinational business; if they are archaeologists, they sit in the dirt performing a kind of fanatic epigraphy. It is the triumph of Axton that he finds a way to "have a grounding in the real world"—to exist in the modern-ancient city, receptive to the perennial human cry in it.

Despite its oblique and parodic nature, *White Noise* can, especially with the sort of background reading suggested here, reveal just as powerfully as any other DeLillo novel his abiding intellectual and moral preoccupations. Let me be more explicit about the formulation of DeLillo's defining ideas that is specific to *White Noise*.

J. M. Coetzee is, like DeLillo, notoriously publicity-shy. It is not that, like J. D. Salinger and Thomas Pynchon (and, for that matter, Bill Gray), Coetzee and DeLillo shrink from all public exposure; rather, they both believe that, in the words of Coetzee, "truth is related to silence, to reflection, to the practice of *writing*" (Sexton). On one level, what both writers have in mind is reflected in an exchange between the Saul Bellow and Allan Bloom characters in Bellow's novel *Ravelstein*. The Bellow figure is trying to explain to his friend why he spends a lot of time in his quiet country house in New Hampshire:

> "It's the stillness all around that attracted me . . ."
> "We've had this conversation before . . ."
> "Because it's important."

> "Life speeding away. Your days fly faster than the weaver's shuttle. Or a stone thrown into the air. . . . [Y]ou'd like time to be as slow as it was when you were a child—each day a lifetime."
>
> "Yes, and to do that you need some reserves of stillness in your soul." (110)

The experience of aesthetic creation or reception is a particularly strong instance of this generative stillness, as Theodor Adorno noted: "Beauty is . . . a curative sickness. It arrests life, and therefore its decay" (*Minima Morali* 77). The attentiveness to the world and to other people that Axton seeks is, as Iris Murdoch argued, an essentially ethical stance—the very opposite of the brain fade from which Jack suffers. Murdoch wrote that in its prompting of "an attentiveness to what is not us, the experience of art moves us toward love, the very basis of human morality" (Conradi 215).

White Noise can be understood and taught as one of contemporary literature's most powerful and nuanced moral explorations of the varieties of silence that surround postmodern Americans. For just as there is debased as well as legitimate noise, so silence can equal (as the ACTUP slogan has it) death.

To make this point clearer, instructors may wish to assign DeLillo's short story "Baader-Meinhof," which focuses on a major, much-discussed New York exhibition of the works of Gerhard Richter, among them his series of large photographic portraits of members of the Baader-Meinhof gang. With this story, DeLillo extends his interest in discriminating between authentic, redemptive art and self-referring, white-noise art. Andy Warhol, whose "execution series" is featured in *Mao II*, and Richter, with his terrorists, are, DeLillo suggests, pseudo-artists, able only to represent in a bland and passive way the terror in our souls and in our world. Implicitly in his story, he echoes what many critics of the Richter exhibit have said, that this sort of art displays merely what Rose calls "the nihilism of disowned emotions" (52). The *New Republic* art critic Jed Perl, for instance, describes Richter's Baader-Meinhof series as "impassively ironic . . . witheringly calculated." He calls Richter "a phony Kafka" whose "radical chic" seems to believe that "deadness is a form of hipness." Fashionable deadness is the deadest form of silence. Like Kafka, DeLillo undeniably inhabits the dying section, but not in order numbly to display morbidity; rather, he creates books that serve, in a famous statement of Kafka's, as "an axe for the frozen sea within us" (*Letters* 16). Axton's name, and the many explorers with pickaxes and other such equipment in *The Names*, literalize this aesthetic imperative to bring the dead city, the dead soul, back to life.

In *White Noise,* Jack's son, Wilder, is the human cry that we hear. The boy at one point begins inexplicably sobbing, then after a long while just as inexplicably stops. The reader, as clueless as the Gladneys, is left to speculate as to the deeper sources of—the symbolic values of—this child's sudden open lament. Supplementing a reading of *White Noise* with more explicitly philosophical excerpts from other DeLillo novels can enrich our understanding of such odd events as well as provide a conceptual framework.

The ultimate point of this lesson in DeLillo's metaphysics, I hope, is the recognition that DeLillo champions above all the aesthetic consciousness, which is to say that he regards art as redemptive, because through art we may most clearly hear the reality-disclosing rhetoric of grief. False rhetoric promises an end to what Rose describes as "the anxiety and ambivalence inherent in power and knowledge" (36). It is particularly urgent for Americans to maintain this anxiety about not only their personal but also their global power; they need to resist the false rhetoric of their "pure and unappreciated good," as Todd Gitlin writes. We know that for DeLillo—whether it expresses itself through Pentecostal Christians, Moonies, terrorists, or angry audiences—false rhetoric always assures us that we are the pure and saved children of God, that we are happy now and do not suffer. "Hell is the place we don't know we're in," says a character in *The Names*. "Is hell a lack of awareness?" (295). DeLillo's characters, writes Vincent Passaro, "live with an unsettling awareness of a world we prefer to ignore."

The virtuous rhetoric of DeLillo is a wholly humanized Blakean soundscape in which, as he writes in *The Names*, "language is the deepest being" and conversation the privileged social mode, since it is in conversation that this dynamic of exchange takes place for the sake of the liberation of the syntax of pathos (307). White noise represents the distracting, numbing, ambient roar postmodern American culture generates to drown out self-generated, shared, and vulnerable discourse. Literature is a privileged locus of meaningful utterance, a kind of counterstatement to white noise. As the Hungarian writer George Konrad says:

> Literature is a slow voice, like the whale's song: it is long vaults and encasements; it is loath to gabble or shout. The thought is neither friend nor foe to the deed; it is separate from it, describing it, understanding it, entering into it, making it its own. (150)

Or, as Michael Wood writes, "In DeLillo, the world is real, but our awareness of it is magnified, as if we could see and think about almost everything we currently miss."

This approach to *White Noise* focuses on both the realistic and transcendental elements in the work of Don DeLillo. Although vague about the extent to which he is lapsed, he makes clear that he was raised a very Catholic Italian American who, like the Irish Catholic Joyce, took his religion seriously for many years. His continued sense of himself as Catholic manifests itself in a variety of ways. He acknowledges a number of Catholic influences, including Joyce and O'Connor, and his work invites comparison with theirs. He regularly signs his name to group letters in the *New York Times* relating to contemporary Catholic issues, he weaves Catholic themes through many of his novels, and he routinely speaks of the ineffability of human life and of the way that a sort of spiritualized art alone seems able to speak this enigma. "I think," he has said,

> there is a sense of last things in my work that probably comes from a Catholic childhood. For a Catholic, nothing is too important to discuss or think about, because he's raised with the idea that he will die any minute now and that if he doesn't live his life in a certain way this death is simply an introduction to an eternity of pain. This removes a hesitation that a writer might otherwise feel when he's approaching important subjects, eternal subjects. (Passaro)

It's unnecessary to invoke DeLillo's Catholicism, at the very least cultural, in order to understand and appreciate his artistic achievement, but his insistent return (most dramatically in *Underworld*) to matters of the spirit does suggest that for him a grounding in reality is not enough: loyalty to reality involves a seriousness about transcendence as well.

CLASSROOM TECHNIQUES AND STRATEGIES

A Burkeian Reading of *White Noise*

David Blakesley

As its title suggests, Don DeLillo's *White Noise* is a babble of discordant voices, a heterogeneity that whitewashes perspectives even as it casts them in relief and irony. The novel lends itself especially well to approaches through dramatism and rhetoric, both of which examine the agency and purpose of language as symbolic action in what Kenneth Burke describes as "the Scramble, the Wrangle of the Market Place, the flurries and flare-ups of the Human Barnyard, the Give and Take, the wavering line of pressure and counterpressure, the Logomachy, the onus of ownership, the Wars of Nerves, the War" (*Rhetoric* 23). The logomachy—literally, "a war of words"—of *White Noise* marks culture as a battleground of competing perspectives and influences, with language compelling our attention, transforming attitude, shielding us from raw terror, leading us astray, making us jump to conclusions, and (perhaps) leading to views that transcend the limitations of individual perspectives.

Naturally, students have a difficult time understanding self-reflexive novels like *White Noise* that complicate transparency or realism by considering language itself as a beguiling or liberating force. With its focus on the power of language for naming and directing attention, the novel can help students understand DeLillo's preoccupation with the power of language for naming the unknown and channeling uncertainty in partisan directions. There is much at stake in *White Noise*, as there is for Burke, in understanding this power of language to persuade and to move.

In this brief overview I show several ways in which students can negotiate a complex work like *White Noise* by using dramatism and rhetoric to gauge its situation and to formulate a response to it. I focus first on the familiar and humorous give-and-take among the Gladneys regarding the airborne toxic event. The characters' responses (or interpretations) reflect the common acts of naming and identification that animate the novel elsewhere. (What is it, after all?) I then examine the themes of white noise and of magic and dread, using the pentad and the rhetorical concept of terministic screens, as well as more-familiar concepts like ideology and hegemony. When allied with traditional concerns of rhetoric, this dramatistic approach helps students understand these intriguing aspects of the novel and DeLillo's more general interest in language as a partisan weapon or unifying force.

The Background: The Dramatistic Pentad and Rhetorical Analysis

Burke's pentad is the set of relational and functional principles that help us understand the cycles or clusters of terms people use to attribute motives in a particular work of philosophy, literature, speech or in more general philosophies of human motivation, such as capitalism, communism, or psychoanalysis. Dramatistic inquiry conceives of language as symbolic action, the word as an act in its own right. Dramatism's two main strategies are the elaboration of act, scene, agent, agency, and purpose as motivational clusters in symbolic action and cluster analysis, a method of systematically tracking down the implications of a terminology, the terministic screen that any symbolic act relies on to focus our attention in unavoidably partisan ways. (A terministic screen is a way of seeing and not seeing.) In the approach to *White Noise* through dramatism, students study the rhetorical processes implicit in human relations. DeLillo explores these processes deeply in many of his works. Students consider textuality in its richest sense, as the system of relations and identities that shape human community.[1]

In their interanimations (ratios or interrelations), the terms of the pentad help us answer the question, "What is involved when we say what people are doing and why they are doing it?" (Burke, *Grammar* xv). Burke's is a deceptively simple question, as are the individual questions he associates with each of the five terms: act (What happened?), scene (Where and when was the act performed?), agent (Who did it?), agency (How was it done?), and purpose (Why was it done?). These questions seem to ask, Why do people do what they do?, and thus prompt us to analyze why we do what we do—or why characters in a novel do what they do. But Burke has the symbolic act in mind (the act of attribution itself) and not necessarily pure motion, which does not involve language or motive (e.g., tripping over a stick). What do people say and thus do when they attribute motives? How might this kind of symbolic action be carried out in a novel like *White Noise*?

As a series of questions, the pentad can teach students what they already know about *White Noise*; more important, it can teach them what to ask of the novel. The method is designed to "*clearly reveal the strategic spots at which ambiguities necessarily arise*" (*Grammar* xviii). Dramatism (like rhetoric) has this capacity to turn on its own creations as a metaperspective, an interpretation of interpretations. In conjunction with rhetoric, then, dramatism shows students when and why our symbol systems sometimes use us by restricting the scope of our action or by reducing the range of our interpretation. Dramatism teases students from the complacency that words and other symbol systems produce as we become accustomed to familiar ways of knowing and seeing.

Students initially have some difficulty grasping how the pentad can be applied, so I focus discussion by charting the variety of ways characters in the novel name and identify their experience, often falling prey to the complacency of naming and identification. *White Noise* makes one of its central themes the struggle to overcome this complacency and to find meaning in the terministic barrage of white noise that is popular consumer culture. How can we see, think, and feel when we have so thoroughly come to rely on the terministic screens of popular culture to structure (or determine) our experience of the world? Such terminologies channel thinking in predictable ways, acting hegemonically and quietly to shape experience at the point of contact, just as the airborne toxic event's symptomology miraculously follows a predictable (and prescribed) path (from sweaty palms to déjà vu). Where is the possibility for action? As with déjà vu, are possibilities inscribed in the range of our available terms from the beginning, precognitions of unanticipated events? Are Waffelos and Kabooms our medicine for muddling through? As Jack wonders in the midst of the airborne toxic event, "Is a symptom a sign or a thing? What is a thing and how do we know it's not another thing?" (126).

A novel like *White Noise* is ripe for dramatistic analysis because it so thoroughly contests its own means of representation, the terministic screen of public memory that gives the novel life, even as it draws on the terministic resources of popular culture and "American magic and dread" (1985 book jacket). These terministic screens—structured in the novel itself or by the wider situation that contains it—function hegemonically to influence, if not script, attitude and behavior, like codes of conduct in a manual of disasters or the broadcast of symptomologies. Words teach us to size up situations in customary ways because we have seen and heard others use them for that purpose. Words articulate public memory through a kind of verbal piety (what goes with what), leading to spontaneous association of signifieds with signifiers, or of symptoms with things, or of dissociation of one thing from another. Students ask questions about these processes as we apply the pentad more systematically to the novel.

The Method

The elements of dramatism may be challenging for students to learn, but the insights they provide can be profound and revelatory, encouraging students to name the world and their shared experiences in new and interesting ways. The best approach is to demonstrate the method with them. Have students freely participate in the rhetorical and interpretive process of elaborating ambiguity. To begin, I provide a visual breakdown of the elements of the pentad, with a brief explanation and question next to each term. I add a sixth term, attitude, which Burke himself added later in his career.

Act: names what took place, in thought or deed. What was done?
Scene: gives the background of the act, the situation in which it occurred. Where and when was the act performed?
Agent: names what person or kind of person or people performed the act. Who did it?
Agency: names what means or instruments the agent used. How and with what was the act performed?
Purpose: suggests why the agent performed the act. What motivated the act?
Attitude: names the state of mind that predisposes the agent to act or that substitutes for an act. What is the agent's attitude toward the act?

The pentad gains utility through the relations across terministic categories (the ratios among terms), so it is important to discuss the possible ratios between terms by asking, for example, "How does the scene influence the act?" Here are the question and all the possible ratios:

How does the ______	influence the ______?
act	scene
scene	agent
agent	agency
agency	purpose
act	agent
scene	agency
agent	purpose
act	agency
scene	purpose
act	purpose

Each ratio can also be reversed. Rather than ask how the act influences the scene, for instance, we can ask how the scene influenced the act. Applying the pentad to *White Noise*, students quickly see how alternative interpretations of an act rest on an associated set of contextual and motivational assumptions. They see how our naming and interpretation of an act is motivated symbolically, ideologically, and psychologically. Any one naming or interpretation may tell only one side of a complex story. The pentad reveals the implicit assumptions people make when they say what people are doing and why they are doing it. It thus draws attention to our own acts of interpretation. As we map various pentadic relations, students quickly see naming itself as the expression of an interpretation, a slant, a rhetorical choice. They see interpretation itself as a rhetorical act. They also generate alternative interpretations by forcing categorical expectations to shift and thus to generate new ways of seeing.

First, we consider how the white noise of consumer culture shapes individual consciousness, working as a terministic screen of brand names, misinformation, and objectification. What fears lurk behind these superficial manifestations of culture? The subject is familiar to students, and the use of brand names is one of DeLillo's most noticeable stylistic techniques. We take a closer look at how this white noise functions hegemonically as a terministic screen. Since it's perhaps the major theme of the novel, we begin by naming the act as "fearing death" or "profound dread." I shift the perspective by introducing a ratio that moves in a different direction. Students can be encouraged to identify important acts, then shown how the rest of the pentad falls into place after an interpretive move. New and interesting insights often leap out and may generate deeper insights or more important questions to ask of the novel.

Pentad 1: Dread
Act: anticipating and fearing death
Scene: a media-saturated culture bent on nurturing (or even creating) such dread on a wide scale, for inscrutable reasons
Agent: Jack Gladney, chair of Hitler studies at the College-on-the-Hill
Agency: persistent observations of death as a common denominator in the events of Gladney's life
Purpose: to rationalize his fascination with Hitler as a cultural icon

Once we define the act as dread, we have choices to make. The agent of dread (who performs the act) could be Jack (as defined here), but it could also be Babette or, more generally, average Americans. We define the scene on a wide social scale, but we could also describe the scene as a typical midwestern university, with somewhat different implications. Agency turns out to be a tricky category. How does Jack dread? Students will notice that throughout much of the novel, he carefully observes others encountering their fear, how they let it glance off them (like Bee, whose indifference to impending doom makes the rest of the family even more self-conscious about it [94]) or how they let it consume them (like Babette, or so Jack believes). Purpose is even more open-ended. We could take a psychoanalytic approach and suggest that such dread is the expression of a death wish; that it is a strange attractor; or that it serves the purpose of uniting the community against a common enemy, not unlike the scapegoat mechanism that can whip a crowd into a furor. Perhaps Jack's fear of death comes from the same ingredients that gave rise to his desire to teach Hitler studies.

Students will find such possibilities interesting, especially when they see how much changes when we rename the act. Deliberately shift the terms of the inquiry so that the cluster of associated motivations and ratios reflect a new perspective. Students are surprised by the insights they generate simply by renaming the act and then reconstructing a new cluster. What would happen, for example, if we named the act the promoting of fear?

Pentad 2: Deliberately Cultivating Fear
Act: promoting fear
Scene: a culture in which the fear of death is used to foster consumption and materialism
Agent: cold-war capitalists
Agency: ritual incantations of inscrutable violence or disaster in the media
Purpose: to make money

Students enjoy exploring the possibilities of this construction and after discussion find it easier to shift the terminology deliberately. Suppose the act were to suppress fear? That possibility immediately raises questions about the function of Dylar in the novel, as well as many other ways people try to handle impending doom.

Scene-Purpose in White Noise

Burke used the pentad to conduct textual analysis of the internal workings of texts and philosophies. The pentad is also useful for analyzing situations more generally, considering events or actions as texts that can be interpreted and that provoke response. People observe the signs around them to make interpretive statements that explain or rationalize their actions or those of others. Burke contends that we should study these interpretations lest we become victimized by our trained incapacity, our inability to interpret such signs in any way other than the familiar or comfortable. This contention is very much in line with the concerns in DeLillo's novel.

In chapter 15 of *White Noise*, Hitler's scene is defined as the family drama, the oedipal situation theorized by Freud. DeLillo focuses attention on Hitler by forcing the analogy between him and Elvis Presley with regard to their personal and familial scene, at the same time inviting questions about how each man became such a cultural force, albeit with different aims and results. That Hitler and Elvis have both become a subject for serious academic study in this imaginary world also comments ironically on the mechanisms of control and manipulation that scholarly inquiry exerts. The scene-purpose ratio is one way to approach this issue.

DeLillo uses Hitler (and Elvis) to comment ironically on the white noise that is consumer culture, ultimately seeing it as yet another manifestation of our fear of death. Jack sees that fear as a possible explanation for the response to Hitler and his "sex murders" (73), which is how people described his rhetorical flourishes (parodied in Chaplin's *The Great Dictator*). With emphasis on the scene-purpose ratio, I ask students to consider DeLillo's act as a writer in a social milieu:

> *Pentad 3:* White Noise
> Act: writing a novel about American magic and dread
> Scene: the mid-1980s, the Reagan era, when the cold war still raged and materialism was the new American religion
> Agent: DeLillo
> Agency: a novel published by a major publishing house (Viking Penguin)
> Purpose: to show the harmful effects and causes of the "babble of brand-name consumerism" (1985 book jacket)

To address how DeLillo's purpose was influenced by his scene, students consider the evidence of *White Noise*, but they can also consider his previous novels (such as *The Names* or *Ratner's Star*). They can consider how the theme of *White Noise* evolves into later novels, such as *Libra* (the story of the John F. Kennedy assassination largely from the perspective of Lee Harvey Oswald), *Underworld* (a sweeping novel about American culture in the cold-war era), or *The Body Artist* (a novella about a woman artist who uses her body as a canvas, like Kafka's protagonist in "A Hunger Artist"). One theme throughout all this work is representation. Western culture encourages us to imagine our experience through the lens—the white noise—of mediated experience, through the slogans, brand names, images, and media of popular culture. Jack and his family are always distracted by this sweep of data. Over time they view all experience through the vocabulary or terministic screen of popular culture. Students will feel compelled to consider the nature of United States culture and politics in the 1980s, which then opens the door to additional questions, such as how the cold war and looming specter of nuclear war shaped American consciousness and fear.

If we describe the purpose in terms of the novel's terministic screen, at the level of the narrative describing Jack's experience, the scene-purpose ratio might look like this:

> *Pentad 4: American Magic and Dread*
> Scene: the world constructed for us by the white noise of consumer culture and behavioral norms
> Purpose: the fear of death
> Agent: popular consumer culture
> Act: shaping individual consciousness (i.e., establishing hegemony)
> Agency: the language that constitutes white noise

Two scenes in the novel illustrate the effects of this scene (white noise) on purpose (the fear of death). In the first, Jack arrives at the airport to pick up his daughter Bee. When she arrives, he discovers that the plane had nearly crashed, that it had suffered from severe turbulence, dropping from thirty-four thousand to twelve thousand feet in a few seconds, with people wailing and falling all over each other. Here is how DeLillo describes the chaos:

> Almost immediately a voice from the flight deck was heard on the intercom: "We're falling out of the sky! We're going down! We're a silver gleaming death machine!" This outburst struck the passengers as an all but total breakdown of authority, competence and command presence and it brought on a round of fresh and desperate wailing.
>
> Objects were rolling out of the galley, the aisles were full of drinking glasses, utensils, coats and blankets. A stewardess pinned to the bulkhead by the sharp angle of descent was trying to find the relevant passage in a handbook titled "Manual of Disasters." (90)

At the moment of crisis, people look to the voices of authority, in this case the people flying the airplane. No one is reassured by the breakdown of "authority, competence and command presence." The stewardess cannot act without reference to the "Manual of Disasters." We see how at the moment of greatest fear, people need to hear the familiar voice (language) of authority, the words that script action and thought.

In the second scene, we learn that Jack's greatest fear is that he won't die before his wife. Babette, however, wants to go first:

> She sounds almost eager. She is afraid I will die unexpectedly, sneakily, slipping away in the night. It isn't that she doesn't cherish life; it's being left alone that frightens her. The emptiness, the sense of cosmic darkness.
>
> MasterCard, Visa, American Express.
>
> I tell her I want to die first. (100)

At the moment of deepest contemplation of his fear, the trademark names intrude unexpectedly. They are distractions typical of what intrudes elsewhere in the novel as Jack struggles to come to terms with Babette's addiction to Dylar (the drug that inhibits the fear of death). The cumulative effect of the terminology of popular consumer culture is narcotic, working by the same principles of hegemony deployed by Hitler. But there is nothing especially magical about it. The characters perceive their lives and their acts through the lens of this terministic screen, which in the flow of media rehearses over and over the ideology that protects people from confronting their fears. *White Noise* foregrounds these interfaces—the mediating function of language and images—that constitute our experience. It makes us aware of this process of representation (or re-presentation). Dramatistic analysis seems especially suited to examining this theme, because it focuses on what we say when we attribute motives, on our interpretations of experience in language.

We could just as well have focused on the scene-agent ratio or any of the others. A writer's situation, for example, can be interpreted as the transformation of personal and public experience into its symbolic equivalents or forms. As a system of symbols, the writer's situation is in turn open to interpretation and, through art, further transformation. Fiction can be seen as writers' attempts to make the world over in their own desire. In what ways are writers propagandists? When we discuss the influence of a writer's scene on the act of making meaning—the scene-act ratio—we consider how circumstances function as motives. As with the other terms of the pentad, how we define the scene is inextricably connected to our definition of each of the other terms in the matrix.

Hegemony and Agency-Purpose in White Noise

The agency-purpose ratio asks, What is the influence of agency on purpose? How does the agency-purpose ratio function as a motive? That question was a central one for Karl Marx, whose most famous proposition was probably that "[l]ife is not determined by consciousness, but consciousness by life" (247). Who we think we are is not merely an act of will but also a consequence of our scene, which functions in turn as an agency that affects purpose: why we do and say as we do. We do not shape something as complex as history or our place in it by an act of conscious purpose, rationality, or desire. Rather, history acts on the agent to shape consciousness, to set the course of a life; it acts as an agency that functions hegemonically. The human struggle has always been to fight against such a process, to exert power over experience and others to shape life. Burke recognizes the problems posed by this conflict, noting that our terminologies can be tracked down to expose the historical forces (the situations) that inscribe them in a cluster of motives. The agency-purpose ratio enables critical perspective by showing us the means by which the agent is motivated by purpose to act.

Hegemony is the "general direction imposed upon social life" (Gramsci 12), a kind of ideological grease. It is what makes common sense common. Its agency is the language and imagery of culture, popular culture especially. Hegemony both guides and reveals attitudes toward and perceptions of the world, functioning much like a terministic screen. Its specific terms are those supplied by ideology. Hegemony is ideological maintenance, an act expressed socially in the language and images of culture. The elements of dramatism work like a counterforce to the persistence of hegemony, causing us to be on guard for its normalizing function and to recognize alternative means of acting. In *White Noise*, hegemony operates in its usual ways to shape and reinforce attitudes, but this process is balanced by attention to the mechanisms of hegemony itself and the cultural noise, the content of ideology that competes for our attention. This content functions hegemonically to motivate action and thought at its inception. From a dramatistic perspective, our explanation of our acts thus becomes a kind of rationalization born of the need to put our experience into familiar terms. We have already seen how experience must be coded to be understood and acted on: the flight attendant consults the "Manual of Disasters" in a total breakdown of command presence.

In *White Noise*, déjà vu is both a consequence and an agency of hegemony. It appears first as a symptom of the airborne toxic event, the result of a train derailment involving tanker cars filled with toxic waste. First reports say that people who breathe the fumes will have "[h]eart palpitations and a sense of *déjà vu*" (116). Jack's children begin to experience déjà vu almost immediately and well after the symptomology has been changed by the authorities. "I saw all this before" (125), says Steffie when they pass a car accident. A bit later, Jack and Babette discuss the déjà vu symptom:

> She spooned some yogurt out of the carton, seemed to pause, deep in thought.
> "This happened before," she said finally.
> "What happened before?"
> "Eating yogurt, sitting here, talking about *déjà vu*."
> "I don't want to hear this."
> "The yogurt was on my spoon. I saw it in a flash. The whole experience. Natural, whole-milk, low-fat." (133)

Murray Jay Siskind has an explanation of the déjà vu phenomenon that he has adapted from Sigmund Freud:

> Why do we think these things happened before? Simple. They did happen before, in our minds, as visions of the future. Because these are precognitions, we can't fit the material into our system of consciousness as it is now structured. This is basically supernatural stuff. We're seeing into the future but haven't learned how to process the experience. So it stays hidden until the precognition comes true, until we come face to face with the event. Now we are free to remember it, to experience it as familiar material. (151)

Here, déjà vu is a precognition of an anticipated event, an amorphous and ephemeral prophecy whereby we project ourselves into an unrealized future. We project ourselves into the future all the time, always one step ahead of ourselves, so it's no wonder that on occasion the future becomes what we'd imagined (or wished or feared) it would be.

In *Language as Symbolic Action*, Burke describes an interesting concept that he calls "prophesying after the event" (83), which has some bearing on déjà vu and can help round out our understanding of the agency-purpose ratio and our notion of dramatism as an interpretive and self-reflexive approach. Prophesying after the event involves specifying principles of development that appear to predict the future manifestation of the symbolic act but have been generated usually (and formally) after it came to be. In more familiar terms, it is a variation of twenty-twenty hindsight, a teleological rationalization of the act. This concept might show students how dread in *White Noise* rationalizes the action of the characters, particularly Jack's. Dread functions as a portent normalizing the act as a precognition, a portent of the end of everything, including meaning. In *White Noise*, as in so much of DeLillo's work (but especially *Libra* and *Underworld*), the future is always anticipated in the present as a type of prophecy, not unlike the self-fulfilling prophecies of the airborne toxic event's symptomology. In focusing on agency-purpose, we see how the mechanism of hegemony—even when so amorphous as free-floating anxiety—shapes consciousness as a species of incantatory magic. These are the sort of complex insights that dramatism and rhetoric can lead us to and that students might find difficult to come on in any other way.

NOTES

This essay is an adaptation and extension of dramatism to *White Noise*, drawing in part from my book *The Elements of Dramatism*, where readers will find many of the concepts discussed in this essay more fully elaborated and applied to different subjects.

[1]Terry Eagleton likely had this function of rhetoric in mind when he called for its return to literary interpretation in *Literary Theory* (205–09).

Homicidal Men and Full-Figured Women: Gender in *White Noise*

Philip Nel

Gender has been all but ignored by scholars of Don DeLillo's work.[1] However, at the time of its publication, *White Noise* offered DeLillo's most sophisticated work on this subject and announced the ways in which the novelist's thinking about gender would develop in subsequent novels (Nel 416–17). Although *White Noise* examines gender predominantly through men and their images of women, the novel does attempt to think critically about gender.

Encouraging students to think critically about gender in *White Noise* first calls for distinguishing between sex and gender. In courses in which I teach *White Noise*—which range from Introduction to Fiction (mostly freshmen) to upper-level courses like Contemporary American Fiction and Don DeLillo (both had a mix of undergraduate and graduate students)—I ask students if they know the difference between sex and gender, and some do. I use the blackboard to clarify the two terms. I write the students' contributions on the board, as well as my own words: "biology," "female," and "male" under *sex*, and "society," "culture," "history," "feminine," and "masculine" under *gender*. As I tell the class, sociologists of gender have explained that, though we are born male or female, we learn how to behave in ways that are masculine or feminine. This process of acculturation begins at an early age. I pass out a cartoon from Lydia Alix Fillingham's *Foucault for Beginners* (1993), in which a nineteenth-century father tells his son, "Take good care of your Mother, Father's off to work." The son thinks, "Daddy work, Mommy stay home" (12). So, as children learn the nouns *mother* and *father*, they learn more than that *mother* means the female parent and *father* the male parent; they also learn social and cultural expectations for fathers and mothers. Children assume that these different gender roles are natural, though they are in fact learned, as evidenced by their variation over time. For example, in the 1880s, experts argued that if women became too educated, their wombs would grow feeble—the energy intended for the womb having been diverted to the brain—and, as a result, women would be unable to produce healthy children. Students generally laugh at this notion. If they don't, I ask, "How many women are worried that their college education is shrinking their wombs? Let's have a show of hands." I say that we think this belief is funny now because we can see it's a prejudice disguised as a scientific fact. But if we had grown up believing it was true, it would be much harder to see this notion as ridiculous. I then summarize: the implication of this past belief is that we learn about gender differences before we are aware that we are doing so; as a result, we may assume that socially constructed differences are natural.

I then ask, Does *White Noise* present gender differences as natural or as products of socialization? And how might we answer this question? I wait as students offer ideas, but if they need prompting, I suggest that they look at the characters Babette, Jack, and Murray. Students' suggestions help determine the order in which I take up particular lines of questioning, but I always borrow from John Berger's *Ways of Seeing* (1972). In his distinction between "surveyor" and "surveyed," Berger points out that a woman learns to

> survey everything she is and everything she does because how she appears to others, and ultimately how she appears to men, is of crucial importance for what is normally thought of as the success of her life. Her own sense of being in herself is supplanted by a sense of being appreciated as herself by another. (46)

In *White Noise* Babette Gladney listens to a woman on the radio say, "I hate my face. . . . Of all the faces you could have given me, lookswise, this one has got to be the worst. But how can I not look? Even if you took all my mirrors away, I would still find a way to look" (263). We might read this scene as an example of how a woman internalizes the scrutiny of others, learning to see herself through an external gaze. In the sentence immediately before she hears the woman on the radio, DeLillo's narrator tells us that "Babette could not get enough of talk radio" (263). This statement suggests that Babette's food-based fixations resonate beyond the novel's preoccupation with aging and death, underscoring how media create the compulsion to lose weight. Perhaps DeLillo is aware that—as Berger, Naomi Wolf, and others have pointed out—women tend to absorb unattainable standards of beauty from media images, and then survey themselves according to those standards.

Judging by his public comments, DeLillo agrees with Berger. To the sole interviewer so far who has asked him about gender, DeLillo said:

> [W]omen are so often the objects of attention, at so many levels. Whether they're in a streetcar, walking down a street or sitting in a restaurant, men look at them constantly and force them at some level to become self-conscious objects of scrutiny. What I mean is that we are all of us made up not only of muscle, brains and blood, but also of the things which others tell us and of the things others see in us.
> ("Interview" [Nadotti] 90)

His words strongly echo Berger's analysis. DeLillo made this remark after the publication of *Mao II* (1991), which offers a more sophisticated analysis of femininity than *White Noise* does; whether his comments also apply to *White Noise* is worth considering.

I tell my students that, before they accept DeLillo's statement as confirmation that *White Noise* presents gender as a cultural construct, they should make sure that the talk-radio moment is not an isolated incident in the novel.

They might, for example, consider Babette. How does she view her body? And what does Jack say about her body? The lunchtime conversation in chapter 2 (7–8) and Jack's comment to Janet Savory in chapter 18 (88) provide excellent examples for the class to examine. Babette intends to eat "yogurt and wheat germ" for lunch and to exercise because "she was not happy with her hips and thighs" (7). Jack, however, likes her plumpness and even views thinner women with suspicion. He distrusts his ex-wives' "high cheekbones" and "[m]arvelous bone structure. Thank God for Babette and her long fleshy face," he says (88). He defends Babette's ultimate decision not to eat yogurt and wheat germ, telling her, "I was the one who needed to show discipline in matters of diet. I reminded her how much I liked the way she looked." He even suggests that "there was an honesty inherent in bulkiness if it is just the right amount. People trust a certain amount of bulk in others" (7). Yet, I ask my class, should we be concerned that Jack's comments merely replace one feminine ideal with another? One answer is that at least a "fleshy" or "bulky" ideal is healthier than the starving-model type popular in the 1980s and 1990s. If, as Wolf writes in *The Beauty Myth*, a "cultural fixation on thinness is not an obsession about female beauty but an obsession about female obedience" (187), then Jack's advocacy of a heavier ideal helps counteract the debilitating effects of a culture that persuades women to strive for too-thin bodies. In this sense, Jack's antidieting arguments encourage Babette to feel comfortable with her body image and with herself.

Nonetheless, Jack's tendency to idealize Babette's plumpness is not always helpful. DeLillo signals the foolishness of some of Jack's comments by undercutting the repeated assumption that larger women are more honest. Jack says that there is "an honesty inherent in bulkiness" and that "[a]mple women" like Babette "lack the guile for conspiracies of the body" (5). If students have read beyond the first two parts of the novel (and certainly if they have read all of it), I ask them if we are supposed to agree with Jack. I read his statements as foreshadowing the fact that Babette does have the requisite guile, as demonstrated by her sex-for-Dylar affair with Willie Mink and by her concealment of both the affair and the Dylar from Jack.

That the novel seems to question Jack's assumptions about femininity leads us to question DeLillo's depiction of masculinity. We should now apply our original question—does *White Noise* present gender differences as natural or as a products of socialization?—to the male characters. Depending on how much of Jack's behavior is intended as comic commentary, we might read the following scenes as either endorsing or skewering macho treatment of women. As I call my students' attention to these scenes, I ask, Should Jack's actions be interpreted as unwanted scrutiny or as tender displays of affection? When Babette runs to the top of the stadium steps, Jack watches as "she leaned into the wall, head down, upper body throbbing" (14); when she reaches the bottom of the steps, he tells us, "I met her at the edge of the playing field and embraced her, putting my hands inside the sweatband of her gray cotton pants. . . . Babette was moist and warm, emitting a creaturely hum" (14–15). In the supermarket, he says to the reader, "I rubbed against Babette in the checkout line. She backed into me and I reached around her and put my hands on her breasts. She rotated her hips and I nuzzled her hair and murmured 'Dirty blond' " (40). During that same scene, "I tried to fit my hands into Babette's skirt, over her belly, as the slowly moving line edged toward the last purchase point" (40). And in the Gladneys' kitchen, "I grabbed her by the inside of the thigh as she passed the table. She squirmed deliciously" (114).

Some students read these scenes and think that Jack is being possessive and is demonstrating that Babette is his woman. He can touch her anytime, anywhere—in the stadium, in the supermarket, or in his home. Others may see him as genuinely affectionate. After all, the moment in the stadium is private: "There was no one around" (14). Even the more public display in the supermarket might simply show that Jack is not worried about expressing his emotions openly. A third reading is to see his behavior as hypermasculine in a way that contrasts with his other, less traditionally masculine traits. If we view these scenes in this final context, then his actions might be parody: he comically overcompensates for his relative lack of stereotypical masculinity. I am inclined to interpret the scenes as both genuinely affectionate and parodic.

Another way to measure the novel's awareness of gender is to ask, Does the novel suggest that masculinity is performance? Or does it imply that masculinity is an essential maleness that all men are supposed to have? To highlight that gender can be performed, when I define sex and gender in class, I often ask for a male and a female volunteer. When the volunteers reach the front of the classroom, I ask the class to help the male volunteer stand as a woman might stand. They tell him, Move your legs closer together, move your hips slightly to one side, put your hand on your hip. Teaching him to sit in a feminine manner, they invariably tell him to cross his legs. However, when directing the female volunteer to sit in a masculine manner, they tell her, Spread out more in the chair and, when standing, take up more space, fold your arms, don't smile. (Holly Devor can be of help here; see 52–53.) I then tell the volunteers that they have been performing gender, pointing out that anyone can act in either a masculine or a feminine way, irrespective of biological makeup.

Since our question concerns the performance of masculinity, I like to borrow Michael Kimmel's "four traditional rules of American manhood":

> (1) No Sissy Stuff: Men can never do anything that even remotely suggests femininity. Manhood is a relentless repudiation and devaluation of the feminine. (2) Be a Big Wheel: Manhood is measured by power, wealth, and success. Whoever has the most toys when he dies, wins. (3) Be a Sturdy Oak. Manhood depends on emotional reserve.

> Dependability in a crisis requires that men not reveal their feelings. (4)
> Give 'em Hell: Exude an aura of manly daring and aggression. Go for it. Take risks. (123)

As Kimmel points out, one problem with this sort of masculinity is that it always has to be proven; men who aspire to this degree of stereotypical masculinity always have to perform it. With this notion in mind, I ask my students to turn to chapter 33 of *White Noise*, in which Jack reflects on his perceived deficiencies as a real man, while comparing himself with his father-in-law, Vernon Dickey. As Jack watches him, Vernon

> glanced around the room, trying to spot something that needed replacing or repair. . . . It put Vernon at an advantage to talk about gaskets and washers, about grouting, caulking, spackling. There were times when he seemed to attack me with terms like ratchet drill and whipsaw. He saw my shakiness in such matters as a sign of some deeper incompetence or stupidity. These were the things that built the world. Not to know or care about them was a betrayal of fundamental principles, a betrayal of gender, of species. What could be more useless than a man who couldn't fix a dripping faucet—fundamentally useless, dead to history, to the messages in his genes? I wasn't sure I disagreed. (245)

After reading this passage, I ask the class, To what degree does Vernon Dickey conform to Kimmel's traditional rules of American manhood? Students should notice that he embodies them all and that the "Dick" in "Vernon Dickey" may not be accidental. The next question is, Does Jack admire Vernon's version of masculinity or mock it? After pointing out that Jack's language both admires and mocks, I ask, Does the novel posit Vernon as an ideal man or parody him? In my view, the description of an inability to fix things as "a betrayal of gender" and of Jack as "dead . . . to the messages in his genes" points to vast insecurities behind Jack's public persona, itself a parody of masculine academic posturing. Vernon is posturing, too: that "he seemed to attack me with terms like ratchet drill and whipsaw" indicates that Vernon uses his expertise to intimidate Jack. In other words, Vernon's masculinity, like Jack's, is an elaborate performance. While Jack may not be fully aware of the extent to which his own masculine persona is an act, Vernon's portrayal of manliness certainly offers an occasion for Jack to think about masculinity as performed.

A similar line of questioning should be applied to Vernon's extended "Don't worry about me" speech (255–56) and to the scenes featuring Orest Mercator (207–08, 182, 298). At the end of his visit, Vernon says:

> Don't worry about me. . . . The little limp means nothing. People my age limp. A limp is a natural thing at a certain age. Forget the cough. It's healthy to cough. You move the stuff around. . . . So the cough's all

right. So is the insomnia. The insomnia's all right. What do you gain by sleeping? (255)

Continuing his monologue, Vernon also says that Babette and Jack should not worry about his casual sex with women, his smoking, his failing teeth, his tendency to get "the shakes," his "sudden and unexplained weight loss," and on and on (255–56). The excessiveness of the "Don't worry about me" list is either Vernon's way of indicating that they should worry or an example of DeLillo's parody of stoic masculinity. Both readings of the speech reveal the inadequacies of the style of manly behavior that Vernon attempts to embody.

Orest Mercator, who is "training to break the world endurance record for sitting in a cage of poisonous snakes" (182), is a younger version of Vernon Dickey. Vernon is an aging, strong, daring, red-blooded man; Orest is a strong-man in training. When Jack asks him, "Why would you want to get killed going for a record?" Orest replies, "What killed? Who said anything about killed?" (207). When Jack says, "They will bite you," Orest says, "They won't bite me" (207). Though Orest will not admit it, these warnings rattle him a bit, as demonstrated by his veiled threats toward Jack (208). Orest's behavior after the snake-sitting stunt goes awry (only three snakes are put in the cage, all nonpoisonous, one of which bites him within four minutes) emphasizes that his macho behavior is all an act. Orest then "dropped out of sight" and "went into complete seclusion" (298), a reaction suggesting that he is not the brave man he pretends to be and that he is not satisfied with his performance.

Jack, while he does not embody the in-your-face masculinity of Vernon and Orest, is still deeply concerned about how people see him. With this in mind, I invite students to consider his professorial outfit and gestures. Told that to gain authority he needs to "become more ugly" and enhance his name (17), Jack adopts the name J. A. K. Gladney ("a tag I wore like a borrowed suit" [16]), wears "glasses with thick black heavy frames," and thinks of himself as "the false character that follows the name around" (17). On campus, he always remains in costume: "I wore an academic gown and dark glasses day and night whenever I was on campus, . . . I carried two hundred and thirty pounds on a six-foot three-inch frame and had big hands and feet" (32). He uses the persona of J. A. K. Gladney, the accomplished and powerful male professor, to conceal his weaknesses. At moments of vulnerability, he hides his fear behind his professor's outfit. After learning the implications of exposure to Nyodene D, he thinks, "I wanted my academic gown and dark glasses" (142). When Eric Massingale confronts an uncostumed Jack off campus, he sees the ordinary man behind the impressive facade. "You look different without your glasses and gown," Massingale tells him (82). "You look so harmless, Jack. A big, harmless, aging, indistinct sort of guy" (83). Unmanned by the encounter, Jack takes his family on a shopping spree and reinflates his ego by spending money (84). Thus his attempts to perform traditional masculinity are neither satisfactory nor entirely successful.

Jack uses Hitler not only to prop up his ego but also to establish a traditionally masculine role by associating himself with a violent man. While guest lecturing on Hitler, he thinks of himself as "secure in my professional aura of power, madness and death" (72), using language that binds him to his subject. He does not disagree when Murray tells him, "Some people are larger than life. Hitler is larger than death. You thought he would protect you. . . . On one level you wanted to conceal yourself in Hitler and his works. On another level you wanted to use him to grow in significance and strength" (287). As I call my students' attention to these passages, I ask, Does Jack's strategy work?

We might argue that *White Noise* treats with great irony what the gender critic Jackson Katz has called "the equation of masculinity with violent masculinity" (136). On the other hand, both Babette and Murray posit violence as innately masculine and not as socially created. So, I ask my students, is it simply biology that inspires Jack's homicidal urges? Or is it the social belief that violence is an appropriate masculine response? If we wanted to support the biological position, we might listen to Babette, who sees that Jack (though he will not admit it) is angry at Willie Mink: "You're a man, Jack. We all know about men and their insane rage. This is something men are very good at. Insane and violent jealousy. Homicidal rage" (225). When Jack brings up his jealousy later, Babette asks, "Does it mean you've turned your male attention to the individual in the motel?" Jack replies, "I didn't say that." Babette says, "You don't have to say it. You're a male. A male follows the path of homicidal rage. It is the biological path. The path of plain dumb blind male biology" (269). Murray agrees with Babette's biological claim (292–93). As Jack says, paraphrasing Murray, "men have tried throughout history to cure themselves of death by killing others" (290). Do these statements confirm a biological basis of masculinity?

The remainder of *White Noise*, however, shows how "the construction of violent masculinity as a cultural norm" (Katz and Jhally) leads men to homicidal behavior. To illustrate this point, I ask my students to look at Jack's confrontation with Mink in chapter 39. When carrying a gun, Jack feels powerful (297). When he shoots Mink, he describes the event as if it were on Jean Baudrillard's TV:

> I fired the gun, the weapon, the pistol, the firearm, the automatic. The sound snowballed in the white room, adding on reflected waves. I watched blood squirt from the victim's midsection. A delicate arc. I marveled at the rich color, sensed the color-causing action of nonnucleated cells. The flow diminished to a trickle, spread across the tile floor. . . . Mink's pain was beautiful, intense. (312)

He experiences the violence as aesthetic: the blood squirts in a "delicate arc" with "rich color," and Mink's pain is not real but "beautiful, intense." Jack fires a second shot just to "relive the experience, hear the sonic waves layering through the room, feel the jolt travel up my arm." He sees himself as the star of his own movie, watching the hero shoot the villain. When the second bullet hits his victim "just inside the right hipbone," he observes that a "claret stain appeared on his shorts and shirt" (312). Blood appears as "claret," the color of spilt wine, not of spilt bodily fluid. Jack's description makes the shooting sound glamorous, as if it were a TV or movie killing, suggesting that his perception of violence issues from popular media—a plausible explanation, given the Gladneys' predilection for watching televised disasters. In contrast, when Mink shoots Jack, the bullet punctures not only his wrist but also the cultural ideal of violent masculinity. After Jack is shot, the "world collapsed inward" and he feels "[h]urt, stunned and disappointed." He asks himself, "What had happened to the higher plane of energy in which I'd carried out my scheme? The pain was searing. . . . I staggered back, moaning, watching blood drip from the tips of my fingers" (313). His own blood is not "claret" or a "rich color"; it is blood. He then sees Mink's blood as blood for the first time. Looking at his target, he sees that Mink's "lap [is] a puddle of blood. With the restoration of the normal order of matter and sensation, I felt I was seeing him for the first time as a person. The old human muddles and quirks were set flowing again. Compassion, remorse, mercy" (313). Mink's shooting back shatters Jack's faith in violent masculinity: when the pain is his own, the pain is real.

If DeLillo invokes homicidal men and full-figured women in the spirit of parodic critique, what of the unrepentant sexist, Murray Siskind? Murray is more difficult to read as parodic because, as the book's main cultural theorist, his point of view is privileged. DeLillo gives Murray some of the novel's best lines, many of which echo DeLillo's public statements,[2] implying that—at least sometimes—Murray acts as the author's mouthpiece. Yet Murray does not appear to be a stand-in for the author when he says, "To plot is to live" (291). DeLillo—echoing Jack (26, 199) and *Libra*'s Win Everett (221, 363)—says, "There is something in the nature of plotting which seems to lead inexorably toward a resolution whose logical end tends to involve death" (Interview [Fender]). So, I ask my students, when Murray is at his most sexist, is he acting as the author's foil or as his stand-in?

Linda Hutcheon's analysis of feminism and postmodernism is helpful here. While feminism is a politics, "[p]ostmodernism is not; it is certainly political, but it is politically ambivalent, doubly encoded as both complicity and critique, so that it can be (and has been) recuperated by both the left and the right, each ignoring half of that double coding" (*Politics* 168). This distinction between feminism and postmodernism prompts the question, Does Murray both inscribe and critique sexist behavior? He says, "What fun it is to talk to an intelligent woman wearing stockings as she crosses her legs. That little staticky sound of rustling nylon can make me happy on several levels" (11). His tendency to fetishize women's bodies also extends to Babette, as when he clutches her "by the left bicep and sidled around her, appearing to smell her hair" (35). While the Gladneys visit his apartment, Murray flirts with Babette and shares a sexual fantasy with her: " 'Don't think I wouldn't appreciate a dramatic visit between two and three in the morning,' he told her, 'from an intelligent woman in spike heels and a slit skirt, with high-impact accessories' " (52). During the airborne toxic event, he chats with a carful of prostitutes and reports, "One of them is dressed in leopard loungewear under her coat. She showed me. Another one says she has a snap-off crotch. . . . I carry a reinforced ribbed condom at all times" (149). Later, he confesses, "My shoulder separates. An old sexual injury" (293). While Murray's detailed descriptions may reinforce sexist beliefs, they appear to be merely talk. For twenty-five dollars, a prostitute is willing to do the "Heimlich maneuver" with Murray (152), but there's no evidence that he participates in even this activity with her. He lives alone, in an "old crumbling" rooming house "near the insane asylum" (10), and refers to himself as "a solitary crank who maroons himself with a TV set and dozens of stacks of dust-jacketed comic books" (52). The novel's representative male chauvinist is a lonely bachelor with an imaginary sex life. If Murray is as heterosexual as he claims to be, then his inability to find female companionship could be read as a rebuke to sexist men: they should treat women with respect or expect to end up like Murray Siskind.

If, in characters like Murray, DeLillo is acknowledging his complicity in what he critiques, how effective is his critique? Hutcheon's analysis of provisional irony provides a way of answering this question. She notes that the pejorative connotations of provisional irony include "evasiveness, . . . hypocrisy, duplicity, and deception" (*Irony's Edge* 51). On the other hand, "irony's doubleness can act as a way of counteracting any tendency to assume a categorical or rigid position of 'Truth' through precisely some acknowledgment of provisionality and contingency"; it offers "an undogmatic alternative to authoritative pronouncements" (51). After contrasting the implications of this type of irony, I ask the students to consider the scene in chapter 7, when Jack and Babette choose erotic texts. Does this chapter's irony evade the political implications of desire? Or does irony's doubleness offer a deconstructive critique? On one level, the range of erotic materials considered by Babette and Jack parodies the proliferation of pornographic choices available to the modern consumer (29). On another, we might see *White Noise* as distinguishing between harmful and beneficial pornography. As Catharine MacKinnon and Andrea Dworkin have shown, pornography that denigrates women demonstrates that "[m]ale power is the raison d'être of pornography" (Dworkin 25). However, as Lisa Palac has argued, pornography can be liberating if it portrays a woman as a three-dimensional character with her own desires (157–63). Jack and Babette use pornography more in Palac's sense—for mutual arousal, not for one's domination of the other. As Babette says, "One person chooses [the work], the other reads. Don't we want a balance, a sort of give-and-take? Isn't that what makes it sexy?" Jack agrees: "A tautness, a suspense. First-rate. I will choose" (29). Both interpretations remain provisional: when Jack returns with family photo albums instead, he and Babette do not have sex after all. Is the chapter a sardonic comment on the erotics of late capitalism, in which the best sex is simulated (or, in this case, only talked about)? Or is *White Noise* suggesting that emancipatory sexual practices can be theorized but never realized? That both readings succeed highlights the trouble with provisional ironies: they seem both to elude and to engage political questions.

Another way to raise these questions is to ask, Is *White Noise* self-consciously satirizing gender roles, or is it satirizing self-consciousness of gender roles? As the following excerpt demonstrates, chapter 7 makes us wonder whether DeLillo is mocking overly sensitive couples or commending them. While they embrace in bed, preparing to have sex, Jack says to Babette:

> "I want to do whatever's best for you."
> "But you please me by letting me please you," she said.
> "As the male partner I think it's my responsibility to please."
> "I'm not sure whether that's a sensitive caring statement or a sexist remark."
> "Is it wrong for the man to be considerate toward his partner?"
> "I'm your partner when we play tennis, which we ought to start doing again, by the way. Otherwise I'm your wife." (28)

In one view, this conversation provides a welcome contrast to Murray and his attitudes toward women. Jack and Babette have a frank discussion about sex, each of them focused on how best to arouse the other. A different perspective might see Jack and Babette as hypersensitive, their language absurdly self-aware. Jack claims his "partner's" orgasm as his "responsibility," and Babette is put off by her spouse's assumption of responsibility and his use of the word "partner." Perhaps DeLillo is mocking political correctness. As Jack observes later in the novel, "It was getting hard to know what you couldn't say to people" (208). The reader, too, may not be sure—to paraphrase Babette—whether this is a sensitive caring couple or a squabbling one. A difficulty of *White Noise* is that it often takes aim at multiple subjects simultaneously, making us wonder about its subject position and ours. The novel's multiple layers of parody create provisional ironies, which can leave readers unsure of where they are supposed to stand in relation to the text. Yet the novel's tendency to send satire in many directions at once is also one of its pleasures. By allowing both readings of gender roles in relationships, Jack and Babette's conversation in the bedroom keeps us slightly off-balance. We find ourselves asking questions and wondering what we should be thinking, which is exactly what DeLillo wants his readers to do.

One final question: How much should we trust Jack's narration? The provisional ironies threaten his authority as narrator, something that the novel also does more explicitly when Babette launches counternarratives. Before she calls Jack on his refusal to admit his "homicidal rage," Babette contests his attempts to take over her story of the affair with Willie Mink. As she begins,

Jack says that "the whole point of Babette" is that "[s]he's a joyous person." She interrupts: "Let me tell it, Jack" (191). The conversation contains many such moments. After Jack says, "The whole point of Babette is that she speaks to me, she reveals and confides," she sets him straight again: "This is not a story about your disappointment at my silence. The theme of this story is my pain and my attempts to end it" (192). Finally, when Jack says he finds it "odd" that Babette was able to "conceal such a thing from a husband and children" (197), Babette corrects him once more. "This is not the story of a wife's deception. You can't sidestep the true story, Jack," she says (197). She refutes the stereotypically gendered narrative of "a wife's deception" in which Jack repeatedly tries to place her. In each of these moments she stresses that it is her story, using the word "story" many times. The emphasis on "story" reminds readers that they are reading a story and that the narrator's point of view—Jack's point of view—dominates that story. That Babette should challenge Jack's story at such a critical moment in the novel dramatizes the importance of who is telling the story and shows that a woman can reveal things that a male narrator may fail to see.

In the novels that follow *White Noise*—especially *Mao II* (1991) and *The Body Artist* (2001)—DeLillo again demonstrates a willingness to imagine the world through a woman's eyes and to make his readers aware of how gender is shaped by culture. *White Noise* and subsequent works begin to think about gender as a social construct because DeLillo's books always register the zeitgeist. As DeLillo observed in his acceptance address for the Jerusalem Prize in 1999, "A novel changes as the decades roll. It takes on new textures . . . depending on the cultural flux around it" ("History" 16). By the 1980s, America had become more aware of how gender orders a person's experience, and *White Noise* acknowledges this change in consciousness. A novelist in tune with the "cultural flux" around him, DeLillo has learned from feminism. If readers of *White Noise* are paying attention, they can learn from feminism too.

NOTES

[1]Thomas J. Ferraro's "Whole Families Shopping at Night!" demonstrates how the marketplace both unifies and disrupts the family unit in *White Noise* but does not address gender specifically. In its chapters on *Players*, *Running Dog*, and *The Names*, Douglas Keesey's *Don DeLillo* offers some analysis of DeLillo's imagining of male-female relationships (88–96, 101–04, 113–15, 123–24). Michael Hardin examines the intersection between masculinity and sexuality in "What Is the Word at Logos College? Homosocial Ritual or Homosexual Denial in Don DeLillo's *End Zone*?" and argues that DeLillo's novel posits football as "one way for men in a homophobic American culture to express desire for other men without having to admit that they are expressing desire for other men" (47).

[2]Describing the Most Photographed Barn in America, Murray says that "[n]o one

sees the barn": "We're not here to capture an image, we're here to maintain one. Every photograph reinforces the aura" (12). Distinguishing Walter Benjamin's notion of aura from his own, DeLillo says that now "there's nothing left but aura. . . . Reality is being diminished, leaving behind the aura that results from tape-recorders, cameras, microphones and all of the technological equipment that we use to consume reality" (Burn 39). Murray's notion that the real barn has been replaced by its aura closely resembles DeLillo's claim that "there's nothing left but aura." In another interview, DeLillo calls children "a form of magic" because "adults are mystified by all the data that flows through their lives, but the children carry the data and absorb it most deeply" ("I Never"). In *White Noise*, Murray offers a comparable analysis when he says that adults "get brain fade . . . because they've forgotten how to listen and look as children. They've forgotten how to collect data" (67). Murray spends time at the Gladney home as "part of his investigation into what he called the society of kids. . . . There were huge amounts of data flowing through the house, waiting to be analyzed" (101). Offering an explanation identical to Murray's diagnosis of Jack's Hitler fixation (quoted earlier in this essay), DeLillo says, "Only Hitler is large enough and terrible enough to absorb and neutralize Jack Gladney's obsessive fear of dying. . . . Jack uses Hitler as a protective device" ("I Never").

"The Natural Language of the Culture": Exploring Commodities through *White Noise*

Mark Osteen

Professors hoping to enlighten students about commodity culture in *White Noise* run the risk of emulating those "movie-mad, trivia-crazed" faculty members from the American Environments Department at Jack Gladney's College-on-the-Hill, with their "Aristotelianism of bubble gum wrappers and detergent jingles" and devotion to reading cereal boxes. Silly and self-absorbed though they may be, these academics have one thing right: commodity messages seem to have become the "natural language of the culture" in postmodern America (9). Even if the relation between this language and nature is more complicated than Jack initially acknowledges, there can be no doubt that commodities speak everywhere in *White Noise*, issuing from the mouths of fringe characters babbling about decongestants, appearing as "psychic data" (51) emanating from supermarket packages, and punctuating the narrative in the form of triadic lists of brand names. Thus *White Noise* provides rare opportunities for instructors to challenge students about our immersion in the world of commodities and its languages and to raise questions about the connections between consumerism and the environment—that is, between nature and culture.

The theme of consumerism shows up in the very first paragraph of the novel, which catalogs the possessions that returning students bring with them to campus. Modulating subtly, this paragraph begins with generic descriptions of seeming necessities (light and heavy clothing, boxes of blankets, boots and shoes, stationery and books); shifts to leisure-time accoutrements such as saddles, skis, and stereos; and finally comes to a comical halt with a particularized list of junk foods: "Waffelos and Kabooms . . . Dum-Dum pops . . . Mystic mints" (3).[1] These brand names attest to ex-adman DeLillo's continuing fascination with American popular culture, but, more important, they reveal the students' infantilization (the Dum-Dum pops) and religious attitude toward commodities (the mints are, we mustn't forget, "Mystic"). Like most of the lists in *White Noise*, this one exemplifies the rhetorical device asyndeton, which refers to an absence of syntactic connections that has become, according to Tony Thwaites, a signal feature of postmodernist writing (5–8) and (I would add) of postmodern thinking. But what is most remarkable about this scene is not Jack's familiarity with this device or these brands but his attitude toward the scene: calling it a "spectacle," he seems detached, faintly condescending, but also impressed, even dazzled. In short, he attends to this cavalcade of consumerism with the eye of a consumer. And no wonder: as Marie-Christine Leps has noted, the students are themselves their parents' most prized commodities (189). Nor are faculty exempt. In an age when universities market themselves to prospective students as a product like any other, faculty members must create compelling brand identities. Jack Gladney has done so, as Murray Siskind reminds him: the Department of Hitler Studies is Jack's successful product line (11).

What unites the characters in the novel and links them to us, then, are not "formal liturgies or laws" (4) but commodities. Indeed, everything in *White Noise* is commodified and prepackaged; even death is reified into risky stunts like Orest Mercator's plan to sit in a cage with snakes (Heinrich, our guide to such matters, refers to it as a "total package" [268]), into Jack's televised dots and numbers, and into the fearsomely tangible yet media-ready Nyodene D cloud (see 158). Having established this fact in class, an instructor can then guide students toward recognizing the "unexpected themes and intensities" beneath its surface (184). There are three related ways of addressing consumerism in *White Noise*: to treat commodities as a language, to view consumerism as a form of sustenance or religion, and to examine the relations between consumerism and the natural environment.

To get at the first aspect, I often begin by asking students, "What is a commodity?" If they have read Karl Marx, they probably have at least a vague notion of the concept of commodity fetishism; even if they haven't read Marx, they possess ample experience with advertising and so can readily grasp the idea that a commodity is an item for sale with a message attached, one related less to use-value than to some intangible benefit that purchasing the item allegedly brings. I follow that question by outlining two extreme positions that academic scholarship has taken toward advertising.

To many on the left, advertising is the instrument that, through constant bombardment and repetition, enables capitalism to extend its sinister power into the psyches of consumers, while also helping to conceal the labor exploited to produce the goods. Ads create desires for products that have little reason to exist other than to maximize profits. The result? Interpellated citizens who conceive of themselves primarily and habitually as consumers. Consequently, consumerist thinking comes to infiltrate all activities, from voting and religion to looking for a mate. Academic writing is rife with variations on this theme.[2] The opposing school pooh-poohs this position. For such scholars, consumer capitalism has created a culture of abundance that democratizes society through freedom of choice. Advertising not only helps eliminate differences in class; it also reassures citizens of their worthiness and uniqueness. Ads are not insidiously hypnotic but artistic and even fun. One such celebrator is James Twitchell, whose book *Adcult USA*, despite its sometimes annoyingly gushy tone, offers useful points about advertising's origins and role in American culture.

Twitchell acknowledges that advertising is ubiquitous and symbiotic (a less friendly writer might use the term *parasitic*), able to transform any cultural artifact into a tool for selling products (16). In other words, advertising remakes culture in its own image, translating all messages into its own idiom.

This won't be news to most college students, who already fancy themselves to be quite savvy about advertising and who can cite examples of advertisements that use pop tunes or high-cultural allusions. They don't think they're dupes and scoff at the extreme-leftist position. Yet they are also suspicious of Twitchell's brand of cheerleading. This ambivalence characterizes their response to *White Noise* as well, partly because, as Murray Siskind suggests, they have arrived at an age when they are "beginning to . . . feel estranged from the products" they consume (50). They are sharp enough to comprehend that DeLillo is satirizing the ways that Americans use commodities to satisfy nonmaterial needs, and as longtime TV watchers they exhibit a fashionable cynicism about the claims of commercials. Yet they are utterly steeped in commercial culture: if few of them can name the sources of "the best lack all conviction, while the worst / Are full of passionate intensity" or even of "two roads diverged in a yellow wood," most can immediately identify "Two scoops!" "Snap, Crackle, Pop," "Still going," and Tony the Tiger. A quick quiz about such psychic data might remind students of their immersion in consumerism; to nudge them further from their reflexive skepticism about the leftist position, one can simply ask them to glance around the classroom and note how many of them are wearing clothes blatantly sporting a brand name.

After these exercises, we move to the second aspect of the theme: consumption as sustenance, religion, or medication. To introduce this portion, I have had reasonable success with a video called *Affluenza*, which comically (if a bit simplistically) portrays the American obsession with shopping and shows its consequences in distorted self-images, bankruptcies, and enormous quantities of trash. Speaking more historically, a link with religion is built into the very origins of advertising. For example, Twitchell notes how twentieth-century advertising grew from the exhortative methods and ethos of perfectibility characteristic of evangelical Protestantism (33–37). Babette Gladney, with her belief that "everything is correctible" (191), exemplifies this creed. To put it another way, advertising promotes magical thinking (Twitchell 16).[3] To support this association, I have asked classes to list five brands or logos that derive from mythology, folklore, or fairy tales. Any student should be able to come up with a solid collection (here's mine: Hermes for FTD, Saturn and Mercury automobiles, the Keebler elves, the Jolly Green Giant). We then focus on two sets of scenes in *White Noise*: the family's first visits to the supermarket (20; 36–38) and the shopping mall vignette (83–84). Why, I ask them, does Jack feel a "sense of replenishment" (20) after going to the grocery store? What kinds of "ceremonial phrases" does a supermarket utter (38)? Is there any truth to Murray's claim that supermarkets resemble temples? Why does Jack feel more like a member of his family when he begins buying things at the mall (83)? How come he grows in self-regard? Why, after shopping, do they all retire to their private rooms?

To accompany these discussions, I use assignments 9 and 10 in the "Research Topics" section of the Viking Critical Library edition of *White Noise*

(523). Although these experiments in "American environments" are not likely to inspire life-altering epiphanies, they can lead students gently toward a more self-critical understanding of their consuming habits. Assignment 10 sends a group to a supermarket to record what they see and hear, then asks them to deliver a presentation to classmates. One group who completed this assignment enthusiastically described familiar "psychic data"—the garish, overwhelming colors in the soft-drink and snack rows, the Muzak and whirr of refrigerators providing soothing background noise—as if they had never noticed them before. I ask students to bring back at least two packages and discuss the messages found on them. One student displayed the Land o' Lakes butter package, humorously noting that it depicts neither cow, milking machine, nor overweight butter eater but rather a slender Native American maiden in a sylvan landscape, thereby associating the product with tradition, health, and natural goodness. With some encouragement, other students will chime in with their own analyses of effective and ineffective packages. We return to the novel with renewed respect for DeLillo's insights.

Many students, I have found, freely admit that they go shopping when they feel depressed. Assignment 9—visiting a mall, noting the atmosphere and people, and distinguishing between needs and desires—is designed to scrutinize this penchant. Their analyses of the shoppers are often astute: they note the slightly glazed-over eyes of small children; the furtive expressions of single men; and the alert, self-conscious posturing of teenagers there to make the scene. But what really ignites discussion is the question of needs: how many items offered in, say, Abercrombie and Fitch are designed to satisfy needs and how many merely fulfill wants? One student claims, "It's a need; everyone needs clothes, don't they?" Another rejoins, "Yeah, but how come they buy them there instead of at, like, Walmart, where they are a whole lot cheaper? It's just to show off the brand name. That's not a need." Students who have been sprawled out in boredom for the whole semester suddenly display the finely honed argumentative skills of seasoned lawyers: "Well, a need can be physical or mental. So if what I buy makes me feel better, that's satisfying a need, too, just a different kind." Others will dispute that definition. But it matters little which side wins, because the point has been made: commodities serve the same functions as drugs or food. Again students perceive that DeLillo's world is their world.

Having discussed the first two aspects of the consumerism theme, we now move to the third—consumerism and the environment. To probe this aspect in class we focus on two scenes in the novel: the descriptions of the toxic cloud (127, 157–58) and the moment when Jack examines his family's compacted garbage. I ask why Jack describes the toxic cloud in the language of advertising. If Nyodene D is a man-made substance, why do they respond to it as a force of nature? What does Jack mean when he wonders if the trash compactor reveals "the dark underside of consumer consciousness" (259)? One real-world assignment can illuminate these issues. Ask two students to monitor and describe their own garbage for three days. What do you throw away? If an outsider were to examine your garbage, what "habits, fetishes, addictions, inclinations" (259) would be revealed? Once again, the data they compile are less important than the exercise itself, which prompts them again to reflect on the differences between needs and wants and to become aware of both the quality and quantity of what they discard.

But we do not need to catalog rubbish to see the connections among consumerism, technology, and the environment in *White Noise*, for the novel dramatizes this association in the way it buzzes with diverse voices, most of them electronic or commodified. These textual intrusions come in four styles. First are the triadic lists, usually of brand names, that periodically interrupt Jack's narration. Second are the words of marginal characters—such as the woman heard muttering, "A decongestant, an antihistamine, a cough suppressant, a pain reliever" (262)—or of external electronic voices (as when the supermarket speaker announces "Dristan Ultra, Dristan Ultra" [167]). Less commodified but equally disturbing are the voices we hear from television interjecting violent or bizarre program excerpts. One might lump this third type of interpolation with the commodity insertions, since, as a character in *Americana* notes, TV is "an electronic form of packaging" (270), except that these voices almost invariably issue from educational shows rather than from network TV. (In the novel's middle section, when the Gladney family is away from home, the radio takes over, providing news, talk, or technology ads.) Finally, the Dylar-popping Willie Mink (who wears Budweiser shorts [305] and resembles not any old nut but a *Planter's* peanut [307]) quotes similar educational television shows during his encounter with the enraged Jack. For this essay, I am concentrating only on the first type of interpolation; the appendix lists them.

Criticism of the interpolations has been relatively light.[4] Like other postmodernist catalogs, these short lists hold out what Thwaites calls "the nagging possibility of connection beyond mere juxtaposition" (1). A diligent instructor can help students unravel the connections and find out where they lead. Indeed, exploring these lists opens a number of windows on the text. They can be enlightening exercises in close reading, as students investigate the narrative context of each interpolation and try to determine its thematic or characterological function and discover its intratextual links; more important, the lists function as tightly wound knots that, when creatively unspooled, expose the physical or environmental consequences of the commodities we enjoy.

In class discussions of these lists I first ask what kind of product comprises each grouping and what is common to them all. We then try to determine how each item in the list is different from the preceding and succeeding ones. An instructor might assign a small group of students to investigate the products in one or two of the triads. First, describe and analyze the use-value of each product. Second, discuss how it is advertised: what aspects of the product do the advertisements emphasize? What do they ignore? Third, find out all you can about this product: its ingredients, its manufacturer, how and where it is manufactured, and so on. Fourth, explore the potential or verified effects of this product's use or manufacture on human health and the environment.[5] The first set of questions probes the triad's textual functions; the second set helps bring together the novel's themes of consumerism and environmental devastation.

Let me give some examples of how this assignment might work. Early in the novel, Jack and Babette dine at Murray's apartment, where he lectures them in faux-innocent glee about the "mantras" and "sacred formulas" to be heard and seen on television (51). Jack and Babette are suspicious, especially after Murray makes sexually suggestive remarks to Babette. Walking home, they glance into closed banks and an optical shop. Then we read, "Dacron, Orlon, Lycra Spandex" (52). Just after this interpolation, Babette begins to allude evasively to her memory loss. What, we might ask, connects these fabric names to what comes before and after them? In one sense, they thread all the way back to the novel's opening paragraph: the caravan of students would likely be carrying Dacron-filled pillows; their sweaters (i.e., "light and heavy clothing") would no doubt contain some Orlon; the women's underclothing and the ski gear would be made of Lycra Spandex. In a more immediate context, perhaps these fabrics make up the "high-impact accessories" that Murray fantasizes Babette's wearing during their erotic encounter (52). Even "Dylar" (apparently causing Babette's memory loss) sounds like the name of a fabric. Is Dylar, which she is taking to lose her fear of death, a kind of artificial fabric created to upholster over the mind's unwanted fears?

DeLillo is particularly fond of brand names like these—synthetic words for synthetic products—which sound like the names of ancient gods but also bear the wide-eyed promise of the early space age, the future as imagined a half century ago. "Dacron," "Krylon," "Dristan," "Celica": these "[s]upranational names, computer-generated, more or less universally pronounceable," are now part of every adult's "brain noise" (155). To use one of his other favorite words, they possess "aura" (12–13; *Mao II* 15). But although Patti White notes that the "raw material, manufacture, and marketing are all implied in the presence of the product on the shelf" (23), actually the conditions of manufacture are concealed by that aura. Puncturing the aura is one goal of this assignment.

A student can learn quite a bit about these products through an Internet search. A cursory skim shows that all three fabrics are manufactured by the DuPont Corporation, whose slogan "Better Things for Better Living through Chemistry" DeLillo employs as a section heading in *Underworld*. The DuPont Web site informs us that Dacron was invented in 1950 as the first commercial polyester fiber ("Dacron: 1950"). A further search reveals that Dacron is made of polyethylene terephthalate (PET), the same substance used in plastic bottles.[6] Orlon, another polymer fabric, was first invented and patented by DuPont in 1941 and officially trademarked in 1948. Lycra is DuPont's brand of Spandex (another polymer fabric) and was first marketed in 1959.

The FiberSource Web site (www.fibersource.com) contains a number of useful educational links. For example, students may want to view the "lifecycle assessment" of a single woman's blouse provided there (www.fibersource.com/f-tutor/LCA-page/htm). The assessment argues that the worst sources of pollution in this garment's manufacture are the oil, gas, or coal used as fuel. It claims that consumers create far more pollution by repeatedly laundering the blouse than producers do when creating it—at least when analyzed on a per-item basis. (Calculating the bulk amounts of pollutants produced each year by factories and individual consumers would, of course, yield a quite different result.) In evaluating these data, one should remind students that the Web site is funded by the American Fiber Manufacturers Association and hence highlights the positive aspects of synthetic fibers and downplays their negative environmental consequences.

Discovering those consequences requires more concentrated research. One might start with the recognition that Dacron, like all forms of PET, is a petroleum product. In addition to the pollutants created by the fuels used in manufacturing it, unrecycled PET (mostly as bottles) contributes almost 2 million tons of garbage per year; in 1997 alone it added 2.76 million cubic yards of solid waste to landfills (*Profiles*). The manufacture of polyesters also creates methanol—a highly toxic form of alcohol—as a by-product. Further, the solvents used to produce polyester fabrics have long been linked with health hazards such as bladder and nasal cancers (masses that are not, unfortunately, "nebulous" [280]; see Hounshell and Smith 572). In fact, DuPont's internal memos from as far back as the 1930s questioned the safety of using the chemical dimethylformamide as a solvent in textile plants producing the fibers later named Orlon. DuPont's Haskell Laboratory warned in 1938 that atmospheric concentrations of this chemical needed to be kept low and admonished employees to avoid all skin contact with it (Hounshell and Smith 398). A bit more digging will turn up the famous Nader report on DuPont (written by James Phelan and Robert Pozen), which in 1973 documented how the company cultivated an environmentally friendly image while working to defeat the Clean Air and Clean Water Acts and denying the toxic effects of tetraethyl lead in gasoline well after scientists had proved its deleterious effects (which is how, by the way, "Leaded" gasoline gave way to "unleaded and super unleaded" [DeLillo, White Noise 199]).[7] The company was also forced to stop selling a fungicide called Ceresan when government scientists learned that the mercury in it was poisoning birds (Phelan and Pozen 42–43). Throughout the 1970s DuPont factories in Delaware were spewing large amounts of sulfur dioxide, sulfuric acid, and hydrochloric acid into the atmosphere and, until the late 1970s, into the Delaware River. Instead of cleaning up, the company moved its dye works to Puerto Rico, thereby exporting the poisons (45–46).

I did much of my research on the World Wide Web, but I encourage students to cast their net more broadly. One should of course caution them that the Internet contains no referees or filters, so they should take everything they read there with a large grain of salt. They should also call information and marketing directors, interview supermarket managers, and read trade journals. With guidance, diligent students can stretch a very brief reference to these fabrics into an essay on the multiple relations between our togs and our toxins: they can learn how, in other words, Dacron, Orlon, and Lycra Spandex are woven not only into our clothes but also into the novel's related themes of consumption and environmental damage. In so doing they may discover how Dacron and Nyodene D are part of the same vast systems, both capitalist and ecological.

Other commodity triads suggest further links. For instance, students could investigate the triad of paints and protectants recited as Jack and family flee the toxic cloud for the second time, when he looks into the rearview mirror and thinks, "Krylon, Rust-Oleum, Red Devil" (159). Although I have suggested elsewhere that, given his exposure to the cloud and the computer forecasting his death, Jack might well feel the need for a synthetic protectant (178), these products do not seem very consoling. Recalling, as they do, the names of 1950s horror-film monsters, they seem nearly as malevolent as the cloud. All three products are, of course, highly toxic, and their manufacture is likely to have marked effects on the environment. Students could also explore the health hazards and environmental effects of the breath mints listed in the interpolation on page 229 or of the dandruff medicines on page 289. In the latter group, a couple of small facts might prompt further discoveries: the active ingredient in Tegrin and Denorex is coal tar, a by-product of the coke ovens used to smelt steel and graphite. Exposure to aerosol coal tar has been shown to cause lung cancer and squamous cell carcinomas in mice (see *Coke Oven Emissions*). In short, all these commodity triads offer excellent opportunities for students to discover how the things we consume come back to haunt us.

One interpolation comments metanarratively on the commodity triads themselves, while also functioning as a bridge between them and the TV and radio voices. This list implicitly summarizes the connections I have been tracing between consumerism and the environment. Chapter 31 opens with a rather chilling set of instructions from Waveform Dynamics that insinuates dreadful consequences if one fails to send payment in full or place a stamp on the envelope. It is followed by a litany in full caps: "CABLE HEALTH, CABLE WEATHER, CABLE NEWS, CABLE NATURE" (231). The interpolation is followed by a scene in which the family devour fast-food chicken in the car while engaging in one of their hilariously misinformed conversations about science and weather (or CABLE WEATHER). One could read their fragmented knowledge as an example of what happens when you get all your information from cable. Likewise, their meal is the dietary equivalent of TV news: chopped up and repackaged, it's not chicken but chicken parts. Beyond the immediate context, this four-part list adumbrates much of what we hear from the novel's television and radio voices: warnings about "[e]xcesses of salt, phosphorus, magnesium" (236) or instructions to "sit half lotus and think about our spines" (18; these messages would be from CABLE HEALTH); the increasingly catastrophic effects of the Nyodene D cloud (reported by CABLE NEWS); bizarre excerpts from nature shows in which surgeons attach an "artificial flipper" (29) or direct us to put feelers on butterflies (96; on CABLE NATURE). In many of these excerpts (and in Willie Mink's "dialogue") human beings arrogantly intervene in nature, which has now been "ineluctably altered by technology" (Phillips 244). Nature is no longer pristine but, like those chicken parts, packaged and processed. Indeed, as Richard Kerridge observes, televised nature is "commodified, paradoxically, as that which is prior to commodification" (187). Yet for the most part *White Noise* dramatizes how nature resists being contained and instead returns to us in altered forms that punish us for manipulating it: it bombards us with a myriad of frighteningly intangible waves and radiation; it chills us by reminding us that, in our bodily death, we are merely animals; it graphically illustrates our technological depredations in spookily garish sunsets and brightly colored poisons.

What, then, can students gain from exploring commodity culture in *White Noise*? The bleak recognition that their brains are, as Joseph Conte argues, no more than another programmable circuit, "an extension of the electronic network in which power and money flow" to the corporation "who most successfully disseminates its" messages (124)? Perhaps. But these assignments may also serve as heartening reminders that there is a nature outside of CABLE NATURE that resists our attempts to make it a slave of our desires; they may demonstrate that what and how we advertise, buy, and consume does not just add to our auras but also affects the physical quality of our lives and that of our planet. Most of all, the assignments can show students that they have the power to make changes: that by learning the real language of commodities, they can gain a more coherent and meaningful purchase on both nature and culture.

NOTES

[1]Waffelos is an artificial maple-syrup cereal made by Ralston-Purina; Kabooms is another sugary kids' cereal. Dum-Dum pops remain a campus favorite: on a couple of occasions students arrived for a class in which we were discussing *White Noise* with Dum-Dum pops stuck in their mouths. If only they had been joking.

[2]A more nuanced version of this approach can be found in Ewen and Ewen. See also Schudson.

[3]A classic statement of this position is R. Williams's "Advertising: The Magic System."

[4]John Frow notes that the interpolations progress from an "apparently impersonal enunciation to more localized points of origin" (428): they seem to issue increasingly from characters. Joseph Conte suggests that they demonstrate Jack's inability to distin-

guish figure from ground in his life's noise (118). David Cowart emphasizes how their triadic structure invokes DeLillo's religious themes, making "all the more poignant the desuetude of that once-ultimate trinity, the three-personed God" (78). Patti White compares them to "narrative toxin" or "commercials and deliveries of junk mail" (14, 12) and offers three possibilities to explain them: that they show Jack's filter breaking down, that they are aimed to "force the reader into noise-reduction strategies," and that they continue or comment on the narrative (15). She concludes that they serve all three functions at once, acting as "effective narrative bridges, capable of carrying themes and transporting action, just as indestructible plastic can be recycled, reformed, and used in construction" (27). In *American Magic and Dread* I also explicate some ways that the textual interpolations—not just the triads but also the television and radio voices—obliquely comment on the passages in which they appear (165–91).

[5]In preparing this essay, I ran across a similar assignment used by Robert J. Brake, a business professor at Concordia University. Students in his Marketing Management course are assigned to discover everything they can about "food products we love to hate," such as Spam or Twinkies, and then create a show about the ones they have chosen. Brake focuses mostly on marketing questions such as line extension, promotion, and pricing rather than on the health or environmental effects of the foods.

[6]See *Polyester Fiber* and "Dacron." The fibers were actually developed almost ten years earlier by Imperial Chemical Industries (Hounshell and Smith 408). For a detailed history of the development of Dacron, see Hounshell and Smith 407–20. For a similar history of Orlon, see Hounshell and Smith 394–407.

[7]Lead additives in gasoline were banned in the United States in 1973, and all cars manufactured after 1975 were required to have catalytic converters. See www.nature.nps.gov/toxic/gasunlea.pdf.

APPENDIX: TEXTUAL INTERPOLATIONS

1. "The Airport Marriott, the Downtown Travelodge, the Sheraton Inn and Conference Center" (15). This phrase occurs as Jack contemplates Babette's running and the question of who will die first. He also observes some running girls and thinks of them as "weightless in their craving, able to land lightly" (15). It is followed by a discussion of Bee's visit: she's nomadic, as is the family itself. See Osteen 169.
2. "Dacron, Orlon, Lycra Spandex" (52). Jack and Babette have just left Murray's place, where Murray has made suggestive remarks about Babette. They are passing by a darkened optical shop. Babette begins to talk about how she is forgetting things. See Osteen 169.
3. "MasterCard, Visa, American Express" (100). Jack and Babette are discussing death; each claims that he/she wants to die first but also suspects that the other is lying. The triad is preceded by Jack's thinking, "it's being alone that frightens her. The emptiness, the sense of cosmic darkness." He follows with "I tell her I want to die first." A little later he confesses, "Given a choice between loneliness and death, it would take me a fraction of a second to decide" (102). As White notes, Babette's notion that one

is safe as long as there are dependent children in the house "constitutes a sort of living-on-credit" (15), an idea that reappears in Murray's exhortations to Jack about storing up "life-credit" (290). Duvall writes, "mastery over death is what [Jack] strives for in his study of Hitler," and the credit cards allow Jack to take a "vacation" from the fear of death ("[Super]Marketplace" 440). See also Osteen 173.

4. "Krylon, Rust-Oleum, Red Devil" (159). Jack and family are fleeing from the toxic cloud, which, having changed direction, seems almost sentiently malicious. The cloud is a devil indeed: a by-product of pesticides used to protect fruits and vegetables from infestation, it has itself become an invader.
5. "Leaded, unleaded, super unleaded" (199). This triad seems clearly to come from Jack's consciousness. It enters just after he and Babette have made love in the aftermath of Babette's confession about Dylar and their funny-grim conversation about death fears. They are feeling competitive about which fears death more, as if sex were a race.

   White writes that this interpolation comments "upon motive force and forward motion, linking fossil fuels to the drives that power human endeavors"; the movements of lovemaking are "contrasted against the brute force of the automobile" (16). See also Osteen 182.
6. As Jack is discussing fear of death with Winnie Richards, he watches "light climb into the rounded summits of high-altitude clouds. Clorets, Velamints, Freedent" (229). See Frow 428; Osteen 170.
7. "CABLE HEALTH, CABLE WEATHER, CABLE NEWS, CABLE NATURE" (231). This interpolation—a quartet, not a triad—comes just after the reminders about paying Waveform Dynamics by check; Jack has entered the system. It is followed by a scene of family fast-food dining in the car—rapid, gluttonous consumption—during which they discuss science. See Osteen 174.
8. Attempting to sleep, Jack can't stop thinking about "Mr. Gray." He thinks of him on TV, as a dominant presence, as an alien. He seems to hear Gray and Babette having sex. "Then gloom moved in around the gray-sheeted bed, a circle slowly closing. Panasonic" (241; the word "Panasonic," ending the chapter, is its own paragraph).
9. Murray and Jack examine products in the supermarket while discussing Jack's fear of death and what to do about it, and one of them (probably Murray) says, "Tegrin, Denorex, Selsun Blue." Immediately before the appearance of this triad, Murray argues that, when plagued by dread, "we resort to repression. . . . This is the natural language of the species" (289).
10. The final triad consists not of brand names but of spelled-out acronyms. As Jack steals the Stovers' car and heads for Iron City, this phrase appears: "Random Access Memory, Acquired Immune Deficiency Syndrome, Mutual Assured Destruction" (303).

Keesey writes that the acronyms designate what Jack wishes to destroy: the violence, unhelpfulness, and insanity of modern technology (147). White argues that the phrases, seen in retrospect, "label Mink's dementia . . . comment upon the contamination of Mink's language processes by reality confusion . . . and predict the mutual attempts at destruction" (18). When converted back to acronyms, RAM, AIDS, MAD suggest Jack's "agitation of the passions" (303).

White Noise as Disaster Movie

Valerie Wee and John Whalen-Bridge

Among its many thematic concerns, Don DeLillo's novel explores disaster at various levels, including the personal, political, and cultural. To grasp these concerns, students must find ways to connect large, public disasters, such as the one DeLillo names the airborne toxic event, to the personal anxieties, such as jealousy and fear of death, that nearly bring Jack Gladney to commit murder. Disaster movies can help. We teach *White Noise* in Imagining Disaster (also known among students as Disaster 101), a cultural studies course at the National University of Singapore that also includes the study of popular disaster movies, documentary and journalistic accounts of disaster, and cinematic responses to the Holocaust and to fears of nuclear holocaust. Our course asks why people are interested in disaster, why disaster films appeal to audiences, and what critical reflection we ought to bring to representations of disaster. Our students learn about American society largely through cultural media, especially Hollywood cinema, and our course is designed to interrogate not only this stream of popular images but also other cultural forms that challenge the representations of commercial cinema. We seek to problematize the artistic representation of disaster, prompting student awareness of how disaster in the contemporary world is amplified and obsessively replayed by various media, including twenty-four-hour cable news networks, free-to-air television, and movies. As Gladney reflects while channel surfing for such footage with his family, this excess of traumatic imagery creates an apparently bottomless appetite: "Every disaster made us wish for more, for something bigger, grander, more sweeping" (64).

Disaster always has an aesthetic effect: when a nationally symbolic space shuttle crashes to the ground or when a famous person with whom many identify is suddenly killed (a Kennedy or a Gandhi), attention is arrested; people remember exactly where they stood when they heard the news. The shock of disaster unifies our perceptions. Despite the contemporary, almost obsessive interest in cultural and aesthetic representations of disaster, disaster first appears to be the antithesis of an aesthetic event. Theodor Adorno famously wrote that "after Auschwitz . . . to write a poem is barbaric" ("Cultural Criticism" 34). Adorno points to a potentially debilitating contradiction between disaster and aesthetic activity. Whether the cultural act in the wake of disaster is barbaric or not, the culture industry exists quite comfortably alongside disastrous events. Imagining Disaster examines a series of texts to show how communities (including producers and consumers) talk about problems and pain in revealing ways, and *White Noise* is a core text because it encourages students to think about the multiple uses of disaster in cultural texts.

One strategy for teaching students how *White Noise* modifies our thinking about disaster is to juxtapose the text with a wide variety of media responses to disaster. To that end, our course focuses on three primary methods through which disastrous events are assimilated into culture. In the first subcategory, "Documenting Disaster," we examine how a work may document a disaster and thus connect directly with a historical referent. A disaster text is shaped by the audience's presumed resistance to face the pain of traumatic events. Unlike texts discussed in "Documenting Disaster," texts in our second category are suspicious of attempts to represent disaster directly. To highlight this critical response to disaster discourse, we focus on how disaster art may satirize either the causes of or responses to an event. Novels and films do not satirize the disasters themselves, of course, but there is a countertradition in which cultural responses parody solemn responses to disaster, exposing the solemn responses as sentimental exploitations of the event. Finally, in the third subcategory we discuss films, novels, and other textual media that present disaster in ways that inspire readers or viewers. Our method is to break up the monolithic nature of disaster art by juxtaposing heterogeneous materials, and for this purpose *White Noise,* which is predominantly a work in the satirical mode, is an ideal summative text.

Documenting Disaster

Students in this lower-level course, designed for nonmajors, are less familiar with the politics of representation than English majors are. Consequently, some initially doubt the notion that the media broadly shape our responses to catastrophic events. Starting with journalism and documentary films, students explore the relation between the media and the real world. The first historical disaster we study is the Holocaust, which, for most of our students, calls to mind such popular films as *Schindler's List* (1993). We play a clip of this film and ask students to compare what happens in the movie with what happened in real life. We juxtapose the film with clips of Claude Lanzmann's nine-and-a-half-hour *Shoah* (1985). After explaining that this film is made up entirely of interviews and excludes any archival documentary film clips, we ask students to begin thinking about why someone would make such a long film and how it differs from a commercially successful one like *Schindler's List*.

Subsequent discussion develops the concept of documenting disasters. We divide our students into groups and assign each group to research different forms of Holocaust memorial projects, including the United States Holocaust Memorial Museum (www.ushmm.org) and the Survivors of the Shoah Visual History Foundation (www.vhf.org). Each group prepares a short presentation of its findings, which should include Web pages or clips from the films. After the presentations, students consider the different forms of historical memory and evaluate the aims and effectiveness of various strategies.

The first complete film we show is Michael Verhoeven's *The Nasty Girl*

(1990; *Das schreckliche Mädchen*), which we screen just before students make presentations on controversial museum exhibitions memorializing the Holocaust. Anticipating later discussions of *White Noise*, we also assign DeLillo's essay "Silhouette City: Hitler, Manson, and the Millennium." We ask, Why is the Holocaust fascinating?, and, What is *fascination*? Having raised the ethical problems inherent in the representation of disaster, we set our examination of *White Noise* alongside documentary evidence of various airborne toxic events to develop contexts for discussion of historical analogues to DeLillo's fictional event. We again divide our class into groups and assign each group a different topic to research. These topics include an actual historical disaster related to the event depicted in the novel; the context—social, political and cultural—surrounding the fictional text's production; and the possible relevance the fictional representation may have to the current era. One group of students collects news and documentary reports on an actual event, such as the Bhopal chemical accident, the post–September 11 anthrax attacks, or the sarin gas attack in Tokyo. A second group researches the cultural, social, economic, and political conditions prevalent in the period *White Noise* was written (if we were teaching this course in the United States, we would encourage our students to interview their relatives, who could provide an added personal perspective on the mid-1980s, the era in which the book is set). The final group considers the book's key messages, ideologies, values, and themes and judges their relevance to contemporary concerns. All these activities are done before the class meeting. During the class, each group presents its findings. To aid discussion, we raise key questions under the following rubrics:

Education versus escapism Does *White Noise* complicate our understanding of actual disasters? Our students note that the novel adopts a fairly cynical and ironic perspective on its disasters, which forces readers to make a decision: does the novel reduce these events to entertainment fodder, or is it the catalyst for a reflection on how the media trivialize disaster?

Media interests What do the media want? Our students know, even before we mention that one discarded title of the novel was *Panasonic* (Champlin), that *White Noise* is in part concerned with examining the increasing media overload that characterizes contemporary American culture and the largely negative impact that this overload has on individuals. Students also consider the role of the media in Singapore and its effect on their perceptions of the world.

Culture as author When *White Noise* was published in 1985, the United States had just experienced a tremendous growth of cable penetration, a development that resulted in an explosion of television channels, including news channels that seemed focused on disasters. The videocassette player then very quickly infiltrated the home, allowing greater access to (disaster) films. DeLillo documents and comments on these developments. Students evaluate DeLillo's concerns and comment on their validity in relation to their own experiences.

Attitudes toward politics In response to a suggestion that he "takes the culture apart" in his fictional treatments, DeLillo corrected the interviewer, saying, "I take the *language* apart" ("I Take"). What is the importance of this distinction? Does the book or its characters participate in any kind of political or socially critical activity? The representation of such activities in DeLillo's text can form the basis for an excellent class discussion.

Text as a cultural benchmark How much has changed culturally, socially, and politically since the mid-1980s? Is there any evidence that DeLillo's concerns should remain ours? Our students note that, with regard to the media, the conditions depicted in *White Noise* have become even more relevant, particularly with the emergence of new media technologies and the further growth of cable, developments that have made it possible to access disaster 24–7.

Some students in Singapore, with its generally conservative Confucian culture, report that, in their experience, people there are much more hesitant to discuss disaster and trauma than are the Americans they read about or see on television. Perhaps they consider it morbid to discuss horrific historical events, and advertisers may prefer to publicize happy news. Often historical disasters have not been adequately memorialized because of such resistance, and so we turn to the artistic and rhetorical strategies that artists deploy to circumvent such instances of aesthetic censorship. To illustrate this issue, we review problems raised in *The Nasty Girl*. This film, which comments on the most serious issues with a darkly comic tone, explores a young girl's attempts to research and write a paper examining her town's role during the Third Reich. Her attempts at uncovering the truth are met with various forms of resistance and rejection by the town's inhabitants. *The Nasty Girl* is a particularly interesting text to compare with *White Noise* because both works address the difficulty of identifying, acknowledging, and documenting disastrous events. While *The Nasty Girl* points to the dangers and problems inherent to a small German community's attempts to ignore and disavow its role in the Holocaust, *White Noise* explores a related set of dangers and problems in a more contemporary setting in which all disasters are either aestheticized, reduced to entertainment, or backgrounded as white noise. Perhaps most emblematically, a cloud of dangerous gas is euphemistically referred to as an airborne toxic event. Debating the importance of remembering traumatic disasters as opposed to the benefits that could come from forgetting or disavowing them, our students present impressive arguments for both points of view. They may also wish to compare and evaluate the similarities and differences that characterize the two accounts of how communities can reject or ignore disaster.

Our students also have more-local frames of reference. For example,

Singapore has its own ongoing disaster discourse, which is tuned mainly to local and international events that directly affect the Singaporean economy. Most recently, SARS and avian flu have been such disasters, causing the government to mobilize the public and take measures to control the spread of disease as well as international perceptions of Singapore's response to the disasters.

World-scale disasters, such as the Bhopal poison cloud or the massacre of students in Tiananmen Square, do not register as full-fledged disasters to quite the same degree that local events do. For students in Singapore during the 1980s, ethnic Chinese and Indian alike, the Bhopal disaster was merely a sad event that occurred in another country, and colleagues remember Singaporean students' response to the massacre in Tiananmen Square as largely indifferent. Such disasters are, as it were, a world apart. Furthermore, the largely state-controlled media tend not to raise questions about the parameters of disaster, and so our students need additional help understanding DeLillo's use of irony. His irony fits in a cultural framework in which the intelligentsia comments ironically on official government and mainstream media claims that a disaster has occurred and that a certain public response is suitable. We point out to students that "white noise" not only refers to the babble on the radio but also comments wryly on the author's manner of cultural critique, which is uncensored yet also completely impotent in terms of guiding the policies or moral values of the culture. Critical white noise is a consolation prize for the irrelevant intelligentsia, which has no direct, meaningful say in the handling of problems like airborne toxic events.

Finally, we help students locate white noise in racial and national identification. That the novel also satirizes the anxieties of the American white male is a point most students will understand quickly, though some have a difficult time imagining that white males in America could ever be anxious about anything. Thus we spend a few minutes reviewing the male midlife crisis, referring to a number of films and texts that explore this cultural strand.

Later in the course, we return to the question of the documentary mode in relation to the domestic and campus satire of DeLillo's first section, "Waves and Radiation." At this point, we propose that students consider seemingly disparate details of *White Noise*, such as "THE MOST PHOTOGRAPHED BARN IN AMERICA" (12) and Gladney's role as founder of Hitler studies, as something of a koan. What does it mean that a completely innocuous barn has become famous for being famous? Do news media that focus on empty celebrity displace attention to disasters and thus shield us from a sense of responsibility?

The Satirical Mode

After having been asked to identify and evaluate the sources of resistance to trauma in the section on documentary, students are better able to understand the uses of satire as an aggressive mode in which the text challenges how a culture assimilates disaster. At this point in the course, we ask our students to compare both straightforward and comic versions of the documentary approach with the fictional account of Hitler studies in *White Noise*. What was DeLillo's intention in having J. A. K. Gladney head such a department? What is the function of the various references to Hitler studies in the book? The most useful aspect of DeLillo's novel for our purposes (getting students to look critically at the media) is that it forces students to consider the source when attempting to locate the meaning of words and pictures. That is, we discuss the narrative and ask why we should or should not collapse DeLillo into his creation, Gladney. For this discussion, we ask students to read Paul A. Cantor's essay "Adolf, We Hardly Knew You," which reviews Bruce Bawer's attack on DeLillo (Bawer accuses DeLillo of failing to judge Hitler's immorality) and argues persuasively that

> we ought to recognize that *White Noise* is not itself an example of Hitler studies, but rather a novel which portrays a professor involved in Hitler studies. . . . In fact, DeLillo could find no better example of the flattening-out of contemporary existence than the routinization of Hitler's charisma at the College-on-the-Hill. (41)

We ask students if they are satisfied with Cantor's defense of the novel. We also have them read Sylvia Plath's poem "Daddy" and review her controversial Holocaust references. We present satire as a risky strategy: an artist may or may not succeed in the attempt to use comedy as an entertaining wake-up call to a community. If satire fails, the artist is accused of having bad taste.

We then focus on DeLillo's use of black humor in "The Airborne Toxic Event." Many of our students are unfamiliar with the notion of black humor. To open up discussion of this form of humor, we mention films such as *Dr. Strangelove; or, How I Learned to Stop Worrying and Love the Bomb* (1964) and explain that merely laughing at someone else's pain is not the point. Students will already have seen journalistic descriptions of the Bhopal disaster, in which a Union Carbide chemical plant leaked a toxic cloud, which has by now killed between ten and twenty thousand people. On an overhead screen, we click through some examples of politically engaged journalism to show how black humor is used to ridicule harmful behavior or inadequate accounts of original disaster, such as Romi Mahajan's attack on Union Carbide's irresponsibility, "Bhopal on $40 a Day." Students quickly connect Mahajan's article title with the travel guides and, reading a bit more, see that forty dollars refers not to the traveler's daily expenses but to the amount of money Union Carbide saved each day by turning off certain safety equipment. Is Mahajan's use of black humor the same as DeLillo's? Both *White Noise* and "Bhopal on $40 a Day" satirize stupidity, but Mahajan's moment of black humor organizes a community of readers against corporate irresponsibility. Clearly DeLillo is not attempting to organize readers politically, at least not in a direct sense. In groups, students are called on to sketch an account of DeLillo's representation of the airborne toxic event in relation to the Bhopal tragedy.

The discussion of Mahajan's journalism and DeLillo's fiction makes clear that disaster can be used in various ways, but many students ask, Why use disaster to produce laughter? After discussing the Cuban Missile Crisis as a historical antecedent, we screen the films *Fail-Safe* (1964) and *Dr. Strangelove* to show how two works with similar content create such different responses in viewers. Most of our discussion develops from the tonal differences between *Fail-Safe* on the one hand and *Dr. Strangelove* and *White Noise* on the other. Seeing straight drama and satirical variation side by side, students better understand how both films exploit audience fears for aesthetic effect, even though the tragic framework of *Fail-Safe* strikes some students as a natural response compared with the giddy extrapolations of *Dr. Strangelove*.

Drawing Inspiration from Disaster

We want a hero, not an uncommon want, since every season Hollywood offers up a new one. For the Hollywood studios with the largest budgets, disaster provides a stage upon which morally mixed characters find their way to heroism: a character who has made moral compromises will, under the pressure of extreme events, experience a clarification of values that produces heroic actions. In *The China Syndrome* (1979), Kimberly Wells (Jane Fonda) begins as a journalist who will frequently compromise her morals. Under the pressure of events, however, Wells and her fellow journalist Richard Adams (Michael Douglas) decide to risk their careers to accurately report the problems at the plant. The plant supervisor, Jack Godell (Jack Lemmon), undergoes a similar transformation, illustrating that disaster art is often about hero-generation. The murky distinction between greed and practicality has been, by the movie's end, clarified in the centrifuge of disaster.

Gladney, the Hitler specialist who does not speak German, is frequently approached as an object of ridicule, but some students will notice that quasi-heroic elements survive the implicitly and explicitly ironic effects of the novel. While students may resist the idea that a satirical work such as *White Noise* can have heroic or inspirational content, they are more able to see the possible continuity when we screen scenes from two recent disaster films, *Independence Day* (1996) and *Mars Attacks!* (1996). These two films can be presented antithetically, since *Mars Attacks!* (like *Dr. Strangelove* and *White Noise*) clearly ridicules the sort of manipulative hero-generation *Independence Day* indulges in, but we also point out that *Mars Attacks!* does not entirely dispense with heroic value. While Jack Nicholson's rendition of President James Dale burlesques the notion of an inspiring leader such as we find in *Independence Day* and *Fail-Safe*, we see in *Mars Attacks!* not an elimination of inspiration but a redirection to where we might find it. It is the clumsy boy Richie Norris (Lucas Haas) who discovers the aliens' secret weakness, not his military-minded brother. In contrast with the completely ridiculous President Dale, the has-been, ex-boxer Byron Williams (Jim Brown) emerges from the satire as a thoroughly inspirational hero. In the film's closing scenes most of civilization is in ruins, but Hollywood's typical patterns of inspirational narrative have survived.

Heroism often runs through DeLillo narratives, albeit in camouflaged forms. While Gladney resists recognizing the danger of the airborne toxic event as long as possible, his son Heinrich, bizarrely and satirically named after Heinrich Himmler to show Gladney's (and American culture's?) strategy of denial through familiarization, is alert to danger:

> When I was halfway down the street I saw Heinrich crouched on a small ledge outside our attic window. He wore his camouflage jacket and cap, an outfit with complex meaning for him, at fourteen, struggling to grow and to escape notice simultaneously, his secrets known to us all. He looked east through binoculars. (109)

At one level, Gladney sensitively perceives the contradiction between Heinrich's self-perception and the world's perception of him, but, on another level, the joke is on Gladney, since his children recognize danger long before he does. Comically, Gladney continues to believe euphemistic radio broadcasts aimed at calming him and others endangered by what is initially called a "feathery plume" (111). Students quickly see that DeLillo's approach is anti-heroic and that Heinrich's contrapuntal heroism and, later, Gladney's insane attempt to hunt down Willie Mink clearly underscore the differences between *White Noise* and such inspiring survival narratives as *Schindler's List*.

Such inspiration as can be found in *White Noise* is an ironic counterpoint to the primary representation of heroism:

> I'm not just a college professor. I'm the head of a department. I don't see myself fleeing an airborne toxic event. That's for people who live in mobile homes out in the scrubby parts of the country, where the fish hatcheries are. (117)

Gladney is the protagonist of *White Noise* rather than the hero, but by approaching the novel as mock form, students may recognize residual shards of heroic or inspirational narrative: certain characters do not deny the realities around them. To consider how disaster highlights ordinary, middle-class life, students reflect on DeLillo's statements from an interview with Anthony DeCurtis: "In *White Noise* in particular, I tried to find a kind of radiance in dailiness. Sometimes this radiance can be almost frightening. Other times it can be almost holy or sacred" ("Outsider" 63). Some students suspect that

DeLillo speaks with tongue in cheek, but others see the use of disaster to redeem seemingly banal everyday life as intriguing, pointing to DeLillo's comment:

> I think it is something we all feel, something we almost never talk about, something that is almost there. I tried to relate it in *White Noise* to this other sense of transcendence that lies just beyond our touch. This extraordinary wonder of things is somehow related to the extraordinary dread, to the death fear we try to keep beneath the surface of our perceptions. (63)

This quotation brings several strands together. "Transcendence" appears frequently in the novel: Murray Jay Siskind is a witty, transparent eyeball as he watches filmed car crashes with his students (40), and Gladney feels "spiritually large" when watching his children (155).

We ask students at this point to reconsider the documentaries, films, works of fiction, and other texts we've discussed in relation to the question of the ethics of representation raised throughout the course. DeLillo's statements can be used to focus the question, What does it mean to use disaster? DeLillo writes:

> I never set out to write an apocalyptic novel. It's about death on the individual level. Only Hitler is large enough and terrible enough to absorb and neutralize Jack Gladney's obsessive fear of dying—a very common fear, but one that's rarely talked about. (C. James)

His claim that "Jack uses Hitler as a protective device; he wants to grasp anything he can" (James) clarifies the distinction between character and author for many students, but some students argue that DeLillo not only satirizes Holocaust studies but also participates in the strategies he satirizes.

Our final discussion of the text involves events from "Dylarama," the third section of the novel, particularly the dialogue between Gladney (who has just dragged Mink by his ankles into the Germantown hospital) and Sister Hermann Marie, the nun who ridicules the idea that she should believe in God, given a world in which one man drags another into a hospital by his ankles: "You would have a head so dumb to believe this?" The sister explains to a shocked Gladney that she does not believe in heaven, angels, and God but that she and her kind perform belief to give comfort to people like him: "It is our task to believe things no one else takes seriously. To abandon such beliefs completely, the human race would die. This is why we are here" (318). Despite Gladney's attempts to eke out an admission of sincere belief in a divine order, the nun mocks him. Her tough-minded realism nonetheless takes the form of social service: "A tiny minority. To embody old things, old beliefs.

The devil, the angels, heaven, hell. If we did not pretend to believe these things, the world would collapse" (318).

We close by considering the dialogue between Gladney and Sister Hermann Marie in the light of the novel's antiheroic subversion. Does her position have any inspirational value in the face of a relativistic, postmodern world in which nothing is sacred and very little seems worthwhile? Or is the nun merely one more object of DeLillo's satire? This consideration can be turned back on other texts studied in the course: is it possible that B-grade disaster movies such as *Independence Day* (movies that, supposedly, no one believes) perform a social role similar to that of Sister Hermann Marie? Do audiences get more enjoyment from melodramatic confrontations with disaster if they think other people actually believe in the inspirational value of stories?

Finally, it is worth pointing out that this novel, in its final pages, resists coming to an end. After Gladney has narrowly avoided ruining his life and after domestic and environmental problems and disasters have settled, DeLillo violates the formulaic happy-ending requirement of American disaster films by having Wilder, shockingly, ride his tricycle across the highway. This conclusion can be approached in many ways. Students are invited to choose whether the return to normality has been revealed as a false hope or whether the nearness of disaster (children dying because of carelessness) is a Romantic redemption from the banality of humdrum everyday life.

When we teach *White Noise* in relation to disaster films and similar cultural by-products of pain and suffering, perhaps the most important lesson is that asteroids, genocide, and other catastrophes—events that seem most impervious to social construction—accrue meaning because of the ways we shape events into story. *White Noise* provides ample opportunity for critical reflection on how textuality conditions our experience in the world, especially because of the ways the novel challenges or even violates rules about how to respond to disaster. As DeLillo wryly remarked in an interview with Charles Champlin, *White Noise* is "about fear, death and technology. A comedy, of course."

NOTES ON CONTRIBUTORS

Michael Bérubé is Paterno Family Professor in Literature at Penn State University. Among his books are *Public Access: Literary Theory and American Cultural Politics*; *The Employment of English: Theory, Jobs, and the Future of Literary Studies*; and, as editor, *The Aesthetics of Cultural Studies*.

Ted Billy, professor of English at Saint Mary's College, is author of *A Wilderness of Words: Closure and Disclosure in Conrad's Short Fiction*, editor of *Critical Essays on Joseph Conrad*, and coeditor of *A Joseph Conrad Companion*. His current projects include a study of nineteenth-century American gothic fiction.

David Blakesley is associate professor of English and director of professional writing at Purdue University and the founder of Parlor Press. He is the author of *The Elements of Dramatism*; the editor of *The Terministic Screen: Rhetorical Perspectives on Film*; and the coeditor, with Julie Whitaker, of *Late Poems, 1968–1993*, by Kenneth Burke. His current projects include "The Thomson Handbook" and "Illuminating Rhetoric."

Theron Britt is associate professor and graduate director for English at the University of Memphis. He has published studies on race and American identity, gender in popular culture, and contemporary American literature. His current manuscript project is "Lawful Fictions: Indeterminacy and Legitimation in Contemporary American Narrative."

John N. Duvall is professor of English at Purdue University and the editor of *MFS: Modern Fiction Studies*. His books include *Faulkner's Marginal Couple*; *The Identifying Fictions of Toni Morrison*; *Don DeLillo's* Underworld; and, as editor, *Productive Postmodernism* and *Faulkner and Postmodernism*. He is currently studying the figurative use of blackness in Faulkner and other southern writers.

Mark A. Eaton is associate professor of English at Azusa Pacific University, where he teaches American literature and film studies. His work has appeared in the *Boston Book Review*, *Modern Fiction Studies*, *Pedagogy*, *Prospects*, and the *Edith Wharton Review*. He is completing a book about the literary uses of mass culture in modern America entitled "What Price Hollywood?"

Tim Engles, associate professor of English at Eastern Illinois University, is coeditor with Hugh Ruppersburg of *Critical Essays on Don DeLillo*. He has written on the work of Tim O'Brien, Chang-rae Lee, and Alice Walker. He is currently studying whiteness and cultural identity in contemporary American literature, film, and the visual arts.

Randall Fuller is associate professor of English at Drury University and editor of the *Gingko Tree Review*. He has published essays on early American literature and several interviews in the *Missouri Review* with contemporary American writers. His current project is entitled "The Haunting of American Literature: Emerson and the Critical Imagination."

Kathleen LeBesco, associate professor of communication arts at Marymount Manhattan College, is author of *Revolting Bodies? The Struggle to Redefine Fat Identity* and coeditor of *The Drag King Anthology* and *Bodies Out of Bounds: Fatness and Transgression.* Among her research and teaching interests are communication theory, feminist and queer theory, politics of popular culture, and disability studies.

Louisa Mackenzie is assistant professor of French and Italian studies at the University of Washington. She has written articles on Pierre de Ronsard, Jean Parmentier, Rabelais, and Michel de Montaigne, and her research and teaching interests include early modern France and Italy, ecocriticism, and science fiction.

Timothy Melley is associate professor of English and American studies at Miami University. He is author of *Empire of Conspiracy: The Culture of Paranoia in Postwar America* and articles in *Contemporary Literature*, *Arizona Quarterly*, *Differences*, and *ESQ*. His stories have appeared in *Threepenny Review*, *Mississippi Review*, *Epoch*, *The Sun*, and *Columbia*. He is working on a book on trauma and memory in contemporary historiographic fiction.

Philip Nel is associate professor of English at Kansas State University. His most recent books are *Dr. Seuss: American Icon* and *The Avant-Garde and American Postmodernity: Small Incisive Shocks*. His articles have appeared in *Children's Literature*, *Comic Art*, *Contemporary Literature*, *Critique*, *Cultural Studies*, *The Lion and the Unicorn*, *Modern Fiction Studies*, and *Mosaic*.

Mark Osteen, professor of English at Loyola College in Maryland, is the author of *American Magic and Dread: Don DeLillo's Dialogue with Culture* and the editor of the Viking Critical Library edition of *White Noise*. He is also the author of *The Economy of Ulysses: Making Both Ends Meet*. Among his research and teaching interests are film, jazz writing, autism, and disability studies.

Margaret Scanlan, professor of English at Indiana University, South Bend, is the author of *Traces of Another Time: History and Politics in Postwar British Fiction* and *Plotting Terror: Novelists and Terrorists in Contemporary Fiction*. She is currently writing a book on contemporary Ireland.

Philipp Schweighauser teaches American literature at the University of Berne. He has published articles on Vladimir Nabokov, Don DeLillo, literary soundscapes, American realism, and concepts of masculinity. His book *The Noises of American Literature, 1890–1984: Toward a History of Literary Acoustics* is forthcoming (Univ. Press of Florida).

Margaret Soltan, associate professor of English at George Washington University, is the author of essays on Don DeLillo's work and other aspects of postmodern American culture. Her current project is a book cowritten with Jennifer Green-Lewis, "The Return of Beauty to Literary Studies." She is also author of the blog *University Diaries* (margaretsoltan.phenominet.com), which describes university life in America and abroad.

Valerie Wee is assistant professor of English language and literature at the National University of Singapore, where she teaches film and media studies. Her publications include studies of television and film. She is currently researching teen culture and the

American culture industries, American science fiction films, and issues of gender and representation in the media.

John Whalen-Bridge is an associate professor of English language and literature at the National University of Singapore. Among his research and teaching interests are American literature, African American literature, and orientalism. He is the author of *Political Fiction and the American Self*. His current project is entitled "American Literary Orientalism, 1945–2000."

Paul Young is assistant professor of English and director of the Film Studies Program at Vanderbilt University. He is the author of articles on film noir and digital-era science fiction and of the forthcoming *The Cinema Dreams Its Rivals: New Media and Hollywood's Public Spheres*. He received the E. Roe Stamps Award for Excellence in Teaching at the Georgia Institute of Technology in 2002.

SURVEY PARTICIPANTS

The editors would like to thank the following teacher-scholars for responding so fully and helpfully to an extensive questionnaire on teaching *White Noise*. Much of the information in the "Materials" section came from their generous contributions. The list indicates the institutional affiliations noted by participants on their questionnaire responses, except when new information was offered.

Laura L. Behling, *Gustavus Adolphus College*
Margaret Boe Berns, *New York University*
Charlie Bertsh, *University of Arizona*
Ted Billy, *Saint Mary's College*
James M. Boehnlein, *University of Dayton*
Cornel Bonca, *California State University, Fullerton*
Jason Camlot, *Concordia University, Sir George Williams Campus*
David Clippinger, *Penn State University*
Lisa Cooper, *Texas Christian University*
Michael Crowley, *University of Georgia*
Christopher Douglas, *Furman University*
Mark A. Eaton, *Azusa Pacific University*
Randall Fuller, *Drury University*
Marni Gauthier, *College at Cortland, State University of New York*
Jennifer Gillan, *Bentley College*
Jeremy F. Green, *University of Colorado, Boulder*
William S. Haney II, *Eastern Mediterranean University (Turkey)*
Ruth Helyer, *Universities of Newcastle and Teeside*
Jesse Kavadlo, *Winona State University*
Henry Laufenberg, *Cascadia Community College, WA*
Kathleen LeBesco, *Marymount Manhattan College*
Louisa Mackenzie, *University of Washington, Seattle*
Timothy Melley, *Miami University, Oxford*
Michelle E. Moore, *State University of New York, Binghamton*
Michael Valdez Moses, *Duke University*
Philip Nel, *Kansas State University*
Stacey Olster, *State University of New York, Stony Brook*
Timothy O'Shannassy, *University of Westminster*
Mark Osteen, *Loyola College*
Timothy B. Powell, *University of Georgia*
Greg Salyer, *Huntingdon College*
Arthur Saltzman, *Missouri Southern State College*
Gary Schneider, *Wayne State University*
Philipp Schweighauser, *University of Berne*
Iliana Semmler, *University at Albany*
Margaret Soltan, *George Washington University*

David L. Vanderwerken, *Texas Christian University*
Alex Vernon, *Hendrix College*
Joseph S. Walker, *Auburn University*
Mark Whalan, *University of Exeter*

WORKS CITED

Adams, Henry. *The Education of Henry Adams*. Ed. Ira B. Nadel. Oxford World's Classics. Oxford: Oxford UP, 1999.

Adorno, Theodor W. "Commitment." 1962. Trans. Francis McDonagh. *Aesthetics and Politics*. Ed. Ronald Taylor. Afterword by Fredric Jameson. London: Verso, 1980. 177–95.

———. "Cultural Criticism and Society." *Prisms*. Trans. Samuel Weber and Shierry Weber. Cambridge: MIT P, 1981. 17–34.

———. *Minima Moralia: Reflections from Damaged Life*. London: Verso, 2000.

Affluenza. Videorecording. Prod. John de Graaf and Viva Boie. Oley: Bullfrog Films, 1997.

American Beauty. Dir. Sam Mendes. DreamWorks SKG, 1999.

Arnold, Matthew. "The Function of Criticism at the Present Time." *The Norton Anthology of Theory and Criticism*. Ed. Vincent B. Leitch. New York: Norton, 2001. 806–25.

The Atomic Café. Dir. Jayne Loader and Kevin Rafferty. Archives Project, 1982.

Babb, Valerie. *Whiteness Visible: The Meaning of Whiteness in American Literature and Culture*. New York: New York UP, 1998.

Barnett, Timothy. "Reading 'Whiteness' in English Studies." *College English* 63 (2000): 9–37.

Barthes, Roland. "The Photographic Message." 1961. *Image/Music/Text*. Trans. Stephen Heath. New York: Noonday, 1977. 15–31.

Baudrillard, Jean. *America*. Trans. Chris Turner. New York: Verso, 1989.

———. "The Ecstasy of Communication." Foster 126–33.

———. *In the Shadow of the Silent Majorities*. Trans. Paul Foss et al. New York: Semiotext(e), 1983.

———. *Jean Baudrillard: Selected Writings*. Ed. Mark Poster. Stanford: Stanford UP, 1988.

———. "The Precession of Simulacra." 1979. *Simulacra and Simulation*. Trans. Sheila Faria Glaser. Ann Arbor: U of Michigan P, 1995. 1–42.

———. *Simulations*. Trans. Paul Foss et al. New York: Semiotext(e), 1983.

———. *The Spirit of Terrorism and Requiem for the Twin Towers*. Trans. Chris Turner. London: Verso, 2002.

Bawer, Bruce. "Don DeLillo's America." *New Criterion* 3.8 (1985): 34–42.

Beech, Jennifer. "Redneck and Hillbilly Discourse in the Writing Classroom: Classifying Critical Pedagogies of Whiteness." *College English* 67 (2004): 172–86.

Begley, Adam. "Don DeLillo: The Art of Fiction CXXXV." *Paris Review* 35 (1993): 274–306.

Bellow, Saul. *Henderson the Rain King*. New York: Penguin, 1987.

———. *Ravelstein*. New York: Viking, 2000.

Benjamin, Walter. *Illuminations: Essays and Reflections*. Ed. Hannah Arendt. Trans. Harry Zohn. 1969. New York: Random, 1988.

———. "The Work of Art in the Age of Mechanical Reproduction." 1936. Benjamin, *Illuminations* 217–52.

Berger, John. *Ways of Seeing*. 1972. London: BBC; Penguin, 1977.

Berger, Peter, ed. *The Desecularization of the World: Resurgent Religion in World Politics*. Grand Rapids: Eerdmans, 1999.

Bergson, Henri. *Laughter: An Essay on the Meaning of the Comic*. Trans. Cloudesley Brereton and Fred Rothwell. Los Angeles: Green Integer, 1999.

Bernstein, Susan Naomi. "Writing and White Privilege: Beyond Basic Skills." *Pedagogy* 4 (2004): 128–31.

Bettelheim, Bruno. "The Ignored Lesson of Anne Frank." 1952. *Literacies: Reading, Writing, Interpretation*. 2nd ed. Ed. Terence Brunk et al. New York: Norton, 2000. 77–88.

Blade Runner. Dir. Ridley Scott. Ladd, 1982.

Blakesley, David. *The Elements of Dramatism*. New York: Longman, 2002.

Bloom, Harold, ed. *Don DeLillo's* White Noise. New York: Chelsea, 2003.

Bonca, Cornel. "*White Noise*: The Natural Language of the Species." *College Literature* 23.2 (1996): 25–44. Rpt. in DeLillo, White Noise: *Text* 456–79.

Bowers, C. A. *Education, Cultural Myths, and the Ecological Crisis: Toward Deep Changes*. Albany: State U of New York P, 1993.

Brake, Robert J. *Researching Food Products We Love to Hate*. Great Ideas for Teaching Marketing: Marketing Research, Cases, and Projects. 13 Aug. 2002. 2003. 21 May 2004 <http://catalog.swlearning.com/marketing.gitm/gitm4e06-02.html>.

Brecht, Bertolt. *The Resistible Rise of Arturo Ui*. Trans. Ralph Manheim. Ed. John Willett and Manheim. New York: Arcade, 2001. Trans. of *Der aufhaltsame Aufstieg des Arturo Ui*.

Brink, Katja van den. "Multimedia in den Schulen: Pediatice." Marquet et al. 257–64.

Brodkin, Karen. *How Jews Became White Folks and What That Says about Race in America*. New Brunswick: Rutgers UP, 1998.

Buell, Lawrence. "Toxic Discourse." *Critical Inquiry* 24 (1998): 639–65.

———. *Writing for an Endangered World: Literature, Culture, and Environment in the U.S. and Beyond*. Cambridge: Harvard UP, 2001.

Burke, Kenneth. *A Grammar of Motives*. 1945. Berkeley: U of California P, 1969.

———. *Language as Symbolic Action: Essays on Life, Literature, and Method*. Berkeley: U of California P, 1966.

———. *A Rhetoric of Motives*. 1950. Berkeley: U of California P, 1969.

Burn, Gordon. "Wired Up and Whacked Out." *Sunday Times Magazine* (London) 25 Aug. 1991: 36+.

Byerly, Alison. "The Uses of Landscape: The Picturesque Aesthetic and the National Park System." Glotfelty and Fromm 52–68.

Campbell, Neil, and Alasdair Kean. *American Cultural Studies*. New York: Routledge, 1997.

Campbell, SueEllen. "The Land and Language of Desire: Where Deep Ecology and Post-structuralism Meet." *Western American Literature* 24 (1989): 199–211.

Cantor, Paul A. "Adolf, We Hardly Knew You." Lentricchia, *New Essays* 39–62.

Carson, Rachel. *Silent Spring*. Boston: Houghton, 1962.

Chambers, Ross. "The Unexamined." Hill 187–203.

Champlin, Charles. "The Heart Is a Lonely Craftsman." *Los Angeles Times* 29 July 1984: 7.

The China Syndrome. Dir. James Bridges. Columbia Pictures, 1979.

Chopin, Kate. *The Awakening*. New York: Dover, 1993.

Cimino, Richard, and Don Lattin. *Shopping for Faith: American Religion in the New Millennium*. San Francisco: Jossey-Bass, 1998.

Civello, Paul. "Don DeLillo." *American Novelists since World War II*. Farmington Hills: Thomson, 1996. 14–36. Vol. 173 of *Dictionary of Literary Biography*.

Clifford, James. *The Predicament of Culture: Twentieth-Century Ethnography, Literature, and Art*. Cambridge: Harvard UP, 1988.

Coke Oven Emissions. 14 Aug. 2002 <http://ntp-server.niehs.nih.gov/htdocs/8_RoC/KC/CokeOven.html>.

Cole, Tim. *Selling the Holocaust: From Auschwitz to Schindler, How History Is Bought, Packaged, and Sold*. New York: Routledge, 1999.

Comte-Sponville, Andre. "The Brute, the Sophist, and the Aesthete: 'Art in the Service of Illusion.' " *Why We Are Not Nietzscheans*. Ed. Luc Ferry and Alain Renaut. Chicago: U of Chicago P, 1997. 21–69.

Conrad, Joseph. *Heart of Darkness*. Ed. Robert Kimbrough. 3rd ed. Norton Critical Ed. New York: Norton, 1988.

Conradi, Peter. *Iris Murdoch: A Life*. New York: Norton, 2001.

Conte, Joseph. *Design and Debris: A Chaotics of Postmodern American Fiction*. Tuscaloosa: U of Alabama P, 2002.

Cowart, David. *Don DeLillo: The Physics of Language*. Athens: U of Georgia P, 2002.

Crane, Stephen. "The Open Boat." *"The Open Boat" and Other Stories*. New York: Dover Thrift, 1993. 57–77.

Crowther, Hal. "Clinging to the Rock: A Novelist's Choices in the New Mediocracy." *South Atlantic Quarterly* 89 (1990): 321–36.

Cunningham, John Christopher. "His Complexion Was of a Tone I Want to Call Flesh-Colored." *Race-ing Masculinity: Identity in Contemporary U.S. Men's Writing*. New York: Routledge, 2002. 95–112.

"Dacron." *CAMEO: Conservation and Art Materials Encyclopedia Online*. Museum of Fine Arts, Boston. 30 Nov. 2004 <http://www.mfa.org/_cameo/frontend>.

"Dacron: 1950." *DuPont Heritage*. 11 Aug. 2002 <http://heritage.dupont.com>.

Daly, Brenda O. "Taking Whiteness Personally: Learning to Teach Testimonial Reading and Writing in the College Literature Classroom." *Pedagogy* 5 (2005): 213–46.

The Day After. Dir. Nicholas Meyer. ABC Circle Films, 1983.

Debord, Guy. *The Society of the Spectacle*. Trans. Donald Nicholson-Smith. New York: Zone, 1994.

Deitering, Cynthia. "The Postnatural Novel: Toxic Consciousness in Fiction of the 1980s." Glotfelty and Fromm 196–203.

Delbanco, Andrew. *The Real American Dream: A Meditation on Hope*. Cambridge: Harvard UP, 1999.

Delgado, Richard, and Jean Stefancic, eds. *Critical White Studies: Looking behind the Mirror*. Philadelphia: Temple UP, 1997.

DeLillo, Don. *Americana*. 1971. Rev. ed. New York: Penguin, 1989.

———. "The Artist Naked in a Cage." *New Yorker* 26 May 1997: 6–7.

———. "Baader-Meinhof." *New Yorker* 1 Apr. 2002: 78–82.

———. *The Body Artist*. New York: Scribner's, 2001.

———. *The Day Room*. New York: Penguin, 1989.

———. *Great Jones Street*. New York: Penguin, 1973.

———. "A History of the Writer Alone in a Room." *The Jerusalem Prize for the Freedom of the Individual in Society*. Jerusalem Intl. Book Fair. Jerusalem: Caspit, 1999. 13–18.

———. "I Never Set Out to Write an Apocalyptic Novel." Interview with Caryn James. *New York Times Book Review* 13 Jan. 1985: 31.

———. Interview with Stephen Fender. *Writers Talking*. BBC Radio 3. 13 Nov. 1988.

———. Interview with Tom LeClair. LeClair and McCaffery 79–90.

———. Interview with Maria Nadotti. Trans. Peggy Boyers. *Salmagundi* 100 (1993): 86–97.

———. "In the Ruins of the Future." *Harper's Magazine* Dec. 2001: 33–40. *Guardian Unlimited*. 22 Dec. 2001. 2004. 6 Jan. 2005 <http://www.guardian.co.uk/saturday_review/story/0,,623666,00.html>.

———. "I Take the Language Apart." Interview with Nora Kerr. *New York Times Book Review* 9 June 1991: 7.

———. *Libra*. New York: Viking, 1988.

———. *Mao II*. New York: Viking, 1991.

———. *The Names*. New York: Vintage, 1989.

———. "An Outsider in This Society." Interview with Anthony DeCurtis. *South Atlantic Quarterly* 89.2 (1990): 281–304. Rpt. in Lentricchia, *Introducing* 43–66.

———. *Players*. 1977. New York: Vintage, 1989.

———. "The Power of History." *New York Times Magazine* 7 Sept. 1997: 60–64.

———. "Silhouette City: Hitler, Manson, and the Millennium." *Dimensions* 4.3 (1989): 29–34. Rpt. in DeLillo, White Noise*: Text* 344–52.

———. *Underworld*. New York: Scribner's, 1997.

———. *White Noise*. New York: Viking, 1985.

———. White Noise: *Text and Criticism*. Ed. Mark Osteen. New York: Viking, 1998.

———. *White Noise*. Penguin Great Books of the Twentieth Century. New York: Penguin, 1999.

DeLillo, Don, and Paul Auster. *Salman Rushdie Defense Pamphlet*. 1994. Rushdie Defense Committee USA. 31 Aug. 1996. 24 Jul. 2002 <http://www.perival.com/delillo/rushdie_defense.html>.

DeLillo, Don, et al. Letter. *New York Times* 26 Feb. 1989, late city final ed., sec. 4: 22. 20 Jun. 2004 <http://www.perival.com/delillo/ddarticles.html>.

DePietro, Thomas, ed. *Conversations with Don DeLillo*. Jackson: UP of Mississippi, 2005.

Derrida, Jacques. *Of Grammatology*. Trans. G. C. Spivak. Baltimore: Johns Hopkins UP, 1976.

Devall, Bill. *Simple in Means, Rich in Ends: Practicing Deep Ecology*. Salt Lake City: Smith, 1988.

Devor, Holly. "Becoming Members of Society: Learning the Social Meanings of Gender." *Gender Blending: Confronting the Limits of Duality*. Bloomington: Indiana UP, 1989. 43–62.

Don DeLillo. Spec. issue of *Critique* 42 (2001): 339–436.

Don DeLillo's America: A Don DeLillo Page. Ed. Curt Gardner. 2002. 24 Jul. 2002 <http://perival.com/delillo/delillo.html>.

Dreiser, Theodore. *The Financier*. New York: Meridian-Penguin, 1995.

———. *Sister Carrie*. Amer. Studies at the U of Virginia. 6 Sept. 2004. 27 Oct. 2005 <http://xroads.virginia.edu/~HYPER/DREISER/carrie.html>.

Dr. Strangelove; or, How I Learned to Stop Worrying and Love the Bomb. Dir. Stanley Kubrick. Columbia Pictures, 1964.

Duvall, John N., ed. *Don DeLillo*. Spec. issue of *Modern Fiction Studies* 45 (1999): 557–851.

———. *Don DeLillo's* Underworld*: A Reader's Guide*. New York: Continuum, 2002.

———. "The (Super)Marketplace of Images: Television as Unmediated Mediation in DeLillo's *White Noise*." *Arizona Quarterly* 50.3 (1994): 127–53. Rpt. in DeLillo, White Noise*: Text* 432–55.

Düx, Sascha. *Internet, Gesellschaft und Pädagogik: Computernetze als Herausforderung für Jugendarbeit und Schule in Theorie und Praxis*. Munich: KoPäd, 2000.

Dworkin, Andrea. *Pornography: Men Possessing Women*. New York: Perigree, 1981.

Eagleton, Terry. *Literary Theory: An Introduction*. 2nd ed. Minneapolis: U of Minnesota P, 1996.

Eck, Diana. *A New Religious America: How a Christian Country Has Now Become the World's Most Religiously Diverse Nation*. San Francisco: Harper, 2001.

Edmundson, Mark. "On the Uses of a Liberal Education: I. As Lite Entertainment for Bored College Students." *Harper's* Sept. 1997: 39–49.

Eisenstein, Elizabeth. *The Printing Revolution in Early Modern Europe*. Cambridge: Cambridge UP, 1983.

Elder, John, and Hertha Wong, eds. *Family of Earth and Sky: Indigenous Tales of Nature from around the World*. Boston: Beacon, 1994.

Eliot, T. S. "The Love Song of J. Alfred Prufrock." *The Complete Poems and Plays, 1909–1950*. New York: Harcourt, 1971. 3–7.

Emerson, Ralph Waldo. "Ode: Inscribed to W. H. Channing." *Selected Prose and Poetry*. New York: Holt, Rinehart, 1969. 433–36.

Engles, Tim. " 'Who Are You, Literally?': Fantasies of the White Self in *White Noise*." *Modern Fiction Studies* 45 (1999): 755–87. Rpt. in Ruppersburg and Engles 171–95.

Enron: The Smartest Guys in the Room. Dir. Alex Gibney. Magnolia Pictures, 2005.

Evans-Wentz, W. Y., and Lama Kazi Dawa-Samdup. *The Tibetan Book of the Dead*. 3rd ed. London: Oxford UP, 1957.

Ewen, Stuart, and Elizabeth Ewen. *Channels of Desire: Mass Images and the Shaping of American Consciousness*. 2nd ed. Minneapolis: U of Minnesota P, 1992.

Fail-Safe. Dir. Sydney Lumet. Columbia Pictures, 1964.

Farrell, Kate, ed. *Art and Nature: An Illustrated Anthology of Nature Poetry*. New York: Metropolitan Museum of Art, 1992.

Fasching, Thomas. *Internet und Pädagogik: Kommunikation, Bildung und Lernen im Netz*. Munich: KoPäd, 1997.

Ferraro, Thomas J. "Whole Families Shopping at Night!" Lentricchia, *New Essays* 15–38.

Fight Club. Dir. David Fincher. Twentieth Century Fox, 1999.

Fillingham, Lydia Alix. *Foucault for Beginners*. Illus. Moshe Susser. New York: Writers and Readers, 1993.

Fine, Michelle, Lois Weis, Linda C. Powell, and L. Mun Wong, eds. *Off White: Readings on Society, Race, and Culture*. New York: Routledge, 1997.

Finkelstein, Norman. *The Holocaust Industry: Reflections on the Exploitation of Jewish Suffering*. New York: Verso, 2001.

Fitzgerald, F. Scott. *The Great Gatsby*. New York: Scribner's, 1995.

Flanzbaum, Hilene. *The Americanization of the Holocaust*. Baltimore: Johns Hopkins UP, 1999.

Forster, E. M. *Aspects of the Novel*. New York: Harcourt, 1985.

———. *A Passage to India*. New York: Harcourt, 1924.

Foster, Hal, ed. *The Anti-Aesthetic: Essays on Postmodern Culture*. New York: New, 1998.

Foucault, Michel. *The History of Sexuality: An Introduction*. Trans. Robert Hurley. New York: Vintage, 1978. Vol. 1 of *The History of Sexuality*. 3 vols. 1978–86.

Fox, Catherine. "The Race to Truth: Disarticulating Critical Thinking from Whiteliness." *Pedagogy: Critical Approaches to Teaching Language, Literature, Composition, and Culture* 2.2 (2002): 197–212.

Frankenberg, Ruth, ed. *Displacing Whiteness: Essays in Social and Cultural Criticism*. Durham: Duke UP, 1997.

———. *White Women, Race Matters: The Social Construction of Whiteness*. Minneapolis: U of Minnesota P, 1993.

Franklin, Benjamin. *The Autobiography of Benjamin Frankin, with Related Documents*. 2nd ed. Ed. Louis P. Masur. Bedford Ser. in History and Culture. Boston: Bedford–St. Martin's, 2003.

Frow, John. "The Last Things before the Last: Notes on *White Noise*." *South Atlantic Quarterly* 89 (1990): 413–29. Rpt. in DeLillo, White Noise: *Text* 417–31.

Gallagher, Charles A. "White Construction in the University." *The Social Construction of Race and Ethnicity in the United States*. Ed. Joan Ferrante and Prince Brown, Jr. New York: Addison, 1998. 167–87.

Gallup, George, Jr., and D. Michael Lindsey. *Surveying the Religious Landscape: Trends in U.S. Beliefs*. Harrisburg: Morehouse, 1999.

Gardaphé, Fred L. *Italian Signs, American Streets: The Evolution of Italian American Narrative*. Durham: Duke UP, 1996.

Gass, William H. "In Defense of the Book." *Harper's Magazine* Nov. 1999: 45–51.

Giroux, Henry. "Rewriting the Discourse of Racial Identity: Towards a Pedagogy and Politics of Whiteness." *Harvard Educational Review* 67 (1997): 285–320.

Gitlin, Todd, "The Ordinariness of American Feelings." 10 Oct. 2001. 12 Mar. 2004 <http://www.opendemocracy.net/debates/article-2-47-105.jsp>.

Glasner, Joanna. "Eerie Image Pulled from CD." *Wired* 13 Sept. 2001. 4 July 2002 <http://www.wired.com/news/culture/0,1284,46771,00.html>.

Glotfelty, Cheryll. "Introduction: Literary Studies in an Age of Environmental Crisis." Glotfelty and Fromm xv–xxii.

Glotfelty, Cheryll, and Harold Fromm, eds. *The Ecocriticism Reader: Landmarks in Literary Ecology*. Athens: U of Georgia P, 1996.

Goffman, Erving. *The Presentation of Self in Everyday Life*. New York: Doubleday, 1959.

Goldhagen, Daniel Jonah. *Hitler's Willing Executioners: Ordinary Germans and the Holocaust*. New York: Vintage-Random, 1997.

Graff, Harvey J. *Early Modern Literacies*. Bloomington: Indiana UP, 1987.

Gramsci, Antonio. *Selections from the Prison Notebook of Antonio Gramsci*. Ed. Quintin Hoare and Geoffrey Nowell-Smith. New York: Intl., 1971.

The Great Dictator. Dir. Charles Chaplin. United Artists, 1940.

Gunn, Giles. *Thinking across the American Grain: Ideology, Intellect, and the New Pragmatism*. Chicago: U of Chicago P, 1992.

Habermas, Jürgen. "Modernity: An Incomplete Project." Foster 3–15.

Hansberry, Lorraine. *A Raisin in the Sun*. Introd. Robert Nemiroff. New York: Modern Lib., 1995.

Happe, François. *Don DeLillo: La fiction contre les systèmes*. Collection Voix Américaines. Paris: Belin, 2000.

Hardin, Michael. "What Is the Word at Logos College? Homosocial Ritual or Homosexual Denial in Don DeLillo's *End Zone*?" *Journal of Homosexuality* 40.1 (2000): 37–50.

Harvey, Anne-Marie. "Students, American Identities, and Whiteness." *Making*

American Literatures in High School and College. Ed. Anne Ruggles Gere and Peter Shaheen. Urbana: NCTE, 2001. 62–71.

Harvey, David. *The Condition of Postmodernity: An Enquiry into the Origins of Cultural Change.* Oxford: Basil, 1989.

Havelock, Eric. *The Literate Revolution in Greece and Its Cultural Consequences.* Princeton: Princeton UP, 1982.

Heidegger, Martin. "The Question concerning Technology." *"The Question concerning Technology" and Other Essays*. Trans. William Lovitt. New York: Harper, 1977. 3–35.

Heise, Ursula. "Toxins, Drugs, and Global Systems: Risk and Narrative in the Contemporary Novel." *American Literature* 74 (2002): 747–78.

Hemingway, Ernest. *The Sun Also Rises*. New York: Scribner's, 1926.

Hill, Mike, ed. *Whiteness: A Critical Reader*. New York: New York UP, 1997.

hooks, bell. "Postmodern Blackness." *Yearnings: Race, Gender, and Cultural Politics*. Boston: South End, 1990. 23–32.

Horkheimer, Max, and Theodor W. Adorno. *The Dialectic of Enlightenment*. Trans. John Cumming. New York: Herder, 1972.

Horstman, Joey Earl. "Fictional Needs, Literary Options: Alternatives to Television in Thomas Pynchon's *Vineland*, Don DeLillo's *White Noise*, and Richard Powers's *Prisoner's Dilemma*." Diss. Purdue U, 1997.

Hounshell, David A., and John Kenly Smith, Jr. *Science and Corporate Strategy: Du Pont R&D, 1902–1980.* Cambridge: Cambridge UP, 1988.

Howells, William Dean. *The Rise of Silas Lapham*. New York: Penguin, 1983.

Hutcheon, Linda. *Irony's Edge: The Theory and Politics of Irony*. London: Routledge, 1995.

———. *A Poetics of Postmodernism: History, Theory, Fiction*. New York: Routledge, 1988.

———. *The Politics of Postmodernism*. London: Routledge, 1993.

Huxley, Aldous. *Brave New World*. New York: Perennial, 1998.

Independence Day. Dir. Roland Emmerich. Twentieth Century Fox, 1996.

Interviews with Don DeLillo. *Don DeLillo's America*. 17 Feb. 2005. 8 June 2005 <http://perival.com/delillo/ddinterviews.html>. Path: 1979–Tom LeClair.

James, Caryn. "I Never Set Out to Write an Apocalyptic Novel." *New York Times Book Review* 13 Jan. 1985: 31.

James, Henry. *The American*. Ed. William Spengemann. Penguin Classics. New York: Penguin, 1986.

Jameson, Fredric. "The Cultural Logic of Late Capitalism." Jameson, *Postmodernism* 1–54.

———. "Postmodernism and Consumer Society." Foster 111–25.

———. *Postmodernism; or, The Cultural Logic of Late Capitalism.* Durham: Duke UP, 1991.

Jenkins, Noel. *Bhopal Investigation*. *Welcome to Geography*. Geography Dept., Hampstead School. 2003. 27 Apr. 2005 <http://www.geography.ndo.co.uk/bhopal.htm>.

Jenkins, Philip. *The Next Christendom: The Coming of Global Christianity*. New York: Oxford UP, 2002.

Joyce, James. *A Portrait of the Artist as a Young Man*. New York: Bedford–St. Martin's, Boston, 1993.

Kafka, Franz. "A Hunger Artist." *"The Metamorphosis," "In the Penal Colony," and Other Stories*. Trans. Willa Muir and Edwin Muir. New York: Schocken, 1948. 243–56.

———. *Letters to Friends, Family, and Editors*. Trans. Richard Winston and Clara Winston. New York: Schocken, 1977.

Katz, Jackson. "Advertising and the Construction of Violent White Masculinity." *Gender, Race, and Class in Media: A Text-Reader.* Ed. Gail Dines and Jean M. Humez. Thousand Oaks: Sage, 1995. 133–41.

Katz, Jackson, and Sut Jhally. "The National Conversation in the Wake of Littleton Is Missing the Mark." *Boston Globe* 2 May 1999: E1.

Kavadlo, Jesse. *Don DeLillo: Balance at the Edge of Belief*. Frankfurt: Lang, 2004.

Kay, Alan C. "Computers, Networks, and Education." *Scientific American* Sept. 1991: 100–07.

Keating, AnnLouise. "Interrogating 'Whiteness,' (De)Constructing 'Race.' " *College English* 57 (1995): 901–18.

Keesey, Douglas. *Don DeLillo*. New York: Twayne, 1993.

Kellner, Douglas. *Jean Baudrillard: From Marxism to Postmodernism and Beyond*. Stanford: Stanford UP, 1989.

Kermode, Frank. *The Sense of an Ending: Studies in the Theory of Fiction*. New York: Oxford UP, 1966.

Kerridge, Richard. "Small Rooms and the Ecosystem: Environmentalism and DeLillo's *White Noise*." *Writing the Environment: Ecocriticism and Literature*. Ed. Kerridge and Neil Sammells. London: Zed, 1998. 182–95.

Kimmel, Michael S. "Clarence, William, Iron Mike, Tailhook, Senator Packwood, Spur Posse, Magic, . . . and Us." *Transforming a Rape Culture*. Ed. Emile Buchwald, Pamela R. Fletcher, and Martha Roth. Minneapolis: Milkweed, 1993. 119–38.

Kincheloe, Joe L. "The Struggle to Define and Reinvent Whiteness: A Pedagogical Analysis." *College Literature* 26.3 (1999): 162–94.

Kincheloe, Joe L., Shirley R. Steinberg, Nelson M. Rodriguez, and Ronald E. Chennault, eds. *White Reign: Deploying Whiteness in America*. New York: St. Martin's, 1998.

Klein, Naomi. *No Logo: Taking Aim at the Brand Bullies*. New York: Picador, 2000.

Koestenbaum, Wayne. *The Queen's Throat: Opera, Homosexuality, and the Mystery of Desire*. New York: Vintage, 1994.

Konrad, George. *The Melancholy of Rebirth: Essays from Post-Communist Central Europe, 1989–1994*. San Diego: Harcourt, 1995.

Kucich, John. "Postmodern Politics: Don DeLillo and the Plight of the White Male Writer." *Michigan Quarterly Review* 27 (1988): 328–41.

Kuechler, Manfred. "Using the Web in the Classroom." *Social Science Computer Review* 17.2 (1999): 144–61.

Lasch, Christopher. *The Culture of Narcissism: American Life in an Age of Diminishing Expectations*. New York: Norton, 1979.

LeClair, Tom. *In the Loop: Don DeLillo and the Systems Novel*. Urbana: U of Illinois P, 1987.

LeClair, Tom, and Larry McCaffery, eds. *Anything Can Happen: Interviews with Contemporary American Novelists*. Champaign: U of Illinois P, 1988.

Lentricchia, Frank. "The American Writer as Bad Citizen." Lentricchia, *Introducing* 1–6.

———. "Don DeLillo's Primal Scenes." DeLillo, White Noise*: Text* 412–16.

———, ed. *Introducing Don DeLillo*. Durham: Duke UP, 1991.

———. Introduction. Lentricchia, *New Essays* 1–14.

———. "*Libra* as Postmodern Critique." Lentricchia, *Introducing* 195–215.

———, ed. *New Essays on* White Noise. Cambridge: Cambridge UP, 1991.

———. "Tales of the Electronic Tribe." Lentricchia, *New Essays* 87–113.

Leps, Marie-Christine. "Empowerment through Information: A Discursive Critique." *Cultural Critique* 31 (1995): 179–96.

Lewis, R. W. B. *The American Adam: Innocence, Tragedy, and Tradition in the Nineteenth Century*. Chicago: U of Chicago P, 1961.

Lewis, Sinclair. *Babbitt*. *Main Street [and] Babbitt*. Ed. John Hersey. New York: Lib. of Amer., 1992. 487–844.

Life Is Beautiful [*La vita è bella*]. Dir. Roberto Benigni. Miramax, 1997.

Lilla, Mark. *The Reckless Mind: Intellectuals in Politics*. New York: New York Rev., 2001.

Lipsitz, George. *The Possessive Investment in Whiteness: How White People Profit from Identity Politics*. Philadelphia: Temple UP, 1998.

Lopez, Ian F. Haney. *White by Law: The Legal Construction of Race*. New York: New York UP, 1996.

Lyotard, Jean-François. *The Postmodern Condition: A Report on Knowledge*. 1979. Trans. Geoff Bennington and Brian Massumi. Minneapolis: U of Minnesota P, 1984.

Mahajan, Romi. "Bhopal on $40 a Day." *Counterpunch* 21 Aug. 2002. 13 Sept. 2003 <http://www.counterpunch.org/mahajan0821.html>.

Manes, Christopher. "Nature and Silence." Glotfelty and Fromm 15–29.

Marquet, Pascal, et al., eds. *Internet-Based Teaching and Learning (IN-TELE) 98: Proceedings of IN-TELE 98*. Frankfurt am Main: Lang, 1990.

Mars Attacks! Dir. Tim Burton. Warner Brothers, 1996.

Marx, Karl. "Excerpts from *The German Ideology*." *Marx and Engels: Basic Writings on Politics and Philosophy*. Ed. Lewis S. Feuer. New York: Doubleday, 1959. 247–60.

McClure, John. "Postmodern/Post-secular: Contemporary Fiction and Spirituality." *Modern Fiction Studies* 41 (1995): 141–63.

McHale, Brian. *Postmodernist Fiction*. New York: Methuen, 1987.

McIntosh, Peggy. "White Privilege and Male Privilege: A Personal Account of Coming to See Correspondences through Work in Women's Studies." *Race, Class, and Gender: An Anthology*. Ed. M. L. Anderson and P. H. Collins. New York: Wadsworth, 1995. 76–87.

McIntyre, Alice. *Making Meaning of Whiteness: Exploring Racial Identity with White Teachers*. Albany: State U of New York P, 1997.

McKinney, Karyn D. "Whiteness on a White Canvas: Teaching Race in a Predominantly White University." TuSmith and Reddy 126–39.

Melville, Herman. *The Confidence-Man: His Masquerade*. Introd. Tony Tanner. Ed. John Dugdale. Oxford World's Classics. Oxford: Oxford UP, 1999.

Messmer, Michael W. " 'Thinking It Through Completely': The Interpretation of Nuclear Culture." *Centennial Review* 32 (1988): 397–413.

Miller, Donald E. *Reinventing American Protestantism: Christianity in the New Millennium*. Berkeley: U of California P, 1997.

Milosz, Czeslaw, ed. *A Book of Luminous Things: An International Anthology of Poetry*. San Diego: Harcourt, 1996.

Mizruchi, Susan L. Introduction. *Religion and Cultural Studies*. Ed. Mizruchi. Princeton: Princeton UP, 2001. ix–xxv.

Moore, R. Laurence. *Selling God: American Religion in the Marketplace of Culture*. New York: Oxford UP, 1994.

Morrison, Toni. *The Bluest Eye*. New York: Knopf, 1993.

———. *Playing in the Dark: Whiteness and the Literary Imagination*. Cambridge: Harvard UP, 1992.

Moses, Michael Valdez. "Lust Removed from Nature." Lentricchia, *New Essays* 63–86.

Mumford, Lewis. *Art and Technics*. New York: Columbia UP, 1947.

Murphy, Patrick D. *Farther Afield in the Study of Nature-Oriented Literature*. Charlottesville: UP of Virginia, 2000.

Naess, Arne. "Deep Ecology and Ultimate Premises." *Ecologist* 18 (1988): 4–7.

The Nasty Girl [*Das schreckliche Mädchen*]. Dir. Michael Verhoeven. Miramax Films, 1990.

A Nation Online: Entering the Broadband Age. Sept. 2004. Natl. Telecommunications and Information Administration. United States Dept. of Commerce. 25 June 2005 <http://www.ntia.doc.gov/reports/anol/>.

Nel, Philip. "*Amazons* in the *Underworld*: Gender, the Body, and Power in the Novels of Don DeLillo." *Critique: Studies in Contemporary Fiction* 42 (2001): 416–36.

Nikelski, Peggy. "Vernetzt—verlinkt—verloren? Lehren und lernen mit hypertext." Marquet et al. 215–22.

Norton, Anne. "The Signs of Shopping." *Signs of Life in the U.S.A.: Readings on Popular Culture for Writers*. Ed. Sonia Maasik and Jack Solomon. Boston: Bedford, 1997. 38–45.

Novick, Peter. *The Holocaust in American Life*. New York: Houghton, 2000.

O'Donnell, Patrick. *Latent Destinies: Cultural Paranoia and Contemporary U.S. Narrative*. Durham: Duke UP, 2000.

Oelschlaeger, Max. *The Idea of Wilderness: From Prehistory to the Age of Ecology*. New Haven: Yale UP, 1991.

Orr, David. *Ecological Literacy: Education and the Transition to a Postmodern World*. Albany: State U of New York P, 1992.

Osteen, Mark. *American Magic and Dread: Don DeLillo's Dialogue with Culture*. Philadelphia: U of Pennsylvania P, 2000.

Palac, Lisa. "How Dirty Pictures Changed My Life." *Next: Young American Writers on the Next Generation*. Ed. Eric Liu. New York: Norton, 1994. 146–63.

Parini, Jay. "The Greening of the Humanities." *New York Times Magazine* 29 Oct. 1995: 52–53.

Passaro, Vincent. "Dangerous Don DeLillo." *New York Times Magazine*. 19 May 1991. 10 March 2004 <http://www.nytimes.com/books/97/03/16/lifetimes/del-v-dangerous.html>.

Perelman, Lewis J. *School's Out: A Radical New Formula for the Revitalization of America's Educational System*. New York: Avon, 1992.

Pérez-Torres, Rafael. "Tracing and Erasing: Race and Pedagogy in *The Bluest Eye*." *Approaches to Teaching the Novels of Toni Morrison*. Ed. Nellie Y. McKay. New York: MLA, 1997. 21–26.

Perl, Jed. "Saint Gerhard of the Sorrows of Painting." *New Republic* 29 Mar. 2002. 10 Mar. 2004 <http://www.tnr.com/showBio.mhtml?pid=31&sa=1>.

Perry, Pamela. *Shades of White: White Kids and Racial Identities in High School*. Durham: Duke UP, 2002.

Phelan, James, and Robert Pozen. *The Company State*. New York: Grossman, 1973.

Philippon, Dan, ed. *@sle Online: The Association for the Study of Literature and Environment*. 28 July 2002. U of Minnesota, Twin Cities. 22 Aug. 2002 <http://www.asle.umn.edu>.

Phillips, Dana. "Don DeLillo's Postmodern Pastoral." *Reading the Earth: New Directions in the Study of Literature and Environment*. Ed. Michael P. Branch, Rochelle Johnson, Daniel Patterson, and Scott Slovic. Moscow: U of Idaho P, 1998. 235–46.

Plath, Sylvia. *The Bell Jar*. Perennial Classics. New York: Harper, 1999.

———. "Daddy." *The Collected Poems: Sylvia Plath*. Ed. Ted Hughes. New York: Perennial-Harper, 1981. 222–24.

Plato. Phaedrus *and the Seventh and Eighth Letters*. Trans. Walter Hamilton. New York: Penguin, 1973.

Polyester Fiber. Fibersource. 23 July 2002 <http://www.fibersource.com/f-tutor/polyester.htm>.

Postman, Neil. *Amusing Ourselves to Death: Public Discourse in the Age of Show Business*. New York: Penguin, 1986.

Prager, Joshua Harris. "Giants '51 Comeback, the Sport's Greatest, Wasn't All It Seemed." *Wall Street Journal* 31 Jan. 2001: A1.

The Producers. Dir. Mel Brooks. MGM, 1968.

Profiles in Garbage: Polyethylene Terephthalate. WasteAge. 12 Aug. 2002 <http://www.wasteage.com/ar/waste_polyethylene_terephthalate/>.

Rodriguez, Nelson M., and Leila E. Villaverde, eds. *Dismantling White Privilege: Pedagogy, Politics, and Whiteness.* New York: Lang, 2000.

Roediger, David R. *Colored White: Transcending the Racial Past.* Berkeley: U of California P, 2002.

Roof, Wade Clark. *Spiritual Marketplace: Baby Boomers and the Remaking of American Religion.* Princeton: Princeton UP, 1999.

Rorty, Richard. *Achieving Our Country: Leftist Thought in Twentieth-Century America.* Cambridge: Harvard UP, 1998.

Rose, Gillian. *Mourning Becomes the Law: Philosophy and Representation.* Cambridge: Cambridge UP, 1996.

Rose, Phyllis. "Shopping and Other Spiritual Adventures in America Today." *Common Culture: Reading and Writing about American Popular Culture.* Ed. Michael F. Petracca and Madeleine Sorapure. Englewood Cliffs: Prentice, 1995. 621–24.

Ruppersburg, Hugh, and Tim Engles, eds. *Critical Essays on Don DeLillo.* New York: Hall, 2000.

Rushdie, Salman. *The Satanic Verses.* London: Viking, 1988.

Safe. Dir. Todd Haynes. Amer. Playhouse and Channel Four Films, 1995.

Saint-Pierre, Jacques-Henri Bernadin de. *Paul and Virginia.* London: Owen, 1982.

Sanders, Scott Russell. "Speaking a Word for Nature." Glotfelty and Fromm 182–95.

Scanlan, Margaret. *Plotting Terror: Novelists and Terrorists in Contemporary Fiction.* Charlottesville: UP of Virginia, 2001.

Schindler's List. Dir. Steven Spielberg. Universal, 1993.

Schlain, Leonard. *The Alphabet versus the Goddess: The Conflict between Word and Image.* New York: Penguin-Arkana, 1998.

Schudson, Michael. *Advertising, the Uneasy Persuasion: Its Dubious Impact on American Society.* New York: Basic, 1984.

Schulmeister, Rolf. *Grundlagen hypermedialer Lernsysteme: Theorie—Didaktik—Design.* Bonn: Addison, 1996.

Sessions, George. *Deep Ecology for the Twenty-First Century.* Boston: Shambala, 1995.

Sexton, David. "Unavailable for Comment." *Scotsman* 8 Dec. 2003. 10 Mar. 2004 <http://news.scotsman.com/features.cfm?id=1344832003>.

Shoah. Dir. Claude Lanzmann. New Yorker Films, 1985.

Slansky, Paul. *The Clothes Have No Emperor: A Chronicle of the American '80s.* New York: Simon, 1989.

Slotkin, Richard. *Regeneration through Violence: The Mythology of the American Frontier, 1600–1860.* Norman: U of Oklahoma P, 1973.

Soltan, Margaret. "Aesthetic Consciousness in *The Names.*" Reading Don DeLillo. Conf. on Don DeLillo. Université d'Orléans. 31 May 2002.

Spender, Dale. *Nattering on the Net: Women, Power and Cyberspace.* North Melbourne, Austral.: Spinifex, 1995.

Spiegelman, Art. *And Here My Troubles Began*. New York: Pantheon, 1991. Vol. 2 of *Maus: A Survivor's Tale*.

———. *My Father Bleeds History*. New York: Pantheon, 1986. Vol. 1 of *Maus: A Survivor's Tale*.

Taylor, Charles. *Varieties of Religion Today: William James Revisited*. Cambridge: Harvard UP, 2002.

Taylor, Mark. *Erring: A Postmodern A/Theology*. Chicago: U of Chicago P, 1987.

"Text: Bush and Daschle Comments on Security and Politics." *New York Times* 26 Sept. 2002. 6 Jan. 2005 <http://www.nytimes.com/2002/09/26/politics/26CTEX.html>.

Thoreau, Henry D. *Walden*. Ed. J. Lyndon Shanley. Princeton: Princeton UP, 1971.

Thwaites, Tony. "Currency Exchanges: The Postmodern, Vattimo, et Cetera, among Other Things (et Cetera)." *Postmodern Culture* 7.2 (1997). *Project MUSE*. Johns Hopkins UP. 29 Dec. 2004 <http://muse.jhu.edu/journals/postmodern_culture/v007/7.2thwaites.html>.

Torres, Alexandra Clarke. "The Resistance to Television: Gender, Genre, and Contemporary Media." Diss. Cornell U, 1991.

Triumph des Willens [*Triumph of the Will*]. Dir. Leni Riefenstahl. Germany, 1934.

TuSmith, Bonnie, and Maureen T. Reddy, eds. *Race in the College Classroom: Pedagogy and Politics*. New Brunswick: Rutgers UP, 2002.

Twain, Mark. *Adventures of Huckleberry Finn*. Ed. Gerald Graff and James Phelan. 2nd ed. New York: St. Martin's, 2004.

———. *A Connecticut Yankee in King Arthur's Court*. Electronic Text Center, U of Virginia Lib. 1994. 20 May 2005 <http://etext.lib.virginia.edu/toc/modeng/public/TwaYank.html>.

Twitchell, James B. *Adcult USA: The Triumph of Advertising in American Culture*. New York: Columbia UP, 1996.

Veblen, Thorstein. *The Theory of the Leisure Class*. New York: Dover, 1994.

Walker, Joseph S. "Don DeLillo: A Selected Bibliography." *Modern Fiction Studies* 45 (1999): 837–51.

Weber, Max. *From Max Weber: Essays in Sociology*. Trans. and ed. H. H. Gerth and C. Wright Mills. New York: Oxford UP, 1946.

Weinstein, Arnold. *Nobody's Home: Speech, Self, and Place in American Fiction from Hawthorne to DeLillo*. New York: Oxford UP, 1993.

Wesley, Marilyn C. "White Epics: Russell Banks's *Continental Drift* and Don DeLillo's *Libra*." *Violent Adventure: Contemporary Fiction by American Men*. Charlottesville: UP of Virginia, 2003. 140–64.

Wharton, Edith. *The House of Mirth*. *Novels*. Ed. R. W. B. Lewis. New York: Lib. of Amer., 1985. 1–348.

White, Patti. *Gatsby's Party: The System and the List in Contemporary Narrative*. West Lafayette: Purdue UP, 1992.

Wilbur, Shawn P. "An Archaeology of Cyberspaces: Virtuality, Community, Identity." *Internet Culture*. Ed. David Porter. New York: Routledge, 1997. 5–22.

Wilcox, Leonard. "Baudrillard, Don DeLillo's *White Noise*, and the End of Heroic Narrative." *Contemporary Literature* 32 (1991): 346–65.

Will, George. "The Great Refutation." *Washington Post* 11 Sept. 2002: A17. 10 Sept. 2003 <http://www.washingtonpost.com/ac2/wp-dyn/A350-2002Sep11?>.

———. "Shallow Look at the Mind of an Assassin." *Washington Post* 22 Sept. 1988: A25. Rpt. in Ruppersburg and Engles 00–00.

Williams, Raymond. "Advertising: The Magic System." *Problems in Materialism and Culture: Selected Essays*. London: Verso, 1980. 170–95.

Williams, Tennessee. *A Streetcar Named Desire*. *The Theatre of Tennessee Williams*. Vol. 1. New York: New Directions, 1990. 239–419.

Wolf, Naomi. *The Beauty Myth: How Images of Beauty Are Used against Women*. New York: Doubleday, 1991.

Wood, Michael. "Post-Paranoid." *London Review of Books* 5 Feb. 1998. 10 Mar. 2004 <www.lrb.co.uk/v20/n03/wood01_.html>.

Wuthnow, Robert. *After Heaven: Spirituality in America since the 1950s*. Berkeley: U of California P, 1998.

Yeats, William Butler. "Sailing to Byzantium." *Selected Poems and Two Plays of William Butler Yeats*. Ed. M. L. Rosenthal. New York: Collier, 1968. 95–96.

Youtt, Harry. "Artists of Denial and Avoidance." Eighth Biannual Conf. of Intl. Soc. for the Study of European Ideas. U of Wales, Aberystwyth. 25 July 2002.

Žižek, Slavoj. "Slavoj Žižek Answers Peter Murphy." 7 Oct. 2001. *Lacanian Ink*. 29 Dec. 2004 <http://www.lacan.com/reflections2.htm>.

———. *Welcome to the Desert of the Real! Five Essays on September 11 and Related Dates*. London: Verso, 2002.

INDEX

Approaches to Teaching DeLillo's *White Noise*